How to Do
Everything
with

Photoshop® CS2

S0-AGC-596

Colin Smith

McGraw-Hill/Osborne

New York   Chicago   San Francisco   Lisbon
London   Madrid   Mexico City   Milan   New Delhi
San Juan   Seoul   Singapore   Sydney   Toronto

The **McGraw·Hill** Companies

McGraw-Hill/Osborne
2100 Powell Street, 10th Floor
Emeryville, California 94608
U.S.A.

To arrange bulk purchase discounts for sales promotions, premiums, or fund-raisers, please contact **McGraw-Hill**/Osborne at the above address.

How to Do Everything with Photoshop® CS2

1234567890 VHN VHN 0198765

ISBN 0-07-226160-9

Vice President &	
** Group Publisher**	Philip Ruppel
Vice President &	
** Publisher**	Jeffrey Krames
Acquisitions Editor	Marjorie McAneny
Project Editor	Emily Rader
Acquisitions Coordinator	Agatha Kim
Technical Editor	Jeff Keyser
Copy Editor	Lisa Theobald
Proofreader	Andrea Fox
Indexer	Rebecca Plunkett
Composition	Lucie Ericksen
Illustrators	Apollo Publishing Services
Series Design	Lucie Ericksen
Cover Series Design	Dodie Shoemaker
Cover Illustration	Colin Smith
Cover Photo	Lise Gagné/Istockphoto.com

This book was composed with Corel VENTURA™ Publisher.

To my parents, the best that anyone could have.
Thanks for your continued support as I pursue my dreams.

About the Author

Colin Smith is a best-selling author, trainer, and award-winning new-media designer who has caused a stir in the design community with his stunning photorealistic illustrations composed entirely in Photoshop. He is founder of the world's most popular Photoshop resource site, PhotoshopCAFE.com, which boasts more than two million visitors.

With over ten years of experience in the design industry, Colin was formerly Senior Editor and Art Director for *VOICE* magazine. He is a regular columnist for *Photoshop User* magazine, PlanetPhotoshop.com, and the official site of the National Association for Photoshop Professionals. He also contributes to a number of other graphic art publications, such as *Mac Design* magazine, *Web Designer* magazine, and *Computer Arts* magazine.

Colin's graphic design work has been recognized with numerous awards, including the Guru awards at Photoshop World 2001 and 2002, for his work in both illustration and web design. He has authored or co-authored more than ten books on Photoshop, including the best-selling *How to Do Everything with Photoshop CS* (McGraw-Hill/Osborne, 2004) and the award-winning *Photoshop Most Wanted: Effects and Design Tips* (A Press/Friends of Ed, 2002). Colin is also creator of the *Photoshop Secrets* Video training series (www.PhotoshopCD.com). He is in high demand across the United States as a lecturer, presenting his Photoshop techniques to web designers and other graphics professionals across the nation.

About the Technical Editor

Jeff Keyser is an award-winning art director, designer, and filmmaker who has produced projects for a variety of high-profile clients, including Nike, ESPN, Billabong, Adidas, Universal, and a host of others. This experience has allowed him to work with a wide group of ad agencies and design houses across the country, spanning the mediums of interactive, broadcast, print, and DVD.

Jeff's work has been honored with numerous awards in shows, including The One Show, Cannes International Advertising Festival, and multiple Flash Film Festivals throughout the United States and Europe. His work can be seen at www.jeffkeyser.com.

Contents

Acknowledgments

A big thank you goes out to Margie McAneny for grabbing the bull by the horns and managing this project. Thanks to Emily Rader and Lisa Theobald for taking care of all of the editing and making me look good. Thanks to the hard-working Lucie Ericksen in production who has made this book look good. Thanks to my friend and technical editor, Jeff Keyser, for your help. Thanks also to Pattie Lee for your vision and direction on the cover. Thanks to Mauriahh for modeling for me once again. Thanks to Jens Karlsson, Bert Monroy, Oliver Ottner, Tim Cooper, Malachi Maloney, and Phil Williams for contributing art to the gallery. You guys rock!

Thank you to the members at PhotshopCAFE and especially the moderators, who have done such an awesome job of running things while I have been otherwise occupied writing this book. Frank (c-fire), Mike, Phil, Sue (Tech chick), Realist, Chris, Christian, DO2, Daz, Matt, and Al— you have made the Café the friendly place that it is.

Thanks to Al Ward for the expensive phone bill. Just kidding, buddy. To the entire crew at NAPP, especially Scott Kelby, Jeff Kelby, Chris Main, Felix Nelson, Dave Cross, and Barbera: I love your spirit of sharing. You are all great to work with. Thanks to Gwyn and Addy at Adobe Systems for all your support.

To my buddies in the "real world"—Jason, Eddie, Frank, George, Michael, Ali, and all the rest—thanks for the friendship and the break from writing all the time. "All work and no play make Colin a dull boy."

Thanks to the people that count the most—my family and friends. To my parents, who brought me into the world and raised me to think for myself and be all that I could be. To my pastors, George and Hazel Hill, thank you for helping me to dream big and do it!

Finally and most important, thanks to God for the gifts he has given me and the opportunity to use them.

Introduction

This book can either be read from cover to cover in a linear fashion or used as a reference. If you are brand new to Photoshop, I urge you to start at the beginning of the book and read all the way through to the end. The extra time invested now will bring many rewards in the future.

You do not need to have any previous experience with Photoshop or image editing to read this book; however, I do assume that you are somewhat familiar with your computer. I will cover a lot of ground, but basic operating system knowledge is assumed and outside the scope of this book.

This book is broken into four parts with an inspirational gallery at the end:

Get to Know Photoshop CS2   In this section, you will learn all the Photoshop basics, such as the tools and workspace. Like an orientation on your first day on the job, I cover the basic elements of the Photoshop program—tools, documents, colors, file types, and resolution.

Beyond the Basics   In this section, you will begin to perform tasks and use features such as layers, channels, paths, and text. You will also learn some efficient work methods that save time.

The Fun Stuff   In this section, you get to do the cool stuff and use selection, filters, and layer styles to produce eye candy and special effects.

The Real World   In this section, you'll use Photoshop for real-world applications. You'll work with photographs, build web pages, and print your work.

Behind the Scenes: A Gallery with Techniques from the Pros   This inspirational gallery features work by some of the biggest names in the graphic design industry. Not only will you see their art, you will learn how to accomplish some of the effects they use.

I have interacted with over three million visitors passing through the virtual doors of PhotoshopCAFE.com, the online Photoshop community I run. One thing I have learned is that not all Photoshop users are the same. In fact, there are few things that draw people from so many different cultures, ethnic backgrounds, ages, and philosophies, uniting them into one common purpose. There are so many types of people using Photoshop, from hobbyists to professionals in the fields of graphic design, web design, photography, architecture, fine art, forensics, medicine, law, and other fields. I am not aware of any other graphics software that has such a diverse user base.

Whether you are brand new to Photoshop or are already comfortable with the program, having picked up this book to brush up your skills and become familiar with the new features of Photoshop CS2, this is the book for you.

Part I

Get to Know Photoshop CS2

Chapter 1

Photoshop CS2 Primer

How to...

- Use palettes
- Use the toolbox
- Use the options bar
- Set rulers, guides, and grids
- Work with windows
- Navigate images
- Choose preset workspaces
- Create custom shortcuts
- Use the Preset Manager
- Set the preferences
- Understand common color modes
- Understand common file types
- Use the status bar
- Change views

At first glance, the interface in Photoshop can seem a bit intimidating, but all those complex-looking windows and palettes are soon going to become your friends. In this chapter, we will tame the interface tiger and quickly have you on your merry way. You see, there is method to the madness in all these palettes. Once you get the hang of one palette, you'll find it easy to conquer all the other palettes, because Adobe has created an intuitive user interface that repeats functionality throughout the program. In other words, once you learn the basics, the rest will start to come naturally to you. The best way to approach learning a program with as many features as Photoshop is as the old saying goes: "How do you eat an elephant?" "One bite at a time." Don't look at everything you need to learn as one huge task; just take one task at a time, and before you know it, you will be soaring with the pros.

The Photoshop Workspace

When you launch Photoshop, you will see the Welcome Screen shown in Figure 1-1.

This screen will direct you to some valuable resources that will help you learn the program. You will find tutorials and techniques that will help you master Photoshop. If you don't want to see this screen every time you open the program, uncheck

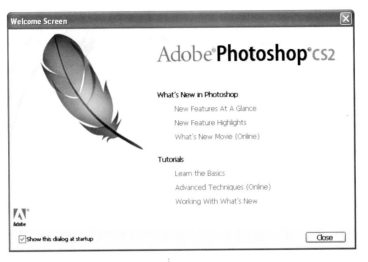

Show This Dialog At Startup. You can access this screen from the Help menu at any time. When you are ready to proceed to the program, click the Close button.

When you are working in Photoshop, you will see an interface similar to Figure 1-2, depending on your platform.

Other than some differences in the onscreen user interface, and some keyboard modifier keys, the Windows and Mac versions of Photoshop features work in exactly the same way. This book will cover both versions and

FIGURE 1-1 The Welcome Screen

FIGURE 1-2 The Photoshop interface

A. In Windows

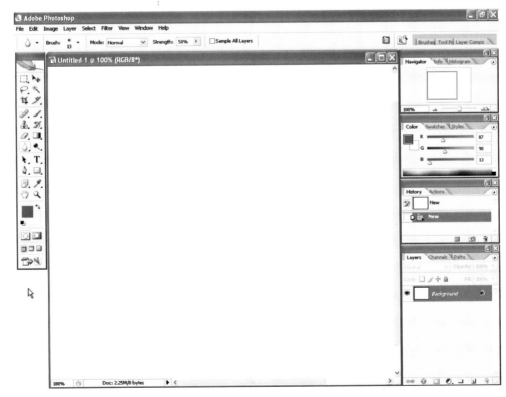

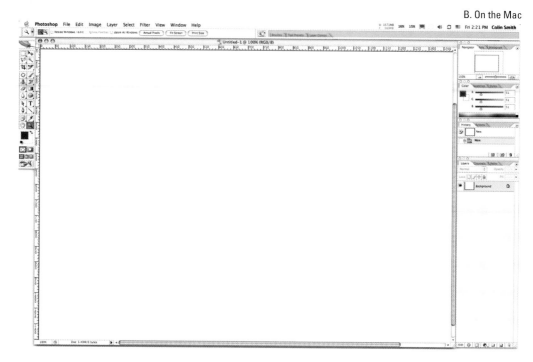

the keyboard commands will be provided for both. The basic differences in keys between the two platforms are listed here:

PC Keyboard	Mac Keyboard
CTRL	CMD (Apple key)
ALT	OPTION
Right-click	CONTROL-click (if you don't have a two-button mouse)
BACKSPACE	DELETE

Palettes

A palette is a movable box that contains a variety of options for a particular tool or for accomplishing a task. Photoshop is a palette-driven program—almost everything you do will involve palettes in one way or another. You can organize palettes in a few different ways. If you need to be able to access more screen space, you can, of course, close all the palettes and use the menus to access and choose information as needed, but there are better ways to get back some of your screen real estate.

A great way to maximize space is to use a two-monitor setup. This setup allows you to extend your workspace to a second monitor. You can drag all your palettes onto the second monitor, freeing up space on the main monitor for your image.

FIGURE 1-3 A group of palettes

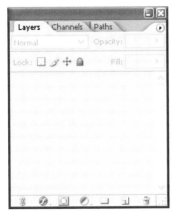

When you first open Photoshop, you will find that related tools are grouped together in palette groups similar to the one shown in Figure 1-3. To activate a palette, click its title tab.

Organizing Palettes

You can easily isolate a palette from the group by clicking and dragging its tab. You can then drop it onto the workspace by releasing the mouse button. The palette will appear exactly where you drop it.

Docking Palettes

You can *dock* columns of palettes together and build a "super palette." When you dock multiple palettes and move the top palette, all the palettes will move with it. Here's how it works:

A.

B.

1. Click and drag the palette's title tab.

2. Drag it over the very bottom of another palette group.

3. You will see a double line appear in the bottom of the palette, as shown at the left in Figure 1-4A.

4. Release the mouse button and the palette will be docked, as shown at the right in Figure 1-4B.

Adding a Palette to a Group

You can also add a palette to a group by clicking and dragging its title bar into a current group, as shown in Figure 1-5.

FIGURE 1-4 Docking the palettes (A) Drag the palette to the bottom of another palette (B) The new palette becomes docked to the group

A.

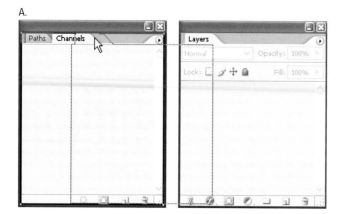

B.

FIGURE 1-5 Adding a palette to the group
(A) Drag the palette
(B) It is added to the group

Expanding and Contracting Palettes

You can also change the size of your palettes. There are four ways that you can expand and contract palettes:

- Expand a palette by dragging the bottom corner (see Figure 1-6A).

- Click the minimize button to shrink the palette the minimum size that is needed to show all of its content (see Figure 1-6B).

- Click the minimize button again; only the options will be visible.

- Click the button once again and the palette will be reduced to just the title bar (see Figure 1-6C). This is as small as it gets.

FIGURE 1-6 Minimizing the palette
(A) Expands a palette
(B) Shrinks to content
(C) Shrinks to title bar

A.

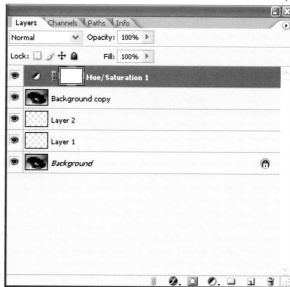

B.

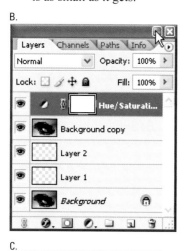

C.

The palette will keep cycling through these views as you click the minimize button.

The Palette Well

You can use the palette well to organize your palettes and free up screen space. You can drop palettes into the palette well, which is located in the top right of the options bar, as shown in Figure 1-7.

Note *The palette well is available only if you are using a screen resolution larger than 800×600.*

Here's how you add a palette to the well:

1. Drag any palette tab to the well, as shown in Figure 1-7A.

2. Release the mouse and it will be added to the well, freeing up precious screen space, as shown in Figure 1-7B.

3. Click the tab in the well, and the palette will open in the well, as shown in Figure 1-7C.

4. You can also add any palette to the well by clicking the little arrow at the upper-right corner of any palette and choosing Dock To Palette Well, as shown in Figure 1-7D.

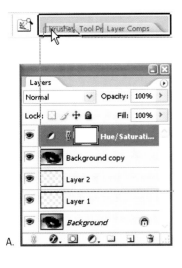

A.

B.

C.

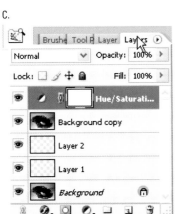

D.

FIGURE 1-7 The palette well
(A) Drag a palette to the well
(B) The palette in the well
(C) Use a palette in the well
(D) Choose the Dock To Palette Well option

Palette Menus

The little arrow at the upper-right corner of all palettes opens the flyout menu called the Palette menu, which provides a quick way to access the most common tasks you will perform with the palette. Figure 1-8 shows the Palette menu for the Layers palette. Particular options available for each palette are described throughout this book when each palette is discussed.

Resetting Palettes

You can reset the palettes to their default positions by choosing Window | Workspace | Reset Palette Locations.

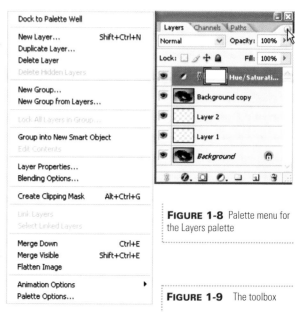

FIGURE 1-8 Palette menu for the Layers palette

FIGURE 1-9 The toolbox

The Toolbox

The toolbox is the vertical bar from which you select all the tools you need to work with in Photoshop. To choose a tool, just click its icon in the toolbox. As shown in Figure 1-9, tools are grouped into four categories:

- **Selection** Use these tools to select objects.
- **Creative** Use these tools to draw objects and retouch photos.
- **Vector** Use these tools to work with vectors.
- **Navigation and Information** Use these tools to view the page and gather information.

Some of the icons in the toolbox show tiny triangles in their lower-right corners. If you click and hold your mouse on an icon with a triangle,

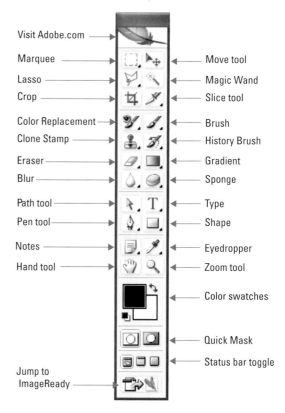

a flyout menu will appear with additional tools. These tools are usually variations of the selected tool.

Figure 1-10 shows you a complete list of all the tools in the toolbox. The single letter to the right of each tool in the group is the keyboard shortcut. Just press the corresponding key on your keyboard to access the tool.

FIGURE 1-10 The toolbox

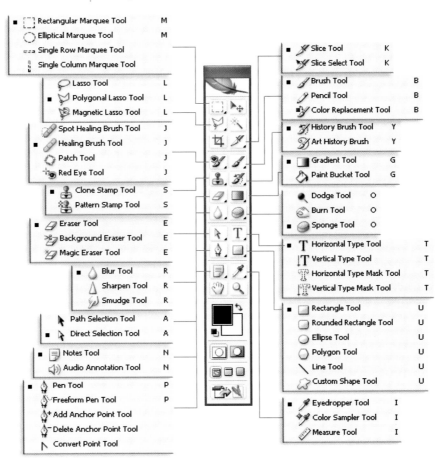

Tools and Information

This section gives you a brief rundown of each tool and tells you where to look for more information regarding use of these tools. Most of the tools are covered in depth throughout the book.

Selection Tools

- **Marquee tools**   Make selections. See Chapter 10 for information.
- **Move**   Drag objects on the page. See Chapter 10.
- **Lasso**   Make irregular shaped selections. See Chapter 10.
- **Magic Wand**   Create a selection based on color. See Chapter 10.

Creative Use Tools

- **Crop**   Crop an image to a chosen size. See Chapter 12.
- **Slice**   Cut an image into smaller pieces for online use. See Chapter 13.
- **Repair tools**   Make repairs and enhance photographs. See Chapter 12.
- **Brushes**   Paint with color and perform special effects in conjunction with other tools. See Chapter 3.
- **Clone Stamp tool**   Sample a portion of the image and then "paint" with the sampled portion of the image. See Chapter 12.
- **History and Art History Brushes**   Paint and make enhancements with a previous version of the working image. See Chapter 3.
- **Eraser**   Delete portions of the image in the same way a traditional eraser works. See Chapter 3.
- **Fill tools**   Fill image areas with color and gradients. See Chapter 3.
- **Blur and Sharpen**   Blur and sharpen precise portions of an image. Good for fixing photos and also for special effects. See Chapter 3.
- **Dodge and Burn**   Lighten and darken select portions of an image. See Chapter 3.

Vector Tools

- **Path Selection**   Manipulate and adjust paths. See Chapter 7.

- **Type**   Create text. See Chapter 8.
- **Pen**   Create paths. See Chapter 7.
- **Shape**   Create paths or predetermined shapes. See Chapters 3 and 7.

Navigation and Information Tools

- **Notes**   Attach notes or audio messages to an image in the same way you would use "sticky notes." Useful for adding instructions for another designer or to remind yourself of some settings or techniques used. Notes will not print, but they will travel with the document.
- **Eyedropper**   Sample colors and other information from images. See Chapter 10.
- **Hand**   Drag the canvas around in a window. You will use this tool when you have zoomed in on an image and need to navigate. See the "Navigating" section later in this chapter.
- **Zoom**   Change the magnification of the working document. You can zoom in or out with this tool. See the "Zooming" section later in this chapter.

Other Tools

- **Color Swatches**   Choose your foreground and background colors here. See Chapter 3.
- **Quick Mask**   Make a selection with a brush. See Chapter 10.
- **View**   Toggle the status bars on and off. See end of this chapter.
- **Jump to ImageReady**   Launch ImageReady, a web design program that ships free with Photoshop. See Chapter 13.

Options Bar

The options bar is a *context-sensitive* menu—whenever you select a tool, the options in the bar will change to the particular options available for that selected tool. Choose another tool and the options will change. This saves a lot of clutter and allows you to see only the options that you need. Whenever you select a tool, glance at the options bar and see what options are available. Figure 1-11 shows the options bar at the top of the screen with the Move tool selected. Notice that more options are available on the options bar, including alignment options, which are covered in Chapter 4.

FIGURE 1-11 The options bar

You can move the options bar to another location on the screen. Click and drag on the dotted line on the far left of the bar, and you can choose to have it floating like the other palettes, or drag it near the bottom and it will snap to the bottom of the screen. The default location at the top should work best for most users, however.

Rulers, Guides, and Grids

When it comes to laying out objects on a page, "eye-balling it" can sometimes be your best bet; however, to be really accurate, you need to use guides. Photoshop comes with rulers, guides, and grids to help make your layouts nice and even. A basic design principle, *alignment* means everything on the page relates to other objects in some way—this gives a sense of balance and order to a page.

Rulers

To help you take measure of a layout, you can choose to show the rulers. The rulers will be visible along the left and top edges of the image. The zero point for both rulers is at the top-left corner of the image.

To show the rulers, press CTRL-R (CMD-R on the Mac) or choose View | Rulers. Figure 1-12 shows an image with the rulers.

You can easily switch among units of measures in your rulers: pixels, inches, centimeters, millimeters, points, picas,

FIGURE 1-12 Showing the rulers

and even percentage. To change the unit of measure, do one of the following:

- Position your mouse over the units on one of the rulers. Right-click (CONTROL-click on the Mac) and choose a new unit of measure from the drop-down list.

- Double-click the ruler and change the unit in the Preferences window that opens.

Guides

You can also use guides to measure and lay out pages. A guide is a nonprinting line that can be positioned on the page to assist you in aligning objects. To add a guide:

1. Show the rulers.

2. Position your mouse over one of the rulers.

3. Click and drag. You will notice that you are dragging a dotted line.

4. Release the mouse to drop the guide on the page. Figure 1-13 shows three guides in place and one guide's placement in process.

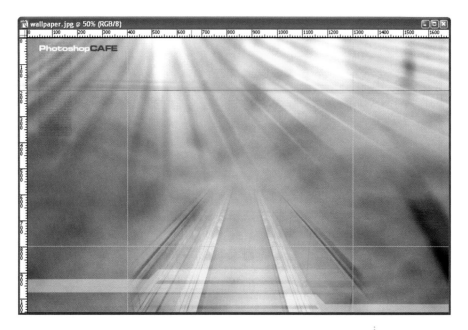

FIGURE 1-13 Adding guides

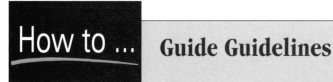 **Guide Guidelines**

Here are a few tips to keep in mind when using guides:

- To add a horizontal guide, drag down from the top ruler.
- To add a vertical guide, drag right from the left ruler.
- To reposition a guide, click it with the Move tool and drag it to another position.
- To remove a guide, drag it off the workspace.
- To hide and show a guide, choose View | Show Guides.
- To lock the guides so that they cannot be moved, choose View | Lock Guides.
- To delete all guides in a document, choose View | Clear Guides.

Snap To Guides

A useful feature to help you lay things out with guides is the Snap To option. To turn it on, choose View | Snap To | Guides.

When the Snap To option is turned on, the guide will act like a magnet that attracts objects as you move them to within a few pixels of the guide. This option is handy if perfect alignment is important to your layout.

Smart Guides

Smart guides are a different kind of guide. They stay invisible until they are needed. When you are dragging a layer, the Smart guides will temporarily appear to indicate that a layer's edge is aligned with another layer's edge or center, as shown in Figure 1-14. This feature saves a lot of time when laying out a design, because you do not have to create manual guides to help align everything on a page. To turn Smart Guides on or off, choose View | Show | Smart Guides.

FIGURE 1-14 Smart guides in action

Grids

When grids are turned on, they provide a visual system that helps you measure, align, and generally keep things in proportion. To turn on grids, as shown in Figure 1-15, choose View | Show | Grids. The grid size can be changed from the

Preferences menu—choose Preferences | Guides, Grids And Slices, and enter new settings in the Grids section.

FIGURE 1-15 Grids visible

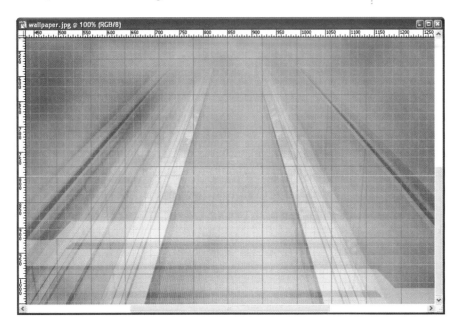

Working with Windows

Whenever you open a new image in Photoshop, it will appear in a window. While working, you can zoom in or out, navigate around the window, and arrange your windows on your screen to make it easier to work.

In Windows, you can maximize your workspace window so that it fills up the entire screen. To do this, click the maximize button. This button is similar to the maximize button that appears in most applications. When you maximize the window, some gray area might appear around the image (Windows only) in your Photoshop workspace window, as shown in Figure 1-16.

This gray area is part of your workspace, but it does not contain any images. You can, however, see bounding boxes in this area when you are scaling and transforming images.

To change the color of the gray pasteboard, choose a foreground color from the Color Picker, select the Paint Bucket tool, and click on the gray area while holding down the SHIFT key.

FIGURE 1-16 Maximized window

Zooming

To zoom in and out of windows, you use the Zoom tool, which looks like a magnifying glass. After you choose the Zoom tool, you can do the following:

- To zoom in, click anywhere within an image window.
- To zoom out, hold down the ALT key (OPTION on the Mac) and click.
- To show 100 percent size, double-click the Zoom tool.

You can also select a portion of the image to zoom into by clicking and dragging the Zoom tool in a rectangle. The image will zoom into the selected area, as shown in Figure 1-17.

Zoom in or out by pressing CTRL-+ *or* CTRL-– *(*CMD-+ *and* CMD-– *on the Mac).*

A.

B.
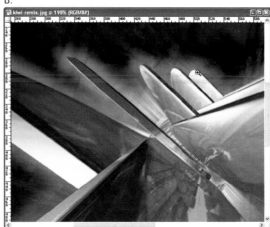

When you choose the Zoom tool, you will notice that the following options appear in the options bar:

FIGURE 1-17 Zooming in to a selected area
(A) The selection is made
(B) The image is zoomed

- **Actual Pixels**   Display images at 100 percent.
- **Fit On Screen**   Fit the entire image on the screen.
- **Print Size**   Show an approximate size of the image if it were to be printed at the current resolution.

 *To display an image at full-screen size, press* CTRL-0 *(*CMD-0 *on the Mac).*

Navigating

Once you have zoomed in on an image, you will notice that scrollbars appear in the window. This means that all the image information cannot be displayed inside the current window size. You can move around the window in a few ways:

- Choose the Hand tool from the toolbox. Click and drag the image around the window.
- Click and drag the scroll bars to reveal other parts of the image.
- Hold down the SPACEBAR. The current tool will temporarily turn into the Hand tool. Click and drag to move the image around onscreen.

Navigator Palette

The Navigator palette allows you to zoom in and out and move your zoomed selections in an image. When you zoom in on an

1

FIGURE 1-18 The Navigator
palette

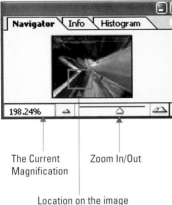

FIGURE 1-18 The Navigator palette

The Current
Magnification

Zoom In/Out

Location on the image

image at a very high magnification, it can be easy to get a bit lost at times and not know where you are in the image as a whole—it's like being lost in a giant maze. The solution would be to have a bird's eye view. That's exactly what the Navigator palette, shown in Figure 1-18, does.

The little red box in the palette shows where the current window area is located on the image. To move to another part of the image, click and drag the red box and the window will follow.

You can also zoom in and out using the Navigator palette. Find the slider that shows a small mountain on the left and a large one on the right. Drag this slider to change the magnification. The amount of magnification will appear in the Percent field.

Arranging Windows

You are not limited to opening just a single image in Photoshop. Sometimes you'll want to have multiple image windows open at the same time—for example, you could be combining images by dragging and dropping or comparing images side by side. Or perhaps you are working on multiple projects at the same time. Whatever the reason, a few tools can help keep you from being overwhelmed by all these windows.

FIGURE 1-19 Cascaded
windows

Cascade

Most of the commands to help you organize windows will be found by choosing Window | Arrange. If you choose Window | Arrange | Cascade, all the open windows will be stacked on top of each other at the current magnification, as shown in Figure 1-19.

Tile

If you choose Window | Arrange | Tile, all the open windows will be tiled on the workspace, as shown in Figure 1-20. This is a good option if you want to see all the open images at once.

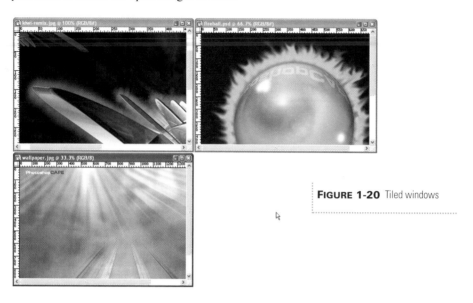

FIGURE 1-20 Tiled windows

Match Zoom

If you choose Window | Arrange | Match Zoom, the magnification of all the open windows will be changed to match the currently selected window. This is a quick way to view all the images at any chosen size. Figure 1-21 shows all the images at 100 percent size.

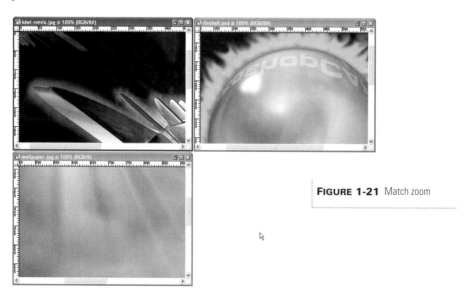

FIGURE 1-21 Match zoom

FIGURE 1-22 Working with multiple windows

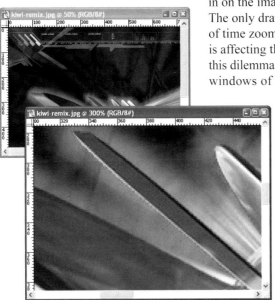

Different Zooms

When you are retouching images, it's a good practice to zoom in on the image so that you can work with precision. The only drawback with this is that you can spend a lot of time zooming out again to see how your retouching is affecting the rest of the image. There is a solution to this dilemma. Photoshop will allow you to open multiple windows of the same image and set each of these at a different magnification. Because the windows all show the same image, you will see a real-time preview as you work. It's common, for example, to open a copy at 100 percent and use it as a reference, while working on an image zoomed up to a maximum of 1600 percent. Figure 1-22 shows working on a zoomed copy of a window.

To open a new working window, choose Window | Arrange | New Window For (the name of your document will appear here).

To snap the new windows to the current working area, as shown in Figure 1-23, choose Window | Arrange | Match Location.

FIGURE 1-23 Match Location

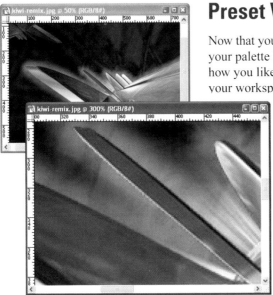

Preset Workspaces

Now that you have gone to all this trouble to customize your palette locations and set up your workspace exactly how you like it, wouldn't it be great to be able to save your workspace and recall it at any time? You can, with the Workspace commands.

To save your settings:

1. Choose Window | Workspace | Save Workspace.

2. A pop-up naming field will open. Type in a name for your workspace.

3. Click OK.

Whenever you want to recall the settings, choose Window | Workspace and choose from a list of named workspaces. This is really helpful if you are using Photoshop for various tasks; you can set up a custom workspace for each task with only the necessary palettes open for each one. Switching between setups is fast.

To remove any of the saved workspaces from the list, choose Window | Workspace | Delete Workspace.

To go back to the original factory settings, choose Window | Workspace | Reset Palette Locations.

Custom Shortcuts and Workspace

Keyboard shortcuts are handy when you're working in Photoshop. You can save time by pressing a keyboard combination instead of working from menus and palettes. Another great thing about shortcuts is that you don't have to wait for the screen to redraw before pressing the next shortcut key. You can press a combination of shortcuts and Photoshop will zip through the tasks.

Creating a New Shortcut

You can assign custom shortcuts using the Keyboard Shortcuts dialog box shown in Figure 1-24. To open the Keyboard Shortcuts and Menus dialog box, choose Edit | Keyboard Shortcuts.

 Even this dialog box has a keyboard shortcut! Press CTRL-ALT-SHIFT-K (CMD-OPTION-SHIFT-K on the Mac).

FIGURE 1-24 Keyboard Shortcuts and Menus dialog box

If you find yourself performing a particular task a lot in Photoshop, first check the list of shortcuts to see whether a current shortcut is already assigned to the task. If not, you can create your own shortcut using this method:

1. Open the Keyboard Shortcuts and Menus dialog box.

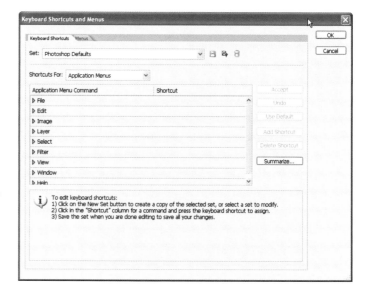

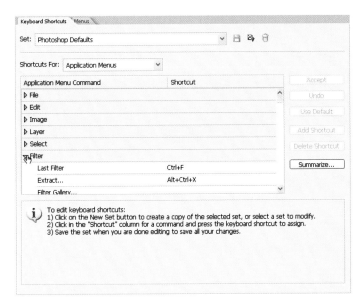

2. Choose the category of shortcut from the Shortcuts For drop-down list.

3. Drill down the list of commands until you find the one you want.

4. Open the chosen group, as shown in Figure 1-25.

5. Click the command you are looking for.

6. Click the Shortcut field, as shown in Figure 1-26.

FIGURE 1-25 Finding the command

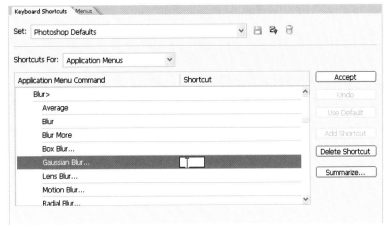

FIGURE 1-26 New Shortcut field

7. Type in the shortcut on your keyboard. You must include the CTRL key (CMD on the Mac) in the combination.

  ▪ If the shortcut is already in use, a warning will appear, as shown in Figure 1-27A. You can try using different keys (recommended) or overwrite the existing shortcut.

■ If the shortcut is not yet in use, it will display without a warning, as shown in Figure 1-27B.

A.

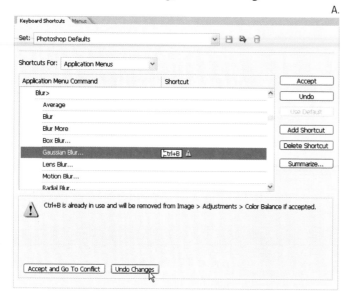

FIGURE 1-27 Choosing shortcuts
(A) An error reports a conflict
(B) The shortcut is assigned

B.

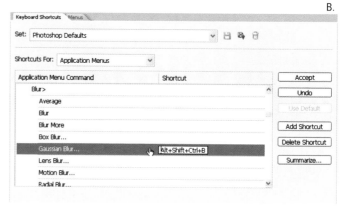

8. Click Accept.

9. Use the shortcut whenever you like.

Three categories of shortcuts can be assigned, as shown in Figure 1-28:

■ **Application Menus**   The menus at the top of the workspace window

■ **Palette Menus**   The menus in the palettes

■ **Tools**   Shortcuts for the tools

FIGURE 1-28 Shortcuts
(application menus already shown)
(A) Palette menus
(B) Tools

A.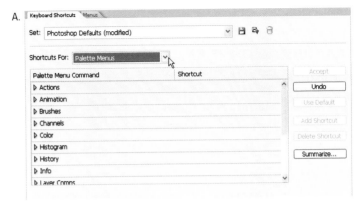

B.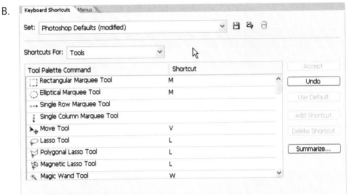

Custom Menus

Menus can also be customized in Photoshop. Colors can be
applied to menu commands and any menu item can be hidden.
This functionality is useful for educators wanting to remove
all the confusion from the menus. Think of it as putting the
students on training wheels. This can also be used in a studio
where color coding items for certain tasks can speed up production.

1. Choose the Menus tab from the Keyboard Shortcuts
   and Menus window, or choose Edit | Menus from the
   application menus.To hide any menu items, click the
   eye icon to toggle it on or off, as shown in Figure 1-29.

2. To color code menu items, click the word None.

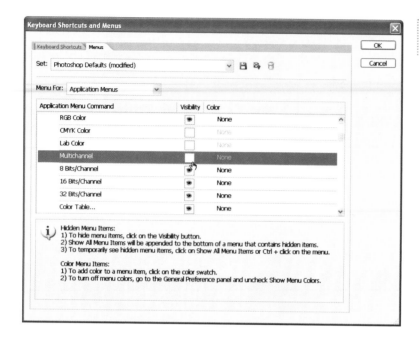

FIGURE 1-29 Hiding menu items

3. Choose a color from the drop-down menu, as shown in Figure 1-30.

FIGURE 1-30 Color coding a menu item

4. Click OK to apply the color.

FIGURE 1-31 The menu with color coding and hidden items

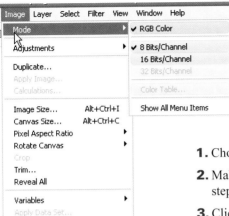

Figure 1-31 shows the menu with the color coding and all the color modes hidden. To show the menu items, click Show All Menu Items. The items will be visible until the menu is closed.

Saving and Loading Menu Sets

To make the menu features really useful, you can load or save menu sets. Educators can now build custom menu sets for each lesson and have the students load them up at anytime. To make a set:

1. Choose Edit | Menus from the application menus.

2. Make your color changes as described in the previous steps.

3. Click the Create A New Set button, as shown in Figure 1-32A.

4. Choose a location for the new set (Program Files\Adobe\ Adobe Photoshop CS2\Presets\Menu Customization by default on Windows, or Applications\Adobe\Adobe Photoshop CS2\Presets\Menu Customization by default on the Mac).

5. Name the file and click Save, as shown in Figure 1-32B.

A.

B.

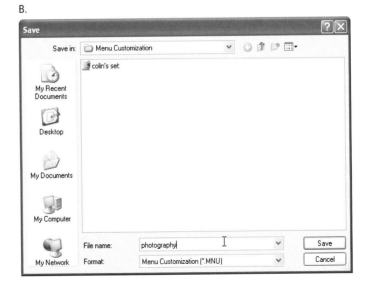

FIGURE 1-32 Saving a custom menu set
(A) Creating a custom menu set
(B) Naming the new set and saving it

To load the set, click the Set drop-down menu in the Keyboard Shortcuts and Menus window and you will see your saved sets (as long as they are in the Menu Customization folder). Click the set to load it, as shown in Figure 1-33.

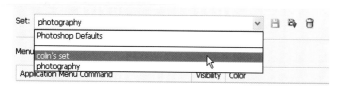

FIGURE 1-33 Loading a custom menu set

To share custom menu sets, they must be copied into the Adobe Photoshop CS2\Presets\Menu Customization folder (on both PC and Mac). You can also copy your sets from the same folder for distribution.

 The same process works for creating custom keyboard shortcuts.

Printing Shortcuts

In the Keyboard Shortcuts and Menus window, you will see a button called Summarize. Click this button to produce a current list of all the shortcuts assigned in Photoshop:

1. Click the Summarize button.

2. Choose a location to which you want to save the list of shortcuts.

3. An HTML document will be generated.

4. To print the list, choose Print from your browser commands.

Preset Manager

As you read this book, you will learn that many of the Photoshop tools have *libraries* attached to them. When Photoshop is loading, a line of text tells you what is loading up. The libraries will need to load before Photoshop is ready for use.

To minimize load time, it's a good idea to keep all the loaded libraries to a minimum. As you progress through the chapters, you'll find tips for loading and saving items from the libraries. All the libraries can be managed from one place, called the Preset Manager, which is accessed from the Edit menu. The Preset Manager is shown in Figure 1-34.

Here is where you'll find more information about each library:

FIGURE 1-34 Preset Manager

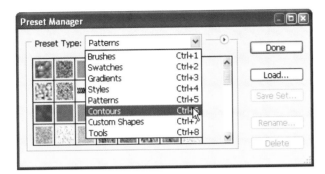

- **Brushes** Chapter 3
- **Swatches** Chapter 3
- **Gradients** Chapter 3
- **Styles** Chapter 11
- **Patterns** Chapter 3
- **Contours** Chapter 11
- **Custom Shapes** Chapter 7
- **Tools** Chapter 9

Preferences

In the Preferences dialog box, you can choose how Photoshop will operate; the default settings are for the average computer, but you'll find it helpful to be able to customize Photoshop for your needs. You may want to make some tweaks if you have a slower or more powerful than average machine.

Rather than discuss each preference, I will focus on those that you should be aware of. I'll make suggestions for changing certain settings.

 If you want a complete rundown of each and every setting, refer to the online help that comes with Photoshop.

To launch the Preferences dialog box, choose Edit | Preferences. You'll see a list of nine categories, beginning with General. Choose any of the categories and then cycle through them all by clicking the Prev and Next buttons.

General

- **History States** This is your "undo memory." If you have a lot of RAM and a fast processor, consider increasing the History States. If you use a slower machine or never use the history options, reduce the History States to 10 or 15 to free up some resources.

You can always use the Edit | Purge command to get back some resources, too.

- **Interpolation** Bicubic is a good multipurpose setting. This setting will be used whenever you are scaling images. If you are reducing images in size, choose Bicubic Sharper; if you are increasing the size of images, choose Bicubic Softer.

- **Export Clipboard** Consider turning off this option unless you are going to paste your images into another program once you close Photoshop.

- **History Log** Turn on this option only if you want to log all your Photoshop use. Otherwise, it will just slow things down for nothing.

File Handling

- **Image Previews** If you are working on the Web only, turn off this option; it will reduce the file size of your images ever so slightly.

- **Enable Large Document Format** Turn on this option if you are working with images larger than 4GB.

- **Recent File List** It's a good idea to increase the Recent File List Contains: (x) files list to 25.

- **Maximize PSD File Compatibility** This saves a composite image (flattened copy) with the layers. This option will increase the file size but allows you to open the images in previous versions of Photoshop and also some other graphics editing programs. Ask is a good option because you will want to allow compatibility only with images that need extra flexibility.

Display and Cursors

The default setting will work well for most cases. You don't need to turn on Precise Cursors because if you press the CAPS LOCK key, the Precise Cursors will be toggled on and off. The Precise Cursors work with the drawing tools and allow for pinpoint accuracy, but they are not always the best option because you cannot see the brush sizes with this option turned on.

- **Normal Tip** Shows the size of the painting area
- **Full Size Tip** Shows the full size of the brush including the feathered area

- **Show Crosshairs in Brush**   Defines the center of the brush with a crosshair

Transparency and Gamut

No changes are needed for transparency unless you prefer to change the indicator for transparency.

The gamut warning tells you an image cannot be printed with the chosen color. Gray is a good color because the "out of gamut" warning will usually appear in bright portions of the image. These can be seen in dialog boxes such as the Variations dialog box.

Units and Rulers

This was covered earlier in the "Rulers, Guides, and Grids" section of this chapter.

Guides, Grids, and Slices

You can change the appearance of your grids and guides. You can also change the appearance of slices. Slices are covered in Chapter 13. No changes are recommended to these options.

Plug-Ins and Scratch Disk

- **Plug-ins**   Specify a location for additional plug-in filters. Choose this option if you are using filters from a previous version of Photoshop. You can enter the serial number in the Legacy field to help you get around serial number verification problems.

- **Scratch Disk**   A scratch disk is your hard drive. When Photoshop runs out of physical RAM, it copies information to the hard drive and processes the images on the drive. You can use up to four drives. If you can afford a separate hard drive or partition a large portion of your main drive to be used as a scratch disk, this will help speed up Photoshop. Generally, Photoshop will need ten times the image size to process a number of tasks.

Memory and Image Cache

- **Cache For Histogram Levels**   If you turn on this option, the histograms will not be accurate in the Levels dialog box. The "Cache" is on by default in the Histogram palette.

- **Memory Usage**   This assigns how much memory is available for Photoshop. If you have a decent amount of RAM (more than 1GB) or you don't use other programs much while Photoshop is running, turn it up to around 75 percent or more.

Type

■ Sets the options for type and the WYSIWYG (What You See Is What You Get) Type menu. The only preference that you may want to change is the font preview size. Uncheck this option to turn off the samples to the right of the font names if this option slows down the menu. Font previews can be set to display in small, medium, or large sizes.

Common Color Modes

A color mode determines the way that Photoshop will process an image. Each color mode has a different color channel configuration. (Channels are covered in Chapter 6.) You can choose different color modes for different tasks. The official name is a *color space*. You can change the color mode by choosing Image | Mode.

■ **Grayscale**   This has only one channel and has a maximum of 256 shades of gray (65,536 in 16-bit mode). No color information appears while in Grayscale. Use this mode for printing black-and-white and duotone images.

■ **RGB (Red, Green, and Blue)**   These are the primary colors used on a monitor, and this is the color space to be used for online and multimedia work. This is also the best working mode for most color images.

■ **CMYK (Cyan, Magenta, Yellow, and Black)**   This is the best color mode for offset printing (commercial printing press). If you are not printing on a commercial press, don't use this mode.

■ **LAB (Luminosity A and B channels)**   This mode puts all the grayscale information on the L channel and splits the colors onto the A and B channels. This is an excellent mode for performing image correction.

Common File Types

Whenever you open or save a file, you are dealing with some kind of file format. When you are saving a file, you will have to choose the best file format for your image. This list will help you decide what to choose.

- **TIFF (Tagged Image File Format)**   This is the most common file format for printing and saving a flattened image without any loss of quality. Photoshop TIFFs support layers and channels.

- **LZW Compression**   Choose this format to compress the TIFF file. It will reduce the file size but will take longer to open and close as well as offer potential compatibility problems with some other programs.

- **EPS (Encapsulated PostScript)**   This is the language designed by Adobe for print. Use this file format if you want to include a clipping path on your image or you are printing to a PostScript printer.

- **PSD (Photoshop Document)**   This is the native working format for Photoshop. Use this for all your working files; it will save all the layers, channels, notes, and color profiles. You can also use this format for printing through Adobe InDesign. (Be sure to convert to CMYK mode for commercial printing.)

- **PSB (Photoshop Large Format)**   Use this format to save an image up to 300,000 pixels. Use this option for images larger than 4GB. This is the default format for Smart Objects.

- **GIF (Graphics Interchange Format)**   This was invented by CompuServe for saving images for the Web; it's limited to 256 colors. This is the best format for images that have repeating patterns or that are cartoon-like. It also supports transparency and animation. GIFs compress images by throwing away colors and repeating simple patterns—this is known as a *lossy* format. (See Chapter 13 for more on the lossy format.)

- **JPG (Joint Photographic Experts Group)**   This is the most popular format for images on the Web. This format reduces the quality of the image (often undetectable to the human eye). This lossy compression can greatly reduce the file size of an image.

■ **PNG (Portable Network Graphics)** Lossless format for the Web that support up to 16 million colors and 256 levels of transparency. This was supposed to be the "miracle" file format, but it hasn't taken off yet because the file sizes are larger than JPG or GIF and older browsers do not support it. (See Chapter 13 for more on the lossless format.)

Status Bar

Along the bottom of the main Photoshop window, you will see a status bar containing useful information. For example, whenever you choose a tool, its description is displayed in the center of the status bar.

The bulk of the information appears on the left side of the bar. At the bottom left is the image magnification. If you type figures here, Photoshop will change the magnification of the image to match. Figure 1-35 shows the status bar at the default settings.

If you click over the document information on the status bar, as shown in Figure 1-36, you will see a print preview that shows how large your image is compared to the default page size of your printer— usually 8.5×11 inches in the United States and A4 in other countries.

If you hold down the ALT key (OPTION on the Mac) and click in the left side of the status bar, you will see the current document information, such as image dimensions, color space, and resolution, as shown in Figure 1-37.

FIGURE 1-35 Status bar

FIGURE 1-36 Print preview

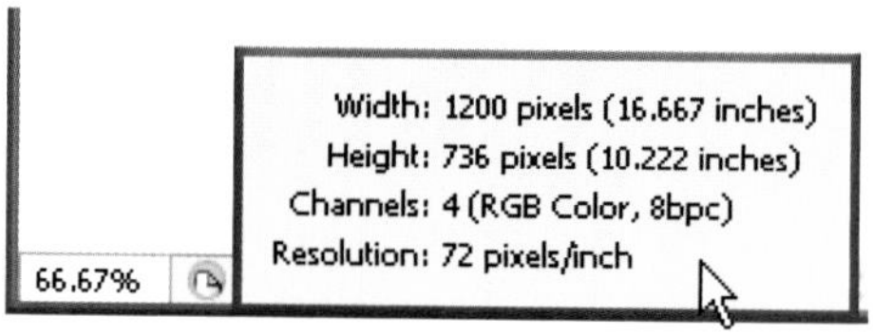

FIGURE 1-37 Image information

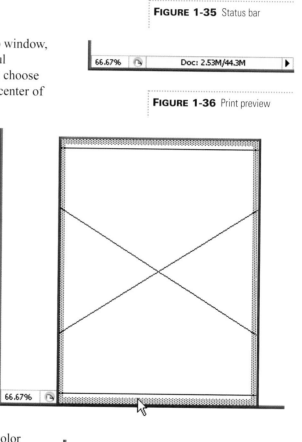

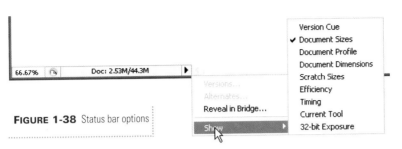

| Version Cue |
| ✔ Document Sizes |
| Document Profile |
| Document Dimensions |
| Scratch Sizes |
| Efficiency |
| Timing |
| Current Tool |
| 32-bit Exposure |

66.67%   Doc: 2.53M/44.3M   ▶

Versions...
Alternates...
Reveal in Bridge...
Show ▶

FIGURE 1-38 Status bar options

Click the arrow and you will see a list of options that control the information that the status bar will display. Figure 1-38 shows the options.

Changing Views

Photoshop has three modes for viewing and working on images:

- **Standard View**   This is the default view, as shown in Figure 1-39A.

- **Full Screen With Menu Bar**   Hides all the window "chrome." All the borders and title bars will be hidden, as shown in Figure 1-39B.

- **Full Screen**   Hides the menu and turns the workspace black, as shown in Figure 1-39C. This is the Presentation mode. Notice that the menu is now available from the top of the toolbox.

FIGURE 1-39 Toggling through the view modes
(A) Standard view
(B) Full screen with menu bar
(C) Full screen

A.

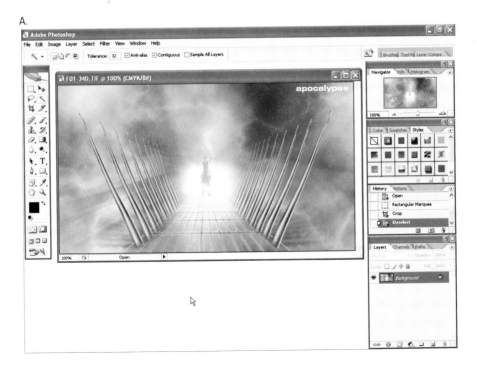

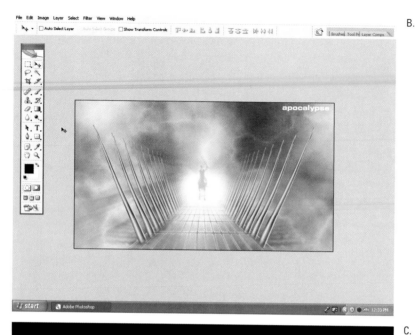

B.

C.

To change the modes, click the View buttons on the bottom of the toolbox, or just press the F key. Each time you press the F key, the view will cycle through the modes. For the ultimate in viewing pleasure, press the TAB key while in Full Screen mode. The TAB key toggles the palettes on and off. You can have a full screen with nothing but your image showing, as shown in Figure 1-39 (turn off rulers for the best effect).

Chapter 2

Documents, Organization, and Resolution

How to...

- Create a new document
- Use preset document sizes
- Open images
- Import PDF images
- Place images
- Scan images
- Use Adobe Bridge
- Rotate and organize images
- Change thumbnail sizes
- Open multiple files at once
- Understand image resolution
- Calculate the output resolution
- Choose different interpolation methods
- Change the size of a picture

We are used to the word *document* when it is used in a text or office setting. A document is also the name given to a Photoshop image. You can bring images into Photoshop in many ways. Documents can be created in Photoshop or in other programs, or images can be brought into Photoshop from a scanner, digital camera, or by opening existing image documents.

In this chapter, we look at the basic Photoshop document.

Creating a New Document

Whenever you open a new document in Photoshop, all the grayed-out options come to life, and you have the opportunity to play around a bit and find your bearings. The best place to start is to create a new document.

1. Choose File | New, and you will see the New dialog box shown in Figure 2-1. Here, you can set up several options for the new document, as shown in the list that follows.

- **Name**   Type in a name for your document.
- **Preset**   Choose an option from the drop-down list of preset document sizes for different types of uses (more on presets in the next section).
- **Width and Height**   You can choose from various measurement units—points, centimeters, and inches.

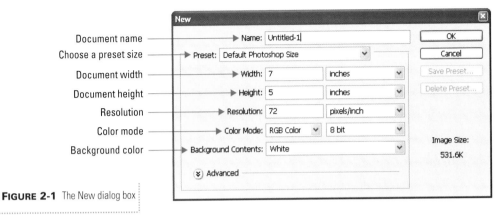

Document name
Choose a preset size
Document width
Document height
Resolution
Color mode
Background color

FIGURE 2-1 The New dialog box

■ **Resolution**   Choose the desired resolution. Typically, 72 pixels/inch (ppi) is fine for online presentation and 300ppi is used for print. (See the section "Understanding Image Resolution" later in this chapter for more information on resolution.)

■ **Color Mode**   Typically, RGB will be the best choice for color images, and Grayscale is fine for noncolor images. Use CMYK for images going to a commercial printing press.

■ **Bit Depth**   By default, images will be 8 bit, but Photoshop also supports 16 and 32 bit images (see Chapter 12).

■ **Background Contents**   Choose a background color or a transparent background.

2. When you're satisfied with your settings, click OK.

 If you are designing for video, click the Advanced button in the New dialog box. In the dialog box that opens, choose a new pixel aspect ratio, because video uses rectangular pixels as opposed to the square pixels used for most graphic uses.

Creating Custom Preset Document Sizes

You may find that you use the same document specifications on a repeated basis. For example, you may want to create a custom preset if you often need to create documents using a particular size and resolution, such as documents used for a PowerPoint presentation or a web page. To save time, you can save the settings as a document preset. Here's how it's done:

1. Choose File | New.

2. In the New dialog box, choose Custom from the Preset drop-down list and enter your custom settings.

3. Click Save Preset.

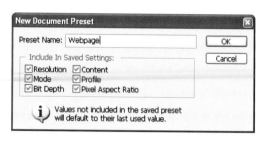

4. In the New Document Preset dialog box, shown in Figure 2-2, type in a name for your document preset.

5. In the Include In Saved Settings area, click to select all the boxes to keep all the settings you set earlier. (These boxes relate to the features explained in Figure 2-1.)

FIGURE 2-2 Saving a preset

6. Click OK.

Your settings are now saved.

Using Presets

In the future, if you want to use the preset, click the Preset field from the new document palette. The list of available presets will display, as shown in Figure 2-3, where you can see that our preset now appears in the list. Select the desired preset and the new document will be created to meet the preset specifications. A number of presets ship with Photoshop, and these can be used to create all kinds of things, from web banners, to 4×6 photos, to letter-sized pages.

FIGURE 2-3 Choosing the custom preset

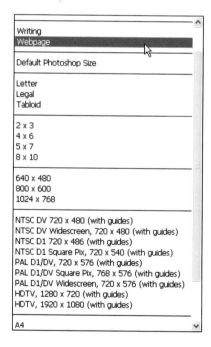

Opening Documents

You can also open an existing document in Photoshop.

1. Choose File | Open. You will see the Open dialog box, shown in Figure 2-4.

2. By default, all file types appear, but if you want to limit the display to one type, choose it from the Files Of Type (Format on the Mac) drop-down list.

A.

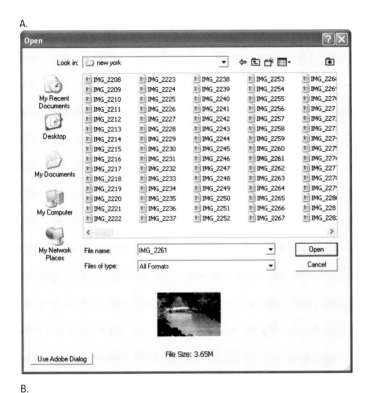

B.

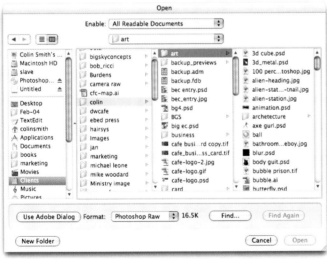

3. Locate your document and select it. You will see a small preview of the image.

4. Click Open.

Using the Adobe Dialog

With the advent of Creative Suite, Adobe has been creating ways for all the Adobe products to work together more closely, such as with Version Cue and Bridge. If you click the Use Adobe Dialog button in the bottom left of the Open dialog box, you will see a different way of browsing for files, as shown in Figure 2-5. This view offers advantages over the operating-system controlled dialog box:

- Different views are available.

- You can see larger thumbnails.

- Version Cue documents can be managed.

- Different file types are available for preview.

FIGURE 2-4 The Open dialog box in Windows (A) and on the Mac (B)

A.

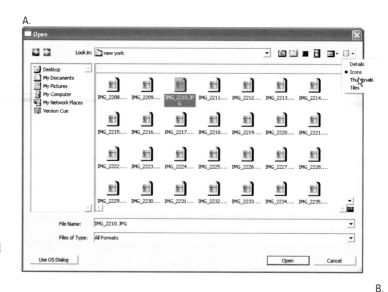

To return to the regular view, click Use OS Dialog.

Working with Images

You can import images into Photoshop—even those created from other applications. Photoshop has a robust set of import filters and can open images created from a variety of sources.

Importing PDF Images

PDF (Portable Document Format) is a growing technology that is fast becoming the standard for e-paper. You can open images from within a PDF document in Photoshop, even if it is a multiple-page document.

1. Choose File | Open.

2. Navigate to the PDF image and click OK.

3. You will see a PDF Image Import dialog box like that shown in Figure 2-6. Choose the page that you want to import by clicking its thumbnail.

4. To open the entire page as an image, click OK; to extract an image, continue with step 5.

B.

FIGURE 2-5 Adobe dialog (A) In Windows, showing the change view menu (B) On the Mac

FIGURE 2-6 Import PDF dialog box

5. Click the Select drop-down box and change it from Page to Image, as shown in Figure 2-7. You can now choose an image from the page.

6. Click OK, and the image will open in Photoshop.

You can use this process to import either a single image or a group of images from a PDF document. You can get some pretty good quality images by importing them from PDF, as shown in Figure 2-8.

FIGURE 2-7 Choosing an image to import

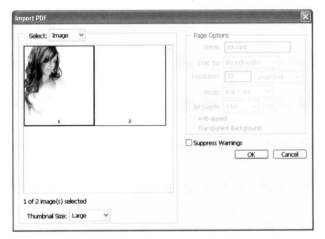

FIGURE 2-8 Image imported from a PDF document

Placing an Image

When images are created solely in programs such as Adobe Illustrator, Macromedia Freehand, or CorelDRAW, they can be placed into a Photoshop document and still retain their sharpness. That is because these types of images are made of *vectors*. (Chapter 7 explains vectors in depth.) These types of images typically use the filename extension *.ai* (native to Illustrator) or *.eps* (Encapsulated PostScript). We use a process called *placing* to transfer images to Photoshop from another program.

When we place an image, it will be shown as a *proxy image* (a low-resolution representation of the final image). A box appears around the image with eight little squares on the corners and edges; these squares are called *handles*. You can drag these handles to enlarge or reduce the image. Once you press the ENTER key, the image will be placed as a *Smart Object*. (See Chapter 5 to learn how to work with Smart Objects.)

Here is how you place an image in Photoshop:

1. Create a blank document at the size you want the final image to be.

2. Choose File | Place.

3. Choose the image you want to place.

4. The image and a bounding box will appear, as shown in Figure 2-9. Make size and position adjustments by dragging the handles. Hold down the SHIFT key to constrain image ratio to original proportions.

5. Click OK to place the Smart Object, as shown in Figure 2-10. To turn the Smart Object into a regular layer, choose Layer | Rasterize | Smart Object. (Chapter 7 explains in depth about rasterizing images.)

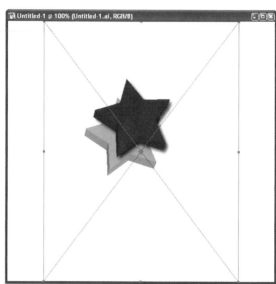

FIGURE 2-9 Placing an image into a Photoshop document

FIGURE 2-10 Resized image

Scanning Images

Because each scanner has its own particular settings and user interface, the explanation in this section will be a bit general and will mainly deal with the Photoshop end of scanning. Before you scan, read the documentation that came with your scanner. You will also have to install the software that comes with the scanner before you can use it. If you have installed Photoshop after installing the scanner, you may need to reinstall your scanner software before it will work with Photoshop.

After installation, your scanner software may have installed a plug-in called Twain. This Twain driver is what allows Photoshop to communicate with many scanners.

To scan an image into Photoshop:

1. Choose File | Import | Twain (or your scanner software name).

2. The scanner's software will open. Make the adjustments according to your scanner's documentation.

3. Click Scan. Your scanner will now scan the image and transfer it to Photoshop.

Scanning Tips

Here are a few tips that should help you achieve better scans:

- Keep the scanner's glass plate clean at all times.
- Scan the images larger than you think you may need. (Enlarging images later will cause loss of quality.)
- Make as many tonal adjustments on the scanner's software as you can before scanning.
- If you are scanning from a magazine or printed page, choose the scanner descreen options or you will see moiré patterns in the scanned image.

Caution   *Moiré patterns are patterns of dots that will appear if you scan an image from a magazine or printed page without using the descreen option on your scanner. If your scanner doesn't support descreen, try scanning the image on an angle to reduce the effects.*

Using Adobe Bridge

Adobe Bridge has replaced the File Browser. This application is more powerful than the File Browser and is the home base where all the Adobe Creative Suite programs work together. Bridge is the place where you browse and organize all the digital assets on your computer, including the images that you will open into Photoshop. It's so useful that I open almost all my files in Bridge.

You can launch Bridge in several ways:

- Choose File | Browse.
- Press CTRL-SHIFT-O (CMD-SHIFT-O on the Mac).
- Click the icon located to the right of the options bar.

Bridge has four main windows, as shown in Figure 2-11.

- **Navigation window**   Navigate to all your disk drives and folders.
- **Preview**   Use this adjustable window to show the currently selected file. To adjust the view, click and drag the windows to the sizes and locations that you want.
- **Image information**   View all the information about the selected image.
- **Image thumbnails**   View the images and their filenames in the current directory.

FIGURE 2-11 Adobe Bridge interface, Thumbnails view

Changing Views

Bridge offers four default views, each designed to help you perform certain tasks more quickly:

2

■ **Thumbnails view (default)**   Provides an overview and allows you to perform most tasks. Main emphasis is given to displaying thumbnails of the images in the chosen folder. Figure 2-11 shows the Thumbnails view.

FIGURE 2-12 Bridge in Filmstrip view (A) and in Details view (B)

■ **Filmstrip view** Shows a strip of thumbnails and displays the selected thumbnail in all its large glory, or not so glorious when the details are revealed in a larger preview. You can click the Previous and Next buttons at the bottom-right of the Preview window to view a slide show, as shown in Figure 2-12A. To change the orientation of the thumbnails from horizontal to vertical, click the Switch Filmstrip Orientation button at the bottom-right of the Preview window.

■ **Details view** Shows the thumbnails in a single column with relevant image information next to each thumbnail, as shown in Figure 2-12B.

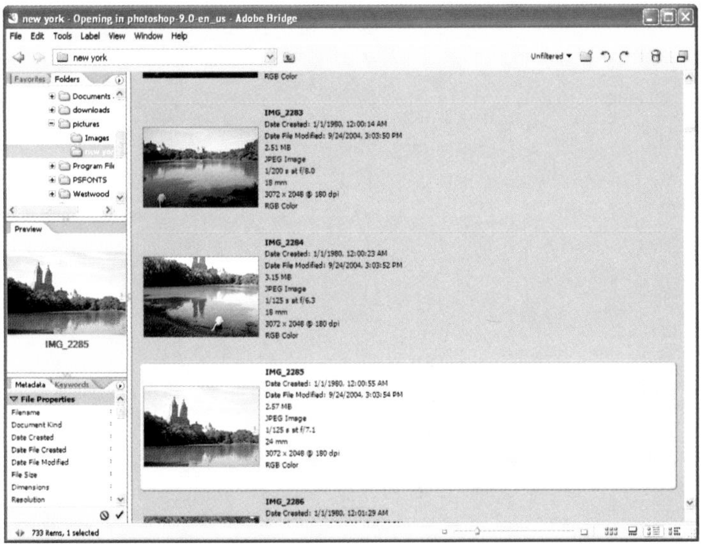

■ **Versions and Alternatives view** Similar to Details view, except it displays different file versions next to each other.

Here's how to open a file in Bridge:

1. Launch Bridge.

2. Navigate to your image directory.

3. Double-click the thumbnail of the image you want to open. (You can also right-click the thumbnail and choose which application you want to use to open the image.)

 To organize the thumbnails, simply click and drag the thumbnails to new locations.

Rotating and Organizing Images

Bridge is more than just a means of opening images. You can organize and rotate your thumbnails there, too. When you take a picture with your camera turned sideways, you will need to rotate the image in Photoshop so that it displays in the correct orientation.

To rotate a thumbnail:

1. Click the thumbnail you want to rotate. To select more than one image, CTRL-click (CMD-click on the Mac) each image.

2. Click either the rotate clockwise or rotate counterclockwise icon, the rounded arrows at the top right of the window.

The source image will not be altered, but every time you view the image in Bridge, it will appear rotated. When you open the image in Photoshop, it will open in the same orientation in which it appears Bridge.

Changing the Thumbnail Sizes

You can change the size of the thumbnails in Bridge by dragging the slider at the bottom of the palette. As you drag, the size of the thumbnails will update in real time. Drag the slider to the left for a smaller view and to the right for a larger view. You'll see two buttons, one on the left and one on the right of the slider. Click the left button to display the smallest possible thumbnails, shown in Figure 2-13A. Click the right button for the largest view, as shown in Figure 2-13B.

FIGURE 2-13
The thumbnails in smallest view (A) and in largest view (B)

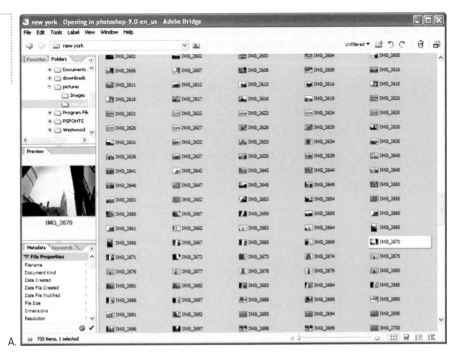

A.

B.

Tip *When you choose small thumbnail view, as shown in Figure 2-13A, all the images are displayed in a column with a tiny thumbnail and the filename next to it. This is a good option to use when you are organizing and renaming groups of pictures.*

Note *To change the name of an image, click its name to highlight it. Then type in a new name.*

Rating Images

I call this the "Siskel and Ebert feature." You can now rate your images by assigning them one to five stars. If you're like me and take hundreds of pictures of everything, this is a useful way to sort through all the confusion. By ranking images, it's easy to weed out all the bad shots and irrelevant images. Ranking doesn't necessarily mean that you rank by quality of images. Creativity is allowed—perhaps you prefer to rank in accordance of relevance of subject or how prominent something is in the photo.

Assigning a Rating

It's easy to assign rankings to an image. It can be fun, too—perhaps you can have a ranking party, where all your friends gather around the computer.

To rank images:

1. Open Bridge and choose an image.

2. Hover your mouse beneath the image. You should see five dots.

3. Click any dot to assign a ranking, as shown in Figure 2-14, where we have just assigned four stars to the image.

FIGURE 2-14 Ranking an image

You can alternatively label an image with a color. (This works like ranking, but without the potential hurt feelings.) Right-click the thumbnail, and choose Label | Assign A Color.

Displaying by Rating and Label

What good is all this ranking stuff? The good news is that you can use it to make Bridge hide certain images and display only certain rankings.

Click the Filtered drop-down box and choose one of the following options, as shown in Figure 2-15:

- **Show All Items**   Ignores all rankings and labels

- **Show Unrated Items Only**   Useful for revealing all the bad images, ready for deletion, if you wish

- **Show *X* Stars**   Filters out how many images are displayed by showing images rated according to your selection

- **Show Labeled Items, Unlabeled Items, *X* Label**   Shows items according to how you've labeled them

FIGURE 2-15 Choosing the filtering options

Automating Options

Choose Tools | Photoshop, and you'll see the various automation options available from within Bridge. You can use these options to apply automatic image processing to folders or images from within Bridge. For a complete rundown of features and instructions, see Chapter 9.

Opening Multiple Files at Once

You can open multiple images at once from Bridge:

1. Launch Bridge.

2. Select the first thumbnail by clicking it.

3. To select a group of contiguous thumbnails, hold down the SHIFT key and click the last thumbnail in the group. For nonadjacent thumbnails, CTRL-click each thumbnail (CMD-click on the Mac). The selected thumbnails are highlighted.

4. Double-click any selected thumbnail to open all the selected images, or press CTRL-O (CMD-O on Mac). The images will open in Photoshop.

FIGURE 2-16 A customized setup

Using Workspaces

Much of Bridge can be customized to suit your tastes or current task. Various views and windows can be dragged around and resized. Even the tabs on the left can be dragged to different windows. Figure 2-16 shows a customized view of Bridge.

It would be a nuisance to set up Bridge, change views, and then have to drag everything back where you want it.

We don't have to do that, because we can save workspaces. A saved workspace remembers the size and position of everything in Bridge.

Here's how to save a workspace:

FIGURE 2-17 Saving a workspace (A) and accessing a workspace (B)

A.

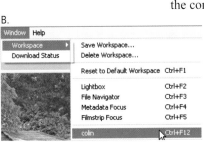

1. Choose Window | Workspace | Save Workspace.

2. In the Save Workspace dialog box, shown in Figure 2-17A, you can assign a keyboard shortcut to the Workspace if you want. Choose a keyboard shortcut key from the Ctrl+ drop-down menu.

3. Enter a descriptive name, and click save.

The Workspace is now saved and can be recalled even after the computer has been restarted:

B.

1. Choose Window | Workspace, and your saved workspace will appear in the menu, as shown in Figure 2-17B.

2. Choose your workspace to revert to that view. Notice that four factory presets all appear for you to use: Lightbox, File Navigator, Metadata Focus, and Filmstrip Focus. By clicking each one, you can see how each configuration would help in different tasks.

To reset the factory defaults, choose Workspace | Reset To Default Workspace, or press CTRL-F1 (CMD-F1 on the Mac).

Understanding Image Resolution

Resolution is one of those words that you hear a lot in the computer world. That is because every digital image displayed has a resolution, whether it be on screen or in print. Understanding and using the correct resolution for your images will ensure the sharpest output for every occasion.

Images created in Photoshop are made up of tiny squares called *pixels*, each a single color. With enough of the tiny colored pixels clustered together, the image appears very smooth. If you view your image on a computer screen, it uses pixels to display the image.

Figure 2-18 shows an image zoomed to 1600 percent, to show the actual pixels that make up the image. Notice that each pixel is uniform in size and shape, and each contains a single color.

FIGURE 2-18 Image zoomed in to see pixels

Image courtesy of Ablestock.com

Resolution refers to how many pixels are present in an image. A typical 17-inch monitor displays pixels at a resolution of 1024×768. To figure out how many pixels are present on the monitor at 1024×768 resolution, you would multiply 1024×768, which comes to 786,432 pixels on your screen. We measure resolution by how many pixels fit into each inch. This is known as *ppi* (pixels per inch). A typical computer monitor displays pixels at 72ppi.

Calculating the Output Resolution

To determine the size of an image in inches, we divide the pixels by the ppi. Here are the sizes of an image 1024 pixels wide at different resolutions:

- **72ppi**   1024 / 72 = 14.2 inches
- **150ppi**   1024 / 150 = 6.9 inches
- **300ppi**   1024 / 300 = 3.4 inches

FIGURE 2-19 Images displayed at different resolutions; from top, 300ppi, 150ppi, and 72ppi

Figure 2-19 illustrates the same image displayed at three different resolutions. Notice that the images appear smaller at higher resolutions. This is because the pixels are packed in much tighter (that is, a higher count of pixels are needed to fill the same space).

Another way to look at it would be to take three images and make them a set size at 3 inches wide. To figure out the pixels present in the image, we would multiply the size by the ppi and this would give us the numbers of pixels in an image:

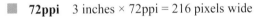

- **72ppi**   3 inches × 72ppi = 216 pixels wide
- **150ppi**   3 × 150 = 450 pixels
- **300ppi**   3 × 300 = 900 pixels

As the image resolution drops, so does the output quality of the image. If the resolution is insufficient for the intended purpose, a problem called *pixelization* occurs. Pixelization occurs when the resolution is so low that the jagged edges of the pixels begin to appear. Figure 2-20 shows an image printed at various resolutions. You can see that the image with the lowest resolution (72ppi) is less sharp than the image at the highest resolution (300ppi).

The more pixels present, the sharper the image will appear. More pixels mean smoother color transitions, more detail, and a sharper output.

The higher the resolution, the larger the file size. At times, you will want to minimize the file size; for instance, an image to be posted on a web page would require the smallest possible file size so that the image loads quicker. Similarly, when you output an image to a printer, a larger file will take a longer time to output and print.

The obvious solution is to use the correct resolution for each task. Here are the most common uses for images and the recommended resolutions:

- ■ **Multimedia**   72ppi
- ■ **Web pages**   72ppi
- ■ **CD-ROM**   72ppi
- ■ **Inkjet printer**   300ppi on high-quality paper
- ■ **Photo printer**   300ppi
- ■ **Commercial printing press** 300ppi (or double the target linescreen)

FIGURE 2-20 Images at 100 percent size; from top, 300ppi, 150ppi, and 72ppi

Resizing

When you enlarge an image in Photoshop, you will lose quality, because less pixels create less detailed images. You can get away with a little bit of enlargement, but it will begin to show pretty quickly. With print resolution it is not so noticeable, but for images used for the web at 72ppi, I would not suggest you use any enlargement at all. You can, however, safely reduce the size of images without losing much, if any, quality.

Interpolation Methods

When you enlarge or reduce an image's size, it's called *resampling*. When the image's dimensions are changed, pixels have to be added or subtracted from the image. When these pixels are altered, Photoshop calculates how the new pixels should look based on the existing pixels. This process is called *image interpolation*. Five interpolation methods are available in Photoshop. When you check the

resample option, as we did in Figure 2-21 in the Image Size dialog box, you will see the following options:

- ■ **Nearest Neighbor**   The quickest method, with the lowest quality

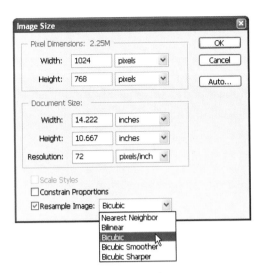

- ■ **Bilinear**   Best for line art
- ■ **Bicubic**   Default mode, high quality and best for most purposes
- ■ **Bicubic Smoother**   Best when you are increasing the size of an image
- ■ **Bicubic Sharper**   Best when you are reducing the size of an image

FIGURE 2-21 Interpolation options in Photoshop

Changing the Size of a Picture

Here is how you change the size of your pictures:

1. Open an image.
2. Choose Image | Image Size. You will see the Image Size dialog box.
3. Check the Resample Image box.
4. Choose Constrain Proportions to maintain the image's proportions. Or, enter the desired sizes into the image fields. (The other fields will adjust automatically if you choose Constrain Proportions, as shown in Figure 2-22.)
5. Click OK. The image will be changed to the desired size.

Changing Image Resolution

Sometimes you may want to change the resolution only, and not change the image's pixel size:

1. Open the image.
2. Choose Image | Image Size. You'll see the Image Size dialog box.
3. Uncheck the Resample Image box and enter the desired resolution, as shown in Figure 2-23. The Height and Width fields will be automatically adjusted to compensate for the new resolution setting.
4. Click OK.

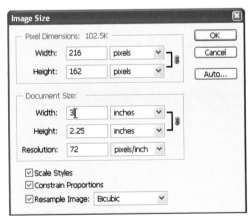

FIGURE 2-22 Changing the image's size

FIGURE 2-23 Changing the resolution of the image

Using the Resize Image Wizard

Another way to resize your images is to use the Resize Image Wizard. This takes care of all the technical resizing issues for you. You just complete a short interview, and based on the answers, Photoshop will make all the decisions for you. Here's how to use the Resize Image Wizard:

FIGURE 2-24 Choose Print or Online in the Resize Image Wizard

1. Open an image.

2. Choose Help | Resize Image. You will see the dialog box shown in Figure 2-24.

3. Choose Print or Online, and then click Next.

4. If you chose Online, enter your pixel dimensions. Then click OK twice. Photoshop

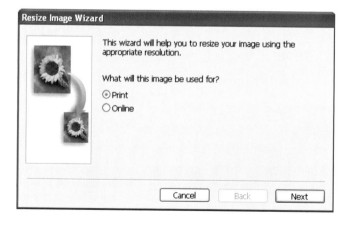

makes a copy of the image for you and leaves the original intact.

If you choose Print in step 3, choose the desired size of the image, and then choose a halftone screen. Hints are displayed in the Description box, as shown in Figure 2-25.

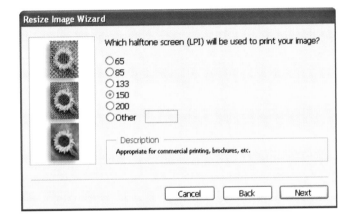

FIGURE 2-25 Choose the halftone screen

5. Choose the image quality, as shown in Figure 2-26. Choose the lowest quality for a draft quality or the highest quality for final print.

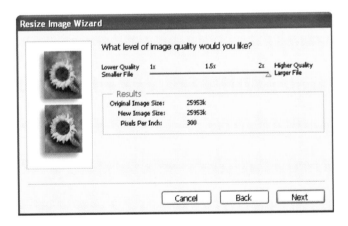

FIGURE 2-26 Choose the quality.

6. Click OK, and you're done.

Chapter 3

Draw, Paint, and Artistry

How to...

- Choose colors and color swatches
- Use the Color Picker
- Use the drawing tools and brushes
- Use the Eraser tool
- Create and modify brushes
- Use the Smudge, Sharpen, and Blur tools
- Use the Dodge, Burn, and Sponge tools
- Apply and create a gradient
- Use the shape tools
- Transform, rotate, and flip
- Use Free Transform
- Warp images
- Use and create patterns
- Use the History palette and History Brush
- Create art with the Art History Brush
- Change the color of objects within a photo

Photoshop includes some powerful drawing tools. Its brushes are packed with features that allow you to touch up photos or even create your own works of art. You can simulate the real world or create fantasy with a host of drawing and painting tools in Photoshop.

Choosing Colors

You can visually choose a color in Photoshop by clicking on a Color Picker; you simply locate the color you want and click it, and it will become your new foreground color. Color Pickers are located in several places in Photoshop, and you'll find yourself using them again and again.

One of the keys to the success of Adobe products is the common user interface. Once you have learned to use one Adobe product, you have a head start on using all the other products. Because of this commonality, if you learn how to use the Color Picker here, you are ready to use every Color Picker in Photoshop— more than that, you are pretty much ready to use the Color Picker in every Adobe product.

Color Swatches

The illustration shows the toolbox with the color swatches highlighted. Most color swatches in Photoshop look this way.

Here is how the color swatches work:

- The top swatch is the foreground color (black by default).
- The bottom swatch is the background color (white by default).
- To switch the foreground and background colors, press the X key.
- To reset the colors to default, press the D key.

Whenever you use the Eyedropper tool, the color in the swatch will be replaced when you click with the eyedropper anywhere inside an image to sample (or pick up) the color.

Color Picker

To choose a new color, double-click any of the color swatches and the Color Picker will open, as shown in Figure 3-1.

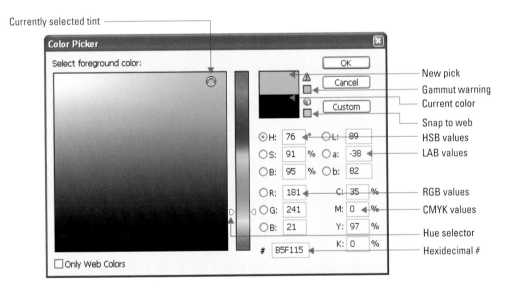

FIGURE 3-1 The Color Picker

You should be aware of the following features in the Color Picker:

- **Hue Selector**   Slide this up and down to choose a color (hue).

- **Currently Selected Tint**   Click and drag to choose a tint of the selected color (hue). This shows the actual color that you are choosing.

- **New Pick**   Shows the color you are choosing from the selected new color.

- **Current Color**   Shows the current color you are replacing.

- **Gamut Warning**   Tells you that the color cannot be reproduced; click the warning icon to choose the closest reproducible color.

- **Snap to Web**   Changes the color to the closest color in the web-safe palette (see Chapter 13).

- **Color Values**   The numerical values of the chosen colors. These values help you identify and reproduce colors. They break down the mix of individual colors to make the final color.

- **Hexadecimal Number**   A six-digit number commonly used for web colors.

- **HSB Values**   Hue, saturation, and brightness values.

- **LAB Values**   Separate luminance and color values that are commonly used for color correction.

- **RGB Values**   Red, green, and blue values that are commonly used for screen and multimedia color.

- **CMYK Values**   Cyan, magenta, yellow, and black values, commonly used for print.

To choose a color:

1. Double-click a color swatch in the toolbox.

2. The Color Picker will open. Click and drag the hue selector to the desired hue.

3. Click and drag inside the Color Picker window to choose the exact tint of the color you want to choose.

4. Click OK. The color swatch displays your new color.

Filling with a Color

You can fill either the entire page or just a portion of an image with color. To fill a portion, you must first make a selection. (See Chapter 10 for more information on selections.)

To apply the color to the image, do one of the following:

- Choose the Paint Bucket tool and click anywhere in the image to apply the current foreground color.

- Choose Edit | Fill and choose either Foreground or Background Color to fill with the currently chosen colors.

Shortcut To open the Fill dialog box, press SHIFT-F5 or SHIFT-BACKSPACE (SHIFT-DELETE on the Mac). To fill with the current foreground color, press ALT-BACKSPACE (OPTION-DELETE on the Mac). To use the background color, press CTRL-BACKSPACE (CMD-DELETE on the Mac).

About Graphics Tablets

Drawing with a mouse has been likened to drawing with "soap on a rope." It can be quite clumsy and requires lots of practice to master. Some people have become extremely efficient at this skill, but if you plan to use Photoshop for a lot of brushwork and freehand drawing, you might consider investing in a graphics tablet.

These tablets are plastic slates that you draw on with specially designed pens. They can help you achieve your artistic vision more easily than using a mouse. The tablets also open up some extra features in Photoshop—the *pressure-sensitive tools*. These tools detect how hard you are pressing with the pen and respond to the pressure by varying the opacity, line thickness, and color of the brush stroke.

Some of the newer tablets even have a feature that allows Photoshop to detect the angle of the pen's tilt and react accordingly. The most popular of these tablets are manufactured by a company called Wacom (www.wacom.com). They range from the $99 Graphire to the Intuos range that costs a few hundred dollars more. Other companies, such as Calcomp, also manufacture graphics tablets.

Drawing Tools

Photoshop comes with various drawing tools. With a little patience and practice, you can master these tools and use them to transform your work from the ordinary to the extraordinary.

Pencil Tool

When it comes to drawing tools, the Pencil tool is about as straightforward as it gets. Choose the Pencil tool, and then click and drag your mouse to draw. As long as you hold your finger on the mouse button, you will continue to draw a trail of pixels. The Pencil tool draws with the current foreground color.

To draw with the Pencil tool:

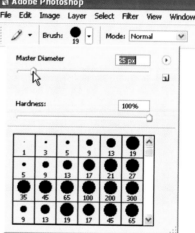

1. Choose the Pencil tool from the toolbox.

2. Choose the foreground color.

3. Choose the pencil tip thickness from the options bar, as shown in Figure 3-2.

4. Click and hold the left mouse button.

5. Drag the mouse with the button still depressed.

You are now drawing freehand with the foreground color. To draw a straight line:

1. Click the mouse.

2. Hold down the SHIFT key.

3. Click the mouse again in a different location. A straight line will be drawn between the two points.

Auto Erase

When you select the Pencil tool, you will see an Auto Erase box in the options bar.

The secret to using this option lies in the location of the mouse pointer when you first click. When you are drawing and click in the background area, the pencil will draw with the foreground color as normal.

If you first click over the foreground color, the Pencil tool will erase to transparent, unless you are working on a background layer. In this case, the tool will draw with the currently selected background color instead.

Brush Tools

Brushes are the main drawing tools that you will use in Photoshop. Because the brushes are versatile and extremely customizable, you will use them for everything—from touching up photos to creating your own works of art from scratch. You can also use brushes in conjunction with other tools, such as the Dodge and Burn tools, Eraser tool, and the Sharpen and Blur tools, for special effects. You can choose from preset brushes or create your own.

Using and Modifying the Brush Tool

When you choose the Brush tool, you will be offered a plethora of options. Figure 3-3 shows the options bar when the Brush tool is selected.

FIGURE 3-3 Brush options bar

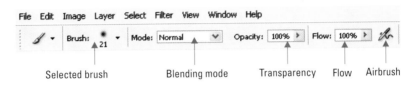

These are the top-level options:

- **Brush**   The currently active brush.

- **Mode**   Choose between blending modes to achieve different effects—see Chapter 5 for more details on these modes. The default is normal.

- **Opacity**   Adjusts the transparency of the brush.

- **Flow**   Controls how fast the paint flows from the brush.

- **Airbrush**   In Airbrush mode, paint will continue to flow as you hold down the mouse button, causing the paint to build up in a layered, airbrushed fashion.

To change the style or type of brush you want to use, click the little arrow to the right of the Brush modifier on the options bar. You will see a drop-down menu, as shown in Figure 3-4, that presents the essential brush options.

FIGURE 3-4 Brush modifier drop-down menu

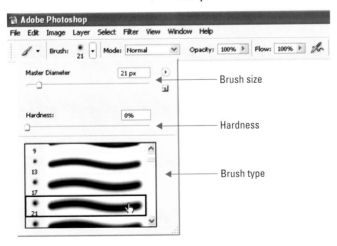

The main options are as follows:

- **Brush Size (Master Diameter)**   Adjust this slider to increase/decrease the diameter of the brush.

- **Hardness**   This adjusts the Hardness of the brush, as shown in Figure 3-5A.

- **Brush Type**   Scroll through the list to choose the brush you want to use. To make it easier, you can switch to Thumbnails view by clicking the arrow at the top-right corner and choosing Thumbnail from the drop-down menu. Figure 3-5B shows the Thumbnails view.

To draw with a brush:

1. Choose the Brush tool from the toolbox.

2. Choose the brush type, size, and hardness.

3. Select the foreground color.

4. Choose the opacity and blending mode.

5. Choose the Airbrush option if desired.

6. Draw with your mouse in the same way you did with the Pencil tool.

 *To adjust the size of a brush while painting, press the [and] keys.*

Modifying and Creating Brushes

Photoshop lets you extensively modify your brushes. This is great news for artists and others who want to have precise control over the tools they are using and will allow them to mimic natural media and thus produce less "digital" looking art.

You will see a couple of terms used often in discussions of the Brushes palette, and we will talk about them briefly before we open the palette.

FIGURE 3-5 Brush options: (A) 0 percent (top) and 100 percent (bottom) (B) Hardness settings, Thumbnails view

A.

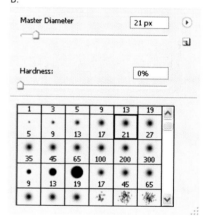

- ■ **Jitter**   Sets the randomness of an attribute. A 0 percent setting has no randomness; as you increase the jitter amount, you will increase the randomness of the chosen attribute of the brush stroke.

- ■ **Control**   Sets how Photoshop will interact with your drawing device. If you are using a drawing tablet, you'll want to turn these options to the pen options to make the most of the pressure-sensitive tools in Photoshop.

- ■ **Off**   Turns off the selected control feature and defaults to the selected setting of the feature.

- ■ **Fade**   Fades the brush tip to transparent at the size you specify.

FIGURE 3-6 The Brushes palette
(A) Tip shape
(B) Texture
(C) Dual brush
(D) Color dynamics
(E) Other dynamics

A.

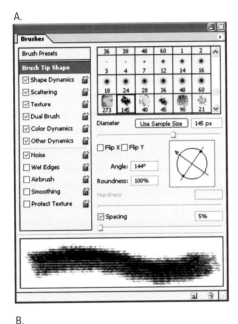

B.

Pen Tilt   As you tilt your pen, changes attributes. (This works only with graphics tablets equipped with tilt ability, such as the Wacom Intuos 2 tablets.)

Pen Pressure   Affects the attributes depending on how hard you press with your pen, just like drawing in the real world. (Only graphics tablets offer this option, such as the Wacom Graphire, Intuos, or Cintiq series.)

Stylus Wheel   Controls the flow of "paint," similar to a traditional airbrush. (Available only for graphics tablets equipped with an airbrush.)

Modifying Brushes

To make modifications to the brush attributes, you will first need to open the Brushes palette. This palette is not the same palette available from the options bar; it's the larger Brushes palette you open by choosing Window | Brushes or by pressing F5. The Brushes palette is shown in Figure 3-6.

You will see quite a few brush options in the palette. To choose a different brush, choose the Brush Presets option. You can scroll through all the available brushes. To make modifications to an attribute, click its name in the Brushes palette and make adjustments. To turn on an attribute, check the box next to the attribute name. If the box is unchecked, that particular attribute will not be applied to the working brush tip.

Brush Tip Shape   Controls style, size, angle, and spacing of brushes.

Shape Dynamics   Controls the shape of the brush.

Scattering   Sprays multiple instances of the brush tip at different sizes.

Texture   Allows you to add texture to your brush tips, as if drawing on a textured surface (see Figure 3-7).

Dual Brush   Allows you to mix two brush tips together.

C.

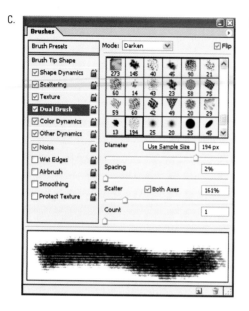

D.

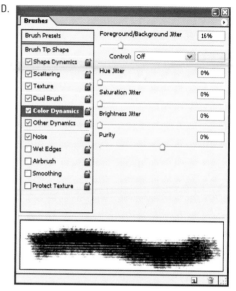

- **Color Dynamics** Allows you to mix the foreground and background together to achieve a two-colored stroke.

- **Other Dynamics** Allows you to adjust the random flow and opacity of the brush tips.

You will also notice five options with checkboxes at the bottom of the palette. These options have no adjustments—they are either on or off:

- **Noise** Speckles the semi-transparent edges of a brush.

- **Wet Edges** Simulates the effect of a wet brush drawing onto a damp surface.

- **Airbrush** Turns on the Airbrush option. Paint will continue to flow as you hold down the mouse button or the pen on a graphics tablet. This causes the paint to build up in an airbrush fashion.

- **Smoothing** Smoothes the curves when you are drawing with the brush.

E.

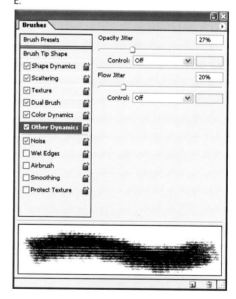

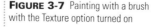

FIGURE 3-7 Painting with a brush with the Texture option turned on

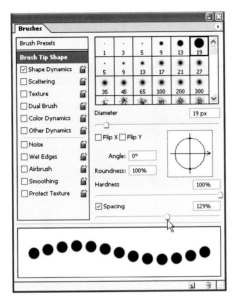

■ **Protect Texture** Keeps consistency across brushes if you are using more than one brush with the Texture option turned on.

Creating a Dotted Line Adjusting the spacing of the brush tips will allow you to create dotted lines. When you change the spacing, you are telling the brush how often to repeat the brush stroke when you are painting. Here's how it works:

1. Choose a brush.

2. Select a brush tip.

3. In the Brushes palette, change the spacing to any number greater than 100 percent, as shown in Figure 3-8.

4. Draw with the brush and you'll see the dotted line.

FIGURE 3-8 Preparing to draw a dotted line

FIGURE 3-9 Maple leaves preset

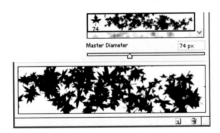

Creating Brushes

Brush tips don't have to be restricted to random shapes and textures; you can use an image or a portion of an image and create a brush shape based on the grayscale information. Brushes cannot be created in color, however. An example of a useful brush shape is the maple leaves preset tip that ships with Photoshop and appears on the Brushes palette, as shown in Figure 3-9.

These types of brushes are excellent to use with scattering and color jitter options. Figure 3-10 shows this brush tip painted as a scatter brush.

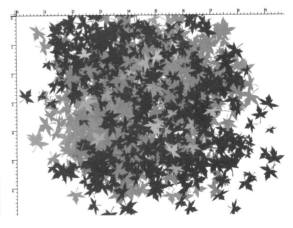

FIGURE 3-10 Maple leaves with the Scatter Brush option

Creating Your Own Brush Tip   Brushes are not limited to basic shapes. You can select portions of images and turn them into custom brushes, too. This can open up a whole new world of creative options.

1. Open an image.

2. Using a Marquee tool, select a portion of an image that you want to use as a brush tip, as shown in Figure 3-11.

3. Choose Edit | Define Brush Preset. The Brush Name dialog box will open.

4. Type in a name for your brush. The brush is now ready for use.

5. Open the image you want to work on, or create a new image file.

6. Choose the Brush tool.

7. Scroll through the brushes in the options bar until you find the new brush you just created.

8. Choose a size, as shown in Figure 3-12.

9. Choose the foreground color.

10. Begin to draw, as shown in Figure 3-13, either by

   - Clicking once in the image to make a single reproduction of the shape

   - Dragging the mouse to make a trail

FIGURE 3-11 Selecting a portion of an image

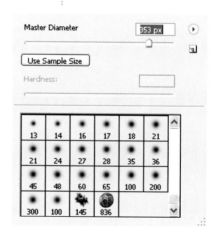

FIGURE 3-12 Choosing the custom brush size

FIGURE 3-13 Drawing with the new brush

Eraser Tool

The Eraser tool functions like the Brush tool, except instead of drawing, you use the Eraser tool for *erasing*. If you are working on a flattened image, the Eraser tool will erase to the current background color. If you are working on a layer, the tool will erase to transparent.

The Eraser tool works in three different modes, as illustrated by Figure 3-14:

- **Brush mode**   Use the currently selected brush as an eraser that takes on the brush's attributes.
- **Pencil mode**   Use the currently selected brush with 100 percent hardness.
- **Block mode**   The eraser is a 15×15 pixel square with hard edges.

FIGURE 3-14 The Eraser tool: (A) Brush mode, (B) Pencil mode, (C) Block mode

A.

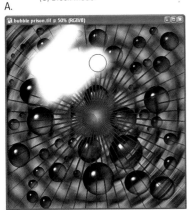

B.

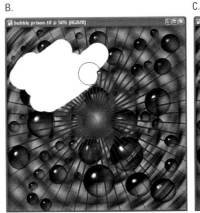

C.

Smudge, Sharpen, and Blur Tools

These three painting tools don't create any paint (with the exception of the Smudge tool with Finger Painting turned on). Instead, these tools simply modify existing pixels in various ways. They are useful drawing tools that, when used in conjunction with the paint brushes, let you create some interesting effects.

The Smudge Tool

The Smudge tool achieves the effect of dragging an object or your finger through wet paint. You can use it in standard mode, in which it will smudge the existing pixels, or you can choose the Finger Painting mode.

When using the Finger Painting mode, some of the foreground color will initially be added to the stroke. The amount will depend on the Strength setting.

Figure 3-15 shows the result of using the Smudge tool to create the illusion of fire. To create this effect, simply make a ring of color and then drag with the Smudge tool, wiggling the mouse on the way out to create the wavy flames.

The Sharpen Tool

The Sharpen tool will sharpen any areas that you brush over. It is best to start with a softer setting and build up the sharpness. Adjust the Strength to change the intensity of the effect.

The Blur Tool

The Blur tool is the exact opposite of the Sharpen tool; you use it to soften pixels you paint over. You can work either on the selected layer or check Use All Layers to work on the entire image. This is a good tool to use for touching up wrinkles or other blemishes on faces. In Figure 3-16, the Blur tool was used to soften lines around the subject's eyes. In a real-word situation, you probably wouldn't want to blur quite as much as I did here, but I wanted to emphasize the effect.

FIGURE 3-15 Fire created with the Smudge tool

FIGURE 3-16 The lines around the eyes, before and after blurring
(A) Before
(B) After

A. 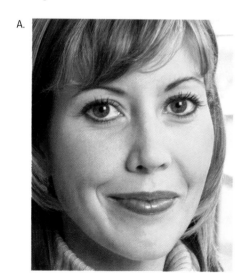   B.

A.

B.

C.

Dodge, Burn, and Sponge Tools

These three tools alter the tonality and color saturation of the pixels to which they are applied. They are favorites for touching up photographs.

The Dodge and Burn tools (shown in Figure 3-17) derive their names from the photographic darkroom. These tools both share the same options and allow you to affect either the highlights, midtones, or the shadows in an image. Use these tools to brush over portions of the image to increase shadow or highlight detail.

- **Burn tool** In the darkroom, photographers will cup their fingers over the light to concentrate it on certain areas to "darken up" parts of the image. You use the Burn tool to darken up areas of images.

- **Dodge tool** In a darkroom, objects are placed in front of the developing light to lighten the images in certain places. When you use the Dodge tool on an image, it will lighten the tonality of the areas to which it is applied.

FIGURE 3-17 Dodging and burning an image:
(A) the original image;
(B) result of the Burn tool;
(C) result of the Dodge tool

3

■ **Sponge tool** The Sponge tool allows you to change the saturation (the amount of color used) of the brushed area of an image. Figure 3-18B shows an image with the tool set to Saturate—notice how the brushed portion of the image has denser color than the rest of the image. In the opposite manner, the rightmost image in Figure 3-18C shows the same image with the option set to Desaturate; notice that virtually no color appears in the brushed areas.

FIGURE 3-18 The Sponge tool: (A) original image, (B) Saturate, and (C) Desaturate

A.

B.

C.

Gradient Tools

Gradients are the gradations between colors or blends that you see. Gradients add a lot of visual interest to images and break up flat color. They can also give the illusion of light falling on a surface.

To use the gradients, click the Gradient tool in the toolbox. The options bar will show all the Gradient options, as shown in Figure 3-19.

■ **Current gradient** Shows a preview of the currently selected gradient.

■ **Linear, Radial, Angle, Reflected, Diamond** Types of gradients. We will look at these in a moment.

■ **Blending modes** Changes the way the color blends with the underlying layers.

■ **Opacity** Indicates how solid or transparent you want to make the gradient.

■ **Reverse** Flips the gradient.

■ **Dither** Adds some "noise" to the gradient to reduce banding. *Banding* occurs when the color changes are abrupt and you can see the bands of separate colors.

■ **Transparency** Makes a part of the gradient transparent.

FIGURE 3-19 Gradient options bar

Linear — Angle — Diamond — Opacity

Mode: Normal   Opacity: 100%   ☑Reverse ☑Dither ☑Transparency

Current gradient — Radial — Reflected — Blending modes

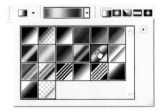

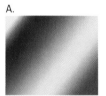

FIGURE 3-20 Gradient chooser

Applying a Gradient

Let's apply a gradient to an image.

1. Choose the Gradient tool from the toolbox.

2. Select the options.

3. Choose a gradient from the options. If you click the gradient preview, you will see the available gradients, as shown in Figure 3-20.

   ▪ Note that two standard options work off the current foreground and background colors. These are "foreground to background" and "background to transparent."

   ▪ The rest of the presets are custom presets based on actual colors.

FIGURE 3-21 Gradients:
(A) Linear; (B) Radial; (C) Angle;
(D) Reflected; (E) Diamond

4. Choose a gradient type. The types are shown in Figure 3-21A–E.

A.   B.   C.   D.   E.

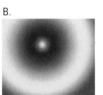 

5. Click and drag the mouse in the direction you want the gradient to flow.

6. Release the mouse and the gradient will be drawn.

Creating a Gradient

You can create your own custom gradients. It's useful to be able to modify gradients and create custom gradients that will work perfectly for your needs.

1. Open the Gradient Editor shown in Figure 3-22 by double-clicking the gradient preview in the options bar.

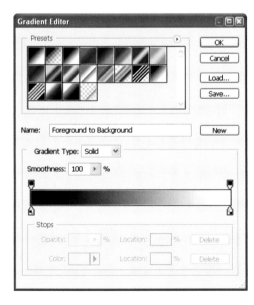

FIGURE 3-22 Gradient Editor

2. Choose a Gradient Type from the drop-down list.

3. The gradients are controlled by *color stops*. Each stop has a color assigned to it. The gradient will produce a smooth blend between the color stops. Create a color stop by clicking anywhere beneath the gradient bar in the middle of the Gradient Editor. In Figure 3-23, a new color is being added.

4. Click the color stop to select it.

5. Click the color swatch next to the word *Color* and choose a color; or choose Other to open the Color Picker.

6. Choose a color from the Color Picker. The color is now applied to the color stop and affects the gradient, as shown in Figure 3-24.

7. Add more color stops and colorize each one, as shown in Figure 3-25. You can also add a transparent stop by reducing the opacity to 0. You can slide the color stops along the gradient by clicking and dragging them.

8. Move the color midpoints to adjust the fall-off on the gradients, as shown in Figure 3-26. The midpoints will appear as small diamonds on each side of the selected color stop. These midpoints control the middle point of the blend.

9. Name your gradient in the Name field.

10. Click New to save your new gradient. You will see your gradient in the thumbnail library.

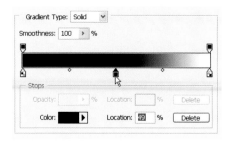

FIGURE 3-23 Adding a color stop

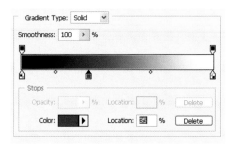

FIGURE 3-24 Changing the color of a stop

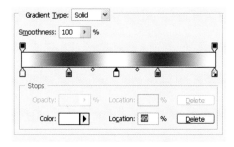

FIGURE 3-25 Creating more color stops

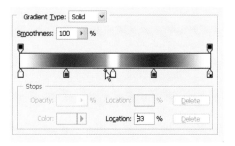

FIGURE 3-26 Adjusting the color midpoints

FIGURE 3-27 The gradient applied multiple times in Difference mode

Using Blending Modes

By using the blending modes, you can create some interesting effects with gradients. See Chapter 5 for more complete information on all the blending modes. Figure 3-27 used the new gradient created in the previous section. The blending mode was set to Difference and the same gradient was applied multiple times in different directions.

Shape Tools

Photoshop lets you draw basic shapes quickly by using the shape tools, which are accessed from the toolbox. After you have selected one of these tools, you can easily switch among different shapes from the options bar, as shown in Figure 3-28. To draw with these tools, click and drag in your document and the shapes will be created using the current foreground color.

FIGURE 3-28 Shape tool options

Five basic shape tools are available:

- **Rectangle**   Produces rectangles and squares.
- **Rounded Rectangle**   Creates a rectangle with rounded corners. You can set the radius of the corners in the options bar. This tool is excellent for creating buttons for web pages.

- **Oval** Creates ovals and circles.
- **Polygon** Draws different polygon shapes; you can draw polygons with three (triangle) to 100 (circle) sides.
- **Line** Draws straight lines; choose the thickness from the options bar. You can also add arrowheads to one or both ends.

Using the Shape Tools

Using the shape tools is a simple process:

1. Choose the foreground color.

2. Choose one of the shape tools.

3. Choose the Pixels option from the options bar.

4. Click and drag inside your image.

5. Release the mouse, and the shape will be drawn in the foreground color.

 Hold down the SHIFT *key to constrain the proportions of the shape tools to draw precise squares and circles.*

Creating Custom Shapes

If you want to create something a bit more complex than the simple shape tools allow, use the custom shape tools. Photoshop ships with a few shapes ready for your use, but you can load more and even create your own. See Chapter 7 for more details and options on shape tools.

FIGURE 3-29 Select a shape

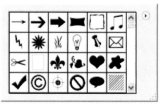

1. Choose the Custom Shape tool.

2. Click the arrow to the right of the Shape box to select a shape, as shown in Figure 3-29.

3. Choose a foreground color.

4. Click and drag the mouse in the document, and you will see an outline of a shape. Release the mouse and the shape is drawn, as shown in Figure 3-30.

A.

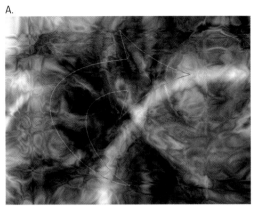

B.

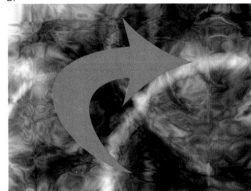

FIGURE 3-30 Drag the mouse to create the shape (A) and release for the finished custom shape (B).

 For more on using shapes, see Chapter 7.

Transform Tool

FIGURE 3-31 The image before any transformations are applied

When you create any object or open an image in Photoshop, you can transform it later using two levels of transformations: basic and advanced.

Basic transformations include scaling, rotating, and flipping. Advanced transformations include skewing, perspective, and distortion. We will look at each of these techniques and how to create them in this section.

Basic: Rotating and Flipping

The controls for rotating and flipping images can be found by choosing Image | Rotate Canvas. We will walk through each of these options, using Figure 3-31 as a visual guide.

Four rotate options are available: three set rotations and one customizable rotation. The main three rotations are used mainly for images that have been scanned upside down or at the wrong orientation:

■ **180** Rotates image 180 degrees, as shown in Figure 3-32

- **90 CW**   Rotates image 90 degrees clockwise
- **90 CCW**   Rotates image 90 degrees counterclockwise

The Arbitrary option lets you enter the angle of the rotation. When you choose this option, you will see the Rotate Canvas dialog box like the one shown in Figure 3-33A.

Choose the angle and the direction you want to rotate the image. Click OK and your image will be rotated, as shown in Figure 3-33B.

The final settings are Flip Canvas Horizontal and Flip Canvas Vertical. Choose these options to flip the image. Figure 3-34 shows the image flipped on the horizontal axis.

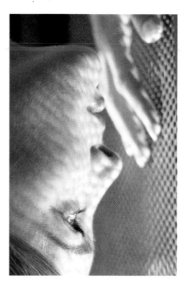

FIGURE 3-32 Rotated 180 degrees

A.

FIGURE 3-33 An image rotated 25 degrees clockwise (A) Enter your settings (B) The result of rotation

B.

FIGURE 3-34 Flipping the canvas horizontally

Free Transform Tool

A more advanced tool for transforming your objects in Photoshop is the Free Transform tool. This tool works only on layered objects. You can do a variety of transformations using the Free Transform tool.

Note   *Refer to Chapter 4 for more information on basic layers.*

Press CTRL-T (CMD-T on the Mac) to enter Free Transform mode. When Free Transform is activated, a *bounding box* appears around your object. You will also see eight little squares on the corners and sides of the bounding box; these are the *adjustment handles*. Figure 3-35A shows the bounding box and adjustment handles. By clicking and dragging these handles, you can perform the following transformations:

FIGURE 3-35 Free transform options
(A) Free Transform mode
(B) Rotate
(C) Scale Side
(D) Scale Corner

- **Rotate**   When you hover your mouse outside the bounding box on one of the corners, you will see a double-sided, curved arrow that indicates that you are ready to rotate. Click and drag your mouse in either a clockwise or counterclockwise direction to rotate the layer, as shown in Figure 3-35B.

- **Scale sides**   Click and drag on any of the side handles to adjust the width or height of the object, as shown in Figure 3-35C.

- **Scale a corner**   If you adjust one of the corner handles, both the height and width will be adjusted at the same time, as shown in Figure 3-35D. This is a good way to resize an image. If you hold down the SHIFT key while dragging, the proportions will remain even.

A.

B.
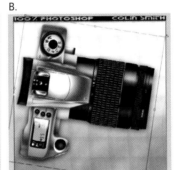

C.
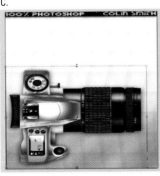

D.

More advanced transform options are also available:

1. Press CTRL-T (CMD-T on the Mac), or choose Edit | Free Transform to enter Free Transform mode.

2. Right-click (CONTROL-click on the Mac) anywhere inside the Free Transform bounding box.

3. You will see the drop-down menu shown in Figure 3-36.

4. Choose any option from the menu to control how the adjustment handles will work.

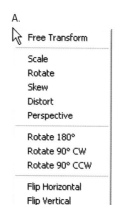

FIGURE 3-36 Advanced Free Transform options
(A) Menu
(B) Skew
(C) Distort
(D) Perspective

■ **Skew**   Drag any of the side handles, and the shape will be distorted into a parallelogram.

■ **Distort**   Choose Distort, and each adjustment handle will operate independently, which allows for a free range of distortion.

■ **Perspective**   Drag one corner, and the opposite corner will also move to mirror your transformation; this creates the perspective effect that is useful to achieve the illusion of size in an object.

■ **Warp**   Use this tool to curve an image to a variety of shapes. Use either the preset shapes or customize the shape. (We will use the Warp tool to fit a logo to a curved surface in the next section.)

B.

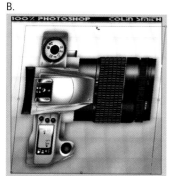

C.

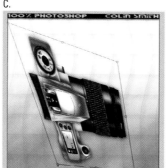

D.

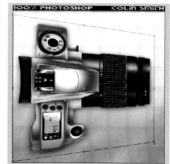

FIGURE 3-37 The glass of water, with the logo on another layer

istockphoto.com, logo Colin Smith

Image Warp Tool

The Image Warp tool allows you to bend and mold your images to almost any shape. This is especially useful for placing logos onto curved three-dimensional surfaces and for photo compositing. Let's wrap a fictitious logo around a glass of water. Begin with a photo of a half-full glass of water.

1. Bring in the image to be warped onto a new layer, and position it above the glass, as shown in Figure 3-37.

2. Press CTRL-T (CMD-T on the Mac) for Free Transform mode.

3. Right-click (CONTROL-click on the Mac) and choose Warp.

4. Choose the closest desired shape from the Warp menu. I chose Bulge for this example.

5. Adjust the settings in the options bar. Rather than enter numbers, move the mouse over the text by the fields in the options bar and click and drag. You will see a double-sided arrow as you slide the settings, as shown in Figure 3-38. This is called *"Scrubby Sliders."*

FIGURE 3-38 Sliding the settings to get the closest match

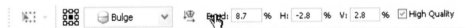

6. You may need to do a little manual tweaking to get the shape just right. Choose Custom from the Warp menu in the options bar, as shown in Figure 3-39.

7. You can now click and drag anywhere on the logo to shape it manually as shown in Figure 3-40. You may also drag the handles on the grid for a more uniform transformation. You don't have to drag the grid; just click and drag the image and it will mold like putty.

8. Press CTRL-H (CMD-H on the Mac) to hide the grid.

9. Press the ENTER key to apply the transformation.

10. In Figure 3-41, I lowered the opacity to 80 percent and chose Hard Light blending mode to make the logo look etched onto the glass.

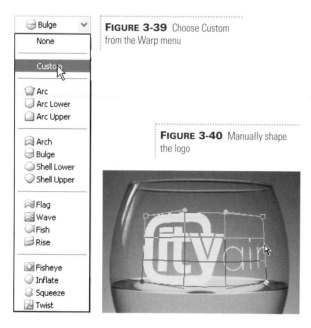

FIGURE 3-39 Choose Custom from the Warp menu

FIGURE 3-41 The logo now follows the curve of the glass.

FIGURE 3-40 Manually shape the logo

Tip

Transformations can also be performed by changing the settings in the options bar; this provides a way for you to achieve precision results.

Patterns

Repeating patterns make a good alternative to color and gradients for filling objects. Any image can be turned into a pattern, and Photoshop ships with a number of patterns. Patterns are fairly simple to use and easy to create.

Using Patterns

The most common place to use patterns is from the Fill dialog box (choose Edit | Fill), shown in Figure 3-42. The available patterns can be seen in the pattern library, which is accessed via the Custom Pattern drop-down list. Here's how you use a pattern.

FIGURE 3-42 The Fill dialog box's pattern library

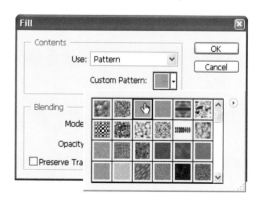

1. If you don't want to apply the pattern to the entire page, make a selection.

2. Choose Edit | Fill.

3. From the Use drop-down box, choose Pattern.

4. Open the Custom Pattern drop-down list by clicking the arrow. You will see the library, as shown in Figure 3-42.

5. To apply a pattern, click any of the thumbnails.

6. Click OK to apply the pattern.

Note *Notice that the pattern repeats and fills the page or the selection in a seamless way. All the patterns that ship with Photoshop will repeat seamlessly.*

FIGURE 3-43 Creating a new document

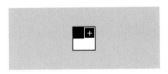

FIGURE 3-44 Creating a pattern

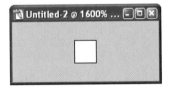

FIGURE 3-45 Defining a pattern

Creating Patterns

You can also create your own patterns. This is a useful way to customize the appearance of objects and backgrounds. By using patterns, you can save a lot of time, because you don't need to re-create the same object or shape over and over again.

Here's how to create your own pattern:

1. Create a new document; for this example, make it 2×2 pixels. This will make a pattern with very fine detail.

2. Zoom into 1600 percent, as shown in Figure 3-43.

3. Create your pattern. For this exercise, the Pencil tool was set to 1 single pixel width and used to create a black-and-white stripe, as shown in Figure 3-44.

4. Press CTRL-A (CMD-A on the Mac) to select the entire document.

5. Choose Edit | Define Pattern.

6. In the Pattern Name dialog box shown in Figure 3-45, enter a name for your pattern.

7. Click OK; your pattern will be saved to the pattern library. Close the pattern document.

Figure 3-46 shows the pattern we created in the Fill dialog box and displayed on a page.

FIGURE 3-46 The pattern in the Fill dialog box (A) and on its own page (B)

A.

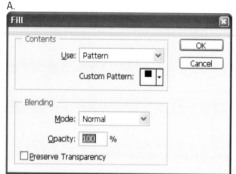

B.

Figure 3-47 shows an example of what you can do with patterns. This grid pattern was created and used for the background.

Loading and Saving Patterns

You can save your pattern sets or load new ones. Extra patterns come with Photoshop, and you can also find them from third-party products, such as on the CD PhotoshopCAFE Live, available from http://www.photoshopcd.com.

FIGURE 3-47 Example of a pattern in use

To manage your patterns (and a lot more), open the Preset Manager by choosing Edit | Preset Manager. You will see the dialog box shown in Figure 3-48.

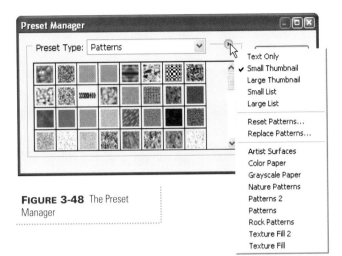

FIGURE 3-48 The Preset Manager

Loading Patterns

Let's load some patterns in the Preset Manager:

1. Choose Edit | Preset Manager to open the Preset Manager.

2. Choose the Patterns Preset Type.

3. To load the sets that come with Photoshop, click the arrow at the top right to open the drop-down menu. Choose any of the pattern sets from the list to load them.

4. To load the sets from an external source, click Load. Navigate to the location of the pattern sets. Then click Load again.

5. Choose Append or Replace. Append will add the pattern to your existing library, and Replace will reset your library with only the new patterns.

You can also perform the same tasks from the Fill dialog box, as shown in Figure 3-49.

Saving Patterns

To save your patterns in the Preset Manager:

1. Open the Preset Manager.

2. Choose the Patterns Preset Type.

3. Select the patterns you want to save. You can CTRL-click

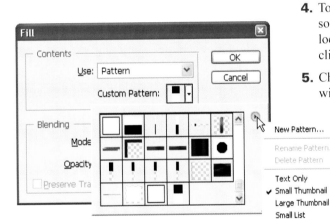

FIGURE 3-49 Managing patterns from the Fill dialog box

(CMD-click on the Mac) to select multiple patterns.

4. Choose Save Set from the menu.

5. Save the pattern set to your hard drive.

 You can also save the patterns from the Fill dialog box; however, you can save only the entire library, you cannot save individual patterns from this dialog box.

History

Who said that time travel isn't possible? It is possible in Photoshop, via the History palette, which saves the most recent versions of the image. Each version is called a *history state*. You can choose the number of history states to save in the Preferences dialog box. Whenever you make any changes to the image, a new state is created with the name of the edit next to it.

History Palette

Figure 3-50 shows the History palette with an image that was opened and then had a Hue/Saturation adjustment applied to it.

The only drawback with the History palette occurs when you have reached the set number of history states: each new edit will replace the oldest state in the palette—in essence, your history states are cycled. Fortunately, a solution to that problem is available. It's called *taking a snapshot*. A snapshot is a state that is saved independently from the revolving history states. In the History palette, click the camera icon and a new "snapshot" of the image will be taken. In the top frame of the History palette, shown in Figure 3-51, you can see the original image and a new snapshot.

To view the history states, click the names of the states, as shown in Figure 3-52. Notice that the current state will be displayed in the main window and the selected state is highlighted in blue in the History palette.

When you have chosen a history state, you can do one of the following:

■ Continue working on the image from the selected history state—in essence, perform a multiple undo.

FIGURE 3-50 History palette

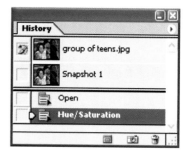

FIGURE 3-51 A new snapshot

Royalty Free Images from Hemera™

FIGURE 3-52 Hue/Saturation history state and original history state

FIGURE 3-53 Choosing a state for the History Brush

History Brush icon

- Take a snapshot of the history state.

- Click the button on the lower-left corner of the History palette to create a new document from the history state. This new document will be totally independent from the working image. All layers will be preserved in this new document.

History Brush

To paint with the History Brush, you will need to choose a history state from which to work. To choose a state, click in the well to the left of the history state in the History palette. You will see an icon of a brush with a circular arrow around it, as shown in Figure 3-53. This indicates that you are painting from this state. You can now paint just as you would with any other brush. Unlike other brushes, though, instead of painting with color, you will be painting with a previous version of the image. This is like the selective undo tool in Photoshop.

Let's do some work with the History Brush:

1. Open an image.

2. Choose Image | Adjust | Hue/Saturation.

3. Click Colorize and slide the Hue slider to the color red.

4. Open the History palette.

5. Choose Create Snapshot of the Hue/Saturation state.

6. Select the original image state with the painting indicator.

7. Choose the History Brush.

8. Select the appropriate size.

9. Begin painting on the image. You should see the full-color image come back to the areas you are painting, as shown in Figure 3-54.

You can use the History Brush for all kinds of things. Experiment with running filters over the image and painting back in portions of the image. Also, try painting from several history states into one image.

FIGURE 3-54 Painting with the History Brush

Art History Brush

This brush works the same as the History Brush except it lets you specify different types of brush strokes that mimic Impressionist-style paintings. This is an amazing tool and a lot of fun to use; anyone can now create convincing Impressionist-style artwork. With a little practice, patience, and creativity, you can create some stunning work.

1. Open an image you want to turn into a painting.

2. If you have resized the image, you will have to create a new snapshot. (The Art History Brush will not work from a resized or rotated image without a new snapshot.)

3. Choose the snapshot as your source image (history state).

4. From the toolbox, choose the Art History Brush, as shown in Figure 3-55.

5. Choose brush options from the options bar shown in Figure 3-56. You can experiment with brush strokes to find the best one to use for your image. The Tight Short setting works well for areas of medium detail.

FIGURE 3-55 The Art History Brush

File Edit Image Layer Select Filter View Window Help

FIGURE 3-56 Choosing a style from the options bar

FIGURE 3-57 Painting with the Tight Short setting

6. Choose a fairly large brush and paint over the areas of less important detail. You should see the image start to form as a painting, similar to the image shown in Figure 3-57.

istockphoto.com

7. The Loose Curl brushes work very well for areas such as the sky and grass. Experiment and find what you like—after all, art does not belong in a box.

8. Choose a smaller brush and paint over the detailed areas. The smaller the brush, the more detail will show in the image. The Dab option works well for areas of detail. Reduce the brush size and the area setting to create more detailed paintwork.

Figure 3-58 shows the completed image.

FIGURE 3-58 Completed painting using the Art History Brush

Try painting the image and then reduce the opacity to a low amount, such as 5 percent. Then go over the top with different brushes to build depth.

Use the Lighten and Darken modes at low opacities and large brush sizes to enhance shadow and highlight detail.

Color Replacement Tool

The Color Replacement tool is a powerful tool that allows you to change the color of objects in a photo while maintaining the luminosity. You could accomplish the same result by painting with any brush using the Color blending mode, if it weren't for some nifty features that we will examine.

Choose the Color Replacement tool from the toolbox. It's hiding under the Brush tool. Figure 3-59 shows the options bar with this tool selected. There are four main features:

- **Mode**   Blending mode, set to Color for most purposes
- **Sampling modes**   Affects the way the tool looks at color
- **Limits**   Determines where the paint will be applied
- **Tolerance**   Controls the sensitivity of the auto detection

FIGURE 3-59 Color Replacement tool options

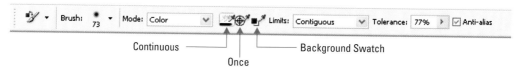

Let's look at the three different modes of the Color Replacement tool. This is where the power of color replacement lies.

Continuous

In Continuous mode, color will be applied wherever you paint; this is just like paining with a normal brush in Color mode.

Once

With the Once option applied, paint will only be applied where a color similar to the sampled color is present. This option is useful for repainting objects within a photo.

1. Choose the Color Replacement tool from the toolbox.

3

2. In the options bar, click the Sampling Once button.

3. Choose a Limits option (in this example, I chose Find Edges):

   ■ **Contiguous**   Affects only similar colors that are touching the sampled area

   ■ **Discontiguous**   Affects similar colors whether or not they are touching

   ■ **Find Edges**   Attempts to find the edge of an object and paint within its bounds

FIGURE 3-60 Replacing the color using sampling once and edge detection

4. Choose the desired color from the Color Picker.

5. Begin to paint on your object. Whenever you click the mouse, the color under the cursor will become the sampled color to replace.

The Color Replacement tool makes it easy to paint without painting out of color boundaries. Figure 3-60 shows this method in operation.

If too much area is painted, reduce the tolerance. If the paint is not flowing freely enough, increase the tolerance.

Background Swatch

The Background Swatch sampling mode works similar to the Once option, except you choose the color to replace before painting.

1. Choose the Eyedropper tool from the toolbox.

2. Hold down the ALT key (OPTION on the Mac) and click the color that you want to change in your image, as shown in Figure 3-61. The background color will now be set to the sampled color. (The ALT/OPTION key chooses the background instead of the foreground color for the sample.)

Note *If the image is grainy and the color varies, change the sampling size to 3×3 or 5×5 in the options bar for the Eyedropper tool. If the color is consistent and the image is smooth, you can use the point; beware, however, because the point sampler is very sensitive and works off only a single pixel.*

3. Choose the Color Replacement tool from the toolbox.

4. Select Background Swatch from the options bar.

5. Choose the new color from the foreground.

6. Begin to paint over the old color; the new color will replace it, as shown in Figure 3-62.

7. Adjust the tolerance as necessary to get it just right.

FIGURE 3-61 Sampling the new background color

FIGURE 3-62 Replacing the background color

Part II

Beyond the Basics

Chapter 4

Use Layers in Photoshop

How To...

- Understand layers
- Change the thumbnail sizes
- Rename layers
- Create and delete layers
- Duplicate layers
- Show and hide layers
- Work with multiple layers
- Link layers
- Align and evenly distribute objects
- Center objects on a page
- Manage layers
- Use layer sets
- Merge layers

In the pre-Photoshop 3 days, artists and designers with change-happy clients had to produce everything without the luxury of using layers. I was one of those unlucky designers who would complete a job, only to have a client then ask something like, "Could you increase the size of the font on the heading?" Before layers, making this kind of change was a major undertaking. Before layers, everything was one, flat image—like a photograph. If you tried to cut and move an object, it would leave a ghastly hole, much as if you were to take a pair of scissors to a photograph. Now that Photoshop uses layers, it takes just a couple of clicks to make such a change.

Layers Explained

Imagine a pile of photographs lying on top of each other—layers of photographs. As you move a photo to the top of the pile, it hides the other photos underneath it. Now imagine each photo in the stack mounted on a sheet of glass a bit larger than the photo. As you move the glass-mounted photos around, you'll notice that even a photo that's not on top may become visible through or around other photos above it, while other photos are still obscured. Think of each photo as being part of a separate layer, and each layer can be moved to hide or show other layers below and around it.

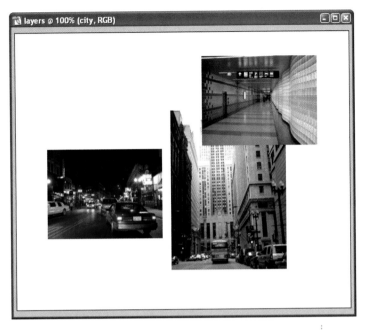

FIGURE 4-1 Three images showing three layers in a Photoshop document Layers window

Now imagine that rather than photos mounted on sheets of glass, you are using images in a Photoshop document, as shown in Figure 4-1. In Photoshop, a layer is always transparent until you put something on it. In this case, we have imported three photos and placed them on three separate layers—"image data" in the form of pixels now appears on each layer. Each layer remains transparent where no image data appears, and other layers will show through.

Using Layers in the Layers Palette

You deal with layers via the Layers palette, which is shown in Figure 4-2. In a nutshell, the order of the thumbnails that appear on the Layers palette represents the order that the layers appear

FIGURE 4-2 The Layers palette

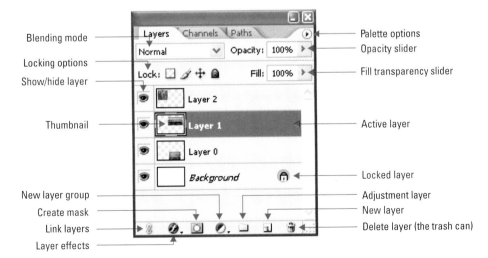

in the layer "stack" in the workspace. Later in this chapter, you'll learn to change the order of the layers by moving a thumbnail image on the palette; as you do this, the image itself will change position on the stack in the workspace.

In the Layers palette, each layer's name appears next to a thumbnail, as shown in Figure 4-2. (Don't worry too much about all the other options, as we will get to them in this and future chapters.)

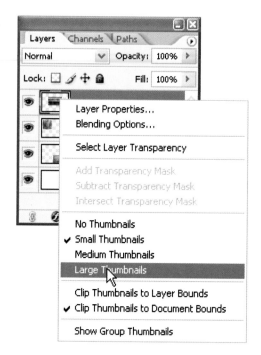

Changing the Thumbnail Sizes

You can adjust the size of the thumbnails in the Layers palette, making them larger so their contents are easier to see and making them smaller if you are working with a lot of layers so that they take up less space. Here's how:

1. Right-click a layer thumbnail in the Layers palette.

2. From the drop-down menu, choose the thumbnail size.

3. The Layers palette appears with large thumbnail previews, as shown in the illustration.

Note *From the Layers palette's options menu, which you open by clicking the arrow in the upper-right corner of the palette, you can choose None to save screen real estate if you are working on a small screen or using a lot of layers. This will default so that only a name appears on the palette, and no thumbnail image will appear.*

Creating and Deleting Layers

You can create new layers in Photoshop in several ways:

■ Click the New Layer button in the Layers palette (see Figure 4-2).

■ From the main menu, choose Layer | New | Layer.

■ From the Layers palette's options menu, choose New Layer.

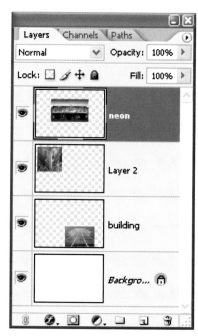

4

- Press SHIFT-CTRL-N (SHIFT-CMD-N on the Mac).
- Drag a layer from another document.

To delete a layer, drag it to the Delete layer (the trash can) at the bottom of the Layers palette.

Renaming Layers

When you create a new layer, it will have the default name "Layer *x*" (*x* being the next incremental number). After you have created ten or more layers in an image, it can be tricky trying to remember what Layer 6 actually contains, even with the thumbnail preview. To help you keep track of your layers, you can give them meaningful names.

To change the name of a layer, simply double-click the layer's name in the Layers palette and type in the new name. Figure 4-3 shows the palette with a rename in process.

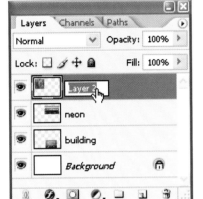

FIGURE 4-3 Naming your layers will help you keep track of them.

Changing a Layer Color

You can also choose colors for layers to help keep track of them. This color coding is useful, for example, if several people are working on the same image—each worker could use a particular color for the image he or she is manipulating. Or you could use the colors to identify revision versions or portions of an image.

To choose a color for a layer:

1. Right-click (CONTROL-click on the Mac) on the layer in the Layers palette.

2. Choose Layer Properties from the pop-up menu.

3. Click the Colors option and choose a color.

4. Click OK.

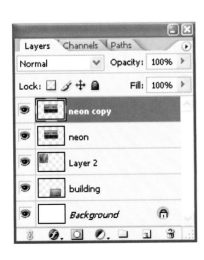

Duplicating Layers

You can duplicate layers in several ways:

- To make an exact copy of a layer, drag the layer to the new layer icon at the bottom of the Layers palette. The duplicate layer will have the same name as the original with the word *copy* appended to the end of its name.

- Use the keyboard shortcut: Highlight the layer on the Layers palette, and then press CTRL-J (CMD-J on the Mac).

- Copy all or part of a layer's contents onto a new layer (discussed in the next section).

- Cut and paste a layer (discussed a bit later).

Copying a Selection of a Layer

You can copy the entire layer or a portion of a layer onto a new layer without changing the contents of the existing layer. (For more information about selections, see the section "Selecting Multiple Layers" later in this chapter.)

1. Choose the target layer (the layer you want to copy) by clicking the layer's name or thumbnail to highlight it.

2. From the document window, make a selection on the layer, using any of the selection tools, as shown in the illustration.

3. Choose Layer | New | Layer Via Copy; or press CTRL-J (CMD-J on the Mac).

Only the selected portion of the layer will be *copied* to a new layer, as you can see in the illustration. (Note that I moved the new layer contents so you could see the result; the copied layer appears in the same position as the original—so you can't really see it until you move it.)

Cutting and Pasting a Duplicate Layer

To cut a selection from a layer, you mark the selection with any Marquee tool and then choose Layer | New | Layer Via Cut.

When you *cut* a selection from a layer, instead of making a *copy* of the selection, it will actually *move* the selected area to a new layer. This means that the pixels are removed from your existing layer and pasted onto a new layer, as shown here.

Changing the Layer Stacking Order

To change the order of layers, just click and drag a layer in the Layers palette.

1. Click and hold down the left mouse button over the name of the layer you want to move.

2. Without releasing the mouse button, drag the layer to the desired location in the palette. Choose the border at the top or bottom of an existing layer to target the new location.

3. Release the mouse button and the layer will move to the desired order in the thumbnail layers and in the stack.

Shortcut *To move a layer up or down the stack in the Layers palette, you can press and hold CTRL (CMD on the Mac) over the layer, and then press the left and right bracket keys on the keyboard.*

Working with the Background Layer

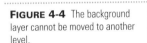

FIGURE 4-4 The background layer cannot be moved to another level.

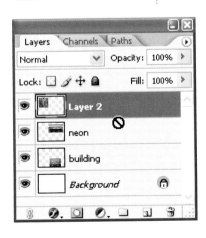

In the Layers palette, the background layer is identified by the word *Background* in italics and displays a small padlock icon. The background layer is flattened by default. Its position is fixed and it does not support any transparency.

The background functions much like other layers, in that you can fill it with color and place images on it. However, the background layer has a few limitations:

■ The background layer is always at the bottom of the stack, and you cannot move it. If you try to move it, you will see the "no" icon, as shown in Figure 4-4.

■ Transparency is not available for the background layer, and you cannot adjust the opacity (transparency).

■ The background is always locked; you cannot change the position of objects on the background.

■ Blending modes may not be applied to the background.

Changing the Background to a Normal Layer

You can change a background layer into a normal layer.

1. Double-click the Background layer in the Layers palette, or right-click the layer and choose Layer From Background.

2. In the New Layer dialog box that opens, click OK or press ENTER.

3. The background will be converted to a regular layer, and you can then manipulate it as a regular layer.

Showing and Hiding Layers

A great feature in Photoshop is the ability to hide layers temporarily without deleting them. This allows for great artistic experimentation, because you can include as many layers as you want (memory/scratch disk permitting) in your project and display only the ones you choose.

The key to hiding or displaying is the little eye icon, called the *layer visibility icon*, that appears to the left of each thumbnail in the Layers palette. To hide or show a layer, you simply click the icon to toggle the layer visibility off and on.

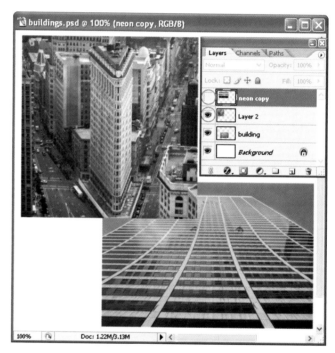

Partially Hiding Layers with the Opacity Slider

You can also change the transparency by using the opacity slider in the Layers palette, shown in Figure 4-5. You can reduce the opacity of a layer to partially hide it.

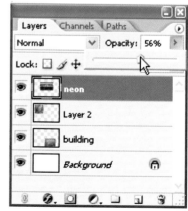

FIGURE 4-5 By dragging the slider, you control the opacity of a layer's contents.

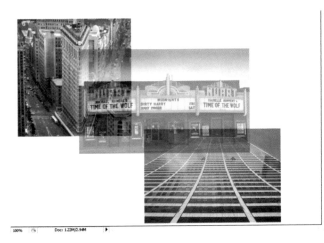

FIGURE 4-6 A layer at 50 percent opacity allows the layers beneath to show through.

Reducing the opacity of layers can have both creative and practical uses. You can use the opacity slider to blend images together in interesting ways. You can also reduce the opacity of an image to "ghost" it for practical purposes. For example, suppose you are working on a layer and need to show a hint of the underlying layers to help you position the layer. Figure 4-6 shows the document window, with the top layer set at 50 percent opacity, and you can see the layers below it.

Note   *Because opacity is the opposite of transparency, the terms are interchangeable as far as the results of the slider go. (That is, 100 percent opacity is the same as 0 percent transparency, 0 percent opacity equals 100 percent transparency, and 50 percent opacity is identical to 50 percent transparency.)*

Tip   *To hide all the layers except for the layer on which you are currently working, right-click the working layer's visibility icon and choose Show/Hide All Other Layers.*

Working with Multiple Layers

In addition to manipulating individual layers, you can also perform tasks on multiple layers at once. Many tools in Photoshop can help you save time by allowing you to work with multiple layers at once.

Selecting Multiple Layers

Once you delve into Photoshop and create more complex images, you may need to reposition, align, and transform more than one layer at a time. Photoshop CS2 lets you select more than one layer at a time, which makes this a snap. If you are used to working with Photoshop CS and earlier versions, it may take a little getting used to this new functionality.

To select multiple layers, click the first layer in the Layers palette to activate it. Then do one of the following:

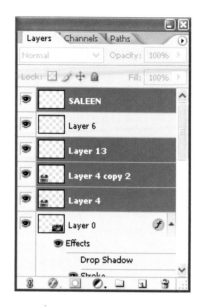

- Hold the CTRL key (CMD on the Mac) and in the Layers palette click any layers you want to add.

- To select several layers in an adjacent stack, hold down SHIFT and click another layer. All the layers between the first and last layers are selected.

- To disconnect a layer, click it while holding down the CTRL (CMD) key.

Figure 4-7 shows the Layers palette with several layers selected.

 You can select layers in the document window by holding down the CTRL key (CMD on the Mac) and clicking the layers object. Alternatively, turn on Auto Select Layers from the Move Tools options in the options bar.

FIGURE 4-7 The Layers palette with several nonadjacent layers selected

Select Layers by Dragging

Layers can also be selected by dragging in the document window with the Select tool (as you can in Adobe Illustrator). All the layers within the marquee area will be added to the selected stack. Here's how it's done:

1. Choose the Move tool.

2. Hold down the CTRL key (CMD on the Mac), or turn on Auto Select Layers in the options bar.

3. Starting outside the image area, drag a selection over the image. Alternatively, hold down SHIFT-CTRL (SHIFT-CMD on the Mac) and click objects to add their layers to the selection.

All the layers within the marquee area will be added to the selected layer stack, as shown in Figure 4-8.

 *You cannot begin dragging on a floating layer, or you will simply move that layer. Either begin selecting on a transparent portion of the image outside the image bounds or lock the layer under the cursor.*

FIGURE 4-8 Selecting multiple layers using a marquee

FIGURE 4-9 The selected layers can be transformed as a single unit.

The selected layers will now be treated as a single layer when you want to work on positioning and transforming. To move the layers at once, click one of the selected images in the document window and drag it to a new location. Notice that the selected layers move as a single layer, as shown in Figure 4-9.

The selected layers can be scaled, rotated, or distorted and they will all be transformed together.

Linking Layers

In previous versions of Photoshop, we needed to link layers together to perform certain tasks. In Photoshop CS2, you can perform most of this functionality by selecting multiple layers. Even so, at times it is useful to link layers. One advantage is that once you link layers, their relationship will be "remembered"; simply choose any of the linked layers to restore the relationship. If you select layers and then deselect them, you would have to choose each layer individually to create a new relationship.

Here's how you link layers:

1. Select all the layers you would like to link from either the Layers palette or from the document.

2. Click the chain icon at the bottom of the Layers palette.

3. Chain icons appear next to the linked layers in the palette, as shown in Figure 4-10.

4. To turn off the links, select the linked layers and click the bottom chain icon again.

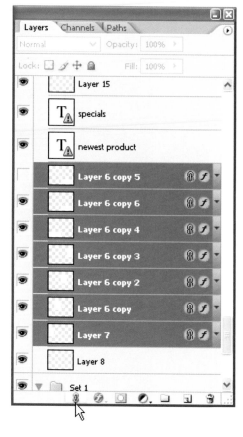

FIGURE 4-10 Linking the layers together

To unlink a layer temporarily from several linked layers, press SHIFT *and click its link icon. You will see a red X indicating that the link is turned off.*

If your file size is getting too big and your work starts to grind to a slow crawl, you can merge some layers to lighten the computer's load a little. Be sure that you have saved a copy of the image first.

Aligning and Evenly Distributing Objects

When you're working with multiple layers, you may find that you need to align several objects or space several objects evenly

4

in the document. You could draw grids and guides and do the math to figure out exactly where to align everything, but a better way is to take advantage of the Align and Distribute tools provided in Photoshop. These options appear in the options bar when the Move tool is active.

These tools are dimmed unless two layers have been selected or linked; at that point, the Align tools are available. At least three layers must be selected to make the Distribute tools available (see Figure 4-11).

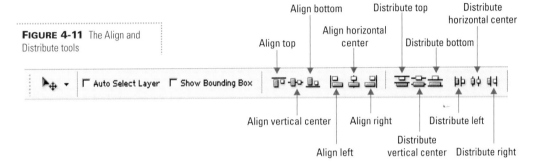

FIGURE 4-11 The Align and Distribute tools

Let's walk through these options.

1. Begin by opening a document with several objects that we can arrange. In this case, we'll use the document shown in the following illustration. We'll align all the DVD boxes horizontally and space them evenly.

2. In the Layers palette, select only the layers that you want to be affected, as shown here.

3. Click the Align Top tool. All the linked objects are now aligned horizontally.

4. To space the boxes evenly, click the Distribute Horizontal Center tool. The DVD boxes in the document are now aligned horizontally and spaced evenly.

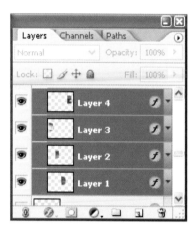

 Being a successful designer requires more than just being good at design. You also have to be fast, and learning to use tools like Distribute and Align will save you lots of time.

Managing Layers

If you're like me, by the end of a working day your desk is covered in clutter—junk mail, notes, and unread mail are strewn all over the place. You start to feel choked by the mess until you clean it up. Some more organized people deal with paperwork by using the two-step rule: either file it or throw it in the trash.

4

To be most effective in managing your projects, you can apply the same rule with your Photoshop documents. You can accumulate many layers in a document: some are failed experiments and others are changes. Fortunately, Photoshop has the tools to help you organize your layers. In this section, you will learn to "file or trash it" with your Photoshop layers.

Deleting Unused Layers

You can easily delete all unused layers in one click in the Layers palette by opening the palette options menu and choosing Delete Hidden Layers. This will trim down the file size and free up your computer's resources.

You can also use a couple of other methods to delete layers:

- Drag individual or multiple selected layers to the trash can at the bottom of the Layers palette.

- Select the unwanted layers and choose Delete Layers from the palette options menu.

 *Before you delete, make sure that you really won't need to use these layers, because once you delete them and turn off your computer, they're gone forever.*

 Empty layers do not take up any space; it is only the content in the layers that adds to the file size.

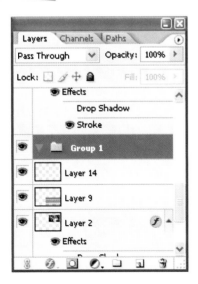

Creating Layer Groups

The Layers palette can be treated much like a file cabinet for your layers. You can create folders called *layer groups* that hold your layers, much like a manila folder holds documents in your file cabinet. Let's create a layer group:

1. On the Layers palette, click the Create a Layer Group button.

2. On the palette, you will see a folder with a downward-facing arrow, named Group 1, as shown in the illustration. This is the new layer group. It is currently empty.

3. To move layers into the group, drag and drop them into the Group 1 folder. Each of the layers in the group will be displayed below the group folder.

4. To change the stacking order in the group, drag the layers up or down. Remember that if you change stacking order, the order of image layers will change in the document.

5. To save space in the Layers palette, you can collapse the expanded layer group. Click the downward-facing arrow, and it will become a right-facing arrow. All the layer thumbnails in the group are hidden away. To expand, just click the arrow again.

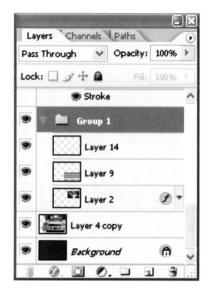

Nesting Layer Groups

By using nested layers, you can drag groups inside other groups to organize your work better. You can also nest groups inside nested groups. You can nest groups up to five levels deep. This will help you keep your files organized in a logical way.

Here's how to nest layer groups:

1. Create several layers.

2. Select the layers you want to include in the group.

3. From the palette options menu, choose New Group From Layers.

4. A new folder will appear in the Layers palette with the layers inside. The folder will be named Group 1.

5. Create new groups of layers.

6. Add or drag the new groups into the existing groups. They will nest under each other in a tree.

You can reposition layer sets in the Layers palette by dragging the entire set, just as you would with a single layer. You can even drag a set into another Photoshop document and the entire set and its contents will be copied there.

Merging Layers

You might want to combine several layers into a single layer. This is called *merging* layers. When you merge layers, the contents of the merged layers become a single image on the *target* layer.

For example, you might find it handy to merge layers as you're linking together the parts of a logo. Figure 4-12 shows an interface and logo used on my design site at www.pixeloverload.com.

FIGURE 4-12 The layered design with the logo

The logo is made up of three separate layers called Pixel, Overload, and Layer 12. Let's merge them into one single logo layer.

1. In the Layers palette, click the Pixel layer to select it.

2. Hold down SHIFT and then click Layer 12. Figure 4-13 shows the layers selected.

3. From the palette options menu, choose Merge Layers.

4. The layers are now combined into one, and they take on the name of the top layer, Pixel, as shown in Figure 4-14.

Merge Down

You can also merge layers by using the merge down option, which combines a layer with the target layer directly beneath it in the stack. To merge two layers, first select a layer in the Layers palette and then, from the palette options menu, choose Merge Down.

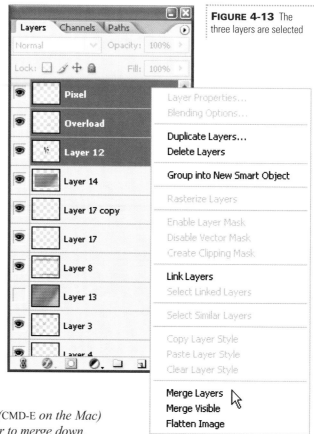

FIGURE 4-13 The three layers are selected

 You can also press CTRL-E *(CMD-E on the Mac) after selecting a target layer to merge down.*

Flatten Layers

At times you may want to flatten the image into a single layer. To flatten an image, select the image in the Layers palette, and then choose Flatten Image from the palette options menu.

FIGURE 4-14 The three layers are merged into a single layer.

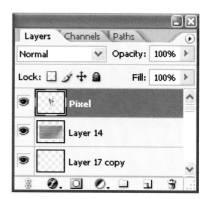

FIGURE 4-15 The image with the logo in layers

Making Selections from Layers

You can also create selections from layers. All the image data inside the selection can be manipulated, while the area outside the selection is protected. Selections operate independently of the layers; after a selection is active, you can switch between layers and the selection will stay active until you turn it off. (Selections are so important that Chapter 10 is dedicated to the subject.)

I created the image shown in Figure 4-15 in Photoshop. Notice the *51* on the door; it's on its own separate layer, and in this example, we'll draw a selection around it.

The easiest way to load the selection is to CTRL-click (CMD-click on the Mac) the layer thumbnail in the Layers palette. Photoshop will automatically create a selection around the opaque areas of the layer in the document window.

When you hover your mouse over the thumbnail in the Layers palette with the CTRL (CMD on the Mac) key pressed, you will notice that a dashed marquee appears around the thumbnail (see Figure 4-16). This indicates that you are about to create a selection. Click the mouse to create the selection.

 To load a selection, you can also right-click the layer thumbnail and choose Select Layer Transparency.

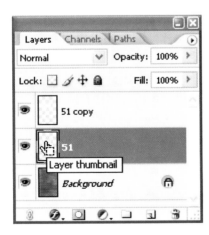

You will now see what Photoshop users affectionately call "marching ants." These ants are not the kind that typically spoil a picnic; they are moving dotted lines that indicate that a selection has been applied to the document as you can see in Figure 4-17A.

Now that we've made a selection, let's explore what we can do with it.

FIGURE 4-16 Making a selection from a layer

1. Create a new layer.

2. Drag the layer to the top of the stack.

3. Fill the layer with gray. To do that, choose Edit | Fill and choose 50 percent gray from the Contents menu.

4. Drag the new layer onto the document, as shown in Figure 4-17B.

Figure 4-17C is another variation using selections and layer styles. Here, I copied the selection to a new layer and added an outer glow and bevel.

We will get more into special effects in Part III of the book, "The Fun Stuff."

Note *For information about making a copy of a selection of a layer, see "Copying a Selection of a Layer" earlier in this chapter.*

A.

B.

C.

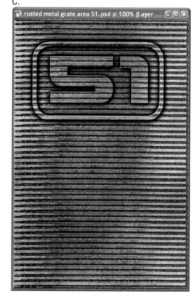

FIGURE 4-17 The selection loaded (A); the filled selection on a new layer (B); and a variation using selections and layer styles (C)

Chapter 5

Work with Advanced Layer Techniques

How to...

- Use special types of layers
- Create text layers
- Use shape layers
- Add adjustment layers
- Use layer masks
- Create clipping groups
- Use Smart Objects
- Use layer comps
- Understand layer blending modes
- Use blending modes for creative results

So far in this book, we have dealt with standard layers. These are all called *raster* layers because they are made out of *pixels*—the tiny squares that fill your screen and make up the images you see.

Photoshop images can be two types: *raster* (or *bitmapped*) and *vector* images. Raster images are made up of patterns of light and dark or various colored pixels arranged in a rectangular array. Vector images contain no pixels; instead, they are made of mathematical instructions that determine the position, length, and direction in which lines are drawn. Images are created with lines rather than with individual pixels. For example, to draw a line, you tell the program, "Place a point here, and now place one there." You then specify how thick you want the line and what color to use, and the line is drawn.

We will be getting deeper into the difference between the two types of images in Chapter 7. For now, you should know the following four points:

- A vector can be scaled without any loss of quality.
- A vector has a very crisp edge.
- The file size of vectors is very small.

- Most of the filters and transformations in Photoshop will not work with vector images.

These points are important to know because layers behave differently, depending on whether they're raster-based layers or vector-based layers. The manipulations you can make to objects on layers depend on their type. Let's look at some special layer types to see how this works.

Special Layer Types

Some Photoshop layers have special features that make them easier to work with. Some of these special features also help produce images of higher quality than those produced using standard layers alone.

Text Layers

A text layer is simply a layer that contains text. These are marvelous little inventions, because they keep the text in an editable vector format. Text layers have three main advantages:

- Vectors are sharp, so the text is clear and printing is sharper.

- You can scale text vectors up and down, with no loss of quality.

- If you make a typo, you can go back and change it later.

FIGURE 5-1 A text layer is indicated by the letter *T.*

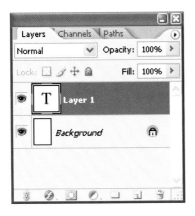

When you add text to a document, Photoshop automatically creates a new layer. The layer is called a text layer and is indicated in the Layers palette by a large *T* in the layer thumbnail, as shown in Figure 5-1. Whatever you type, up to 256 characters, becomes the layer name. A text layer can be linked, moved, and grouped exactly like a regular layer in Photoshop. It cannot have certain transformations and filters applied to it because it is in vector format, but you can apply the text warp and type on a path.

 *If you merge a text layer with other layers, it will cease to be a text layer and the contents will be merged just like any other layer. This means you won't be able to edit misspellings or change any particular characters in the text.*

Converting a Text Layer to a Regular Layer

As we already discussed, type in Photoshop is a vector object and is *resolution independent*. That means you can change the type size at any time without getting *jaggies* (pixelization or jagged edges). The type also remains editable as long as it's in a text layer. If you want to change the font, color, or your text characters, you can do that even after the document has been saved and re-opened.

When you rasterize type, it changes it from the mathematical vectors into pixels. The text layer changes to a *regular* layer. To rasterize the text, right-click the layer name in the Layers palette and choose Rasterize Layer from the pop-up menu. Once rasterized, the text layer will perform exactly like a regular layer, and the *T* indicator will be replaced by a regular thumbnail image.

Some effects can be applied only to rasterized layers. These kinds of effects change the pixels, and they include the majority of plug-ins, filters, and shape transformations available in Photoshop.

If you always rasterize a duplicate of your text layer and keep the original text layer intact as a vector, you can hide the original and work with the copy. You could make a layer set and store all the original text in the folder. Then if you need to change the text in any way later, you will always have the original to go back to (more on text in Chapter 8).

Shape Layers

Shape layers are similar to text layers in that they use vectors, and the same vector rules apply. A variety of tools can be used to draw vector shapes—from predefined shapes to custom shapes. Figure 5-2 shows the tools in the toolbox that can be used to create shape layers. To access these options, click and hold your mouse on the shape icon in the toolbox and the flyout menu will open.

FIGURE 5-2 The vector shape drawing tools

Note *We look into all the features of shapes in Chapter 7.*

When one of the shape tools is selected, the options bar at the top of the Photoshop window will display all the options for the particular shape. The following illustration shows the available options.

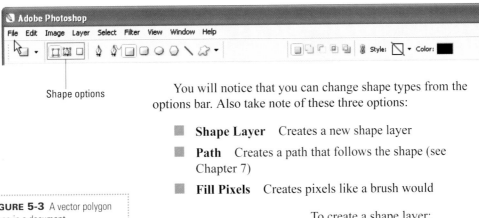

Shape options

You will notice that you can change shape types from the options bar. Also take note of these three options:

- **Shape Layer**   Creates a new shape layer
- **Path**   Creates a path that follows the shape (see Chapter 7)
- **Fill Pixels**   Creates pixels like a brush would

To create a shape layer:

1. Choose a shape tool from the toolbox.

2. Select the Shape Layer icon in the options bar.

3. Draw in the image area as you would using the regular tools.

FIGURE 5-3 A vector polygon shape in a document

A new layer will automatically be created. Figure 5-3 shows a shape created with the Polygon tool. The shape will be filled with the foreground color, and the edges will appear as a thin stroke. The stroke will not print and disappears when you select another layer. It appears only when the shape layer is active.

Note   *You can also create rectangles, rounded rectangles, lines, circles, and custom shapes with the shape tools. These are covered in detail in Chapter 7.*

When you create a shape with the shape tools, the Layers palette will display a special type of layer called a *shape* layer. Figure 5-4 shows a shape layer in the Layers palette.

A shape layer has two main parts:

- **Background** This contains the color of the object. This is an adjustment layer, and you can use a gradient, pattern, or any adjustment for this layer. To change the Background to a different type of adjustment, in the application menu choose Layers | Change Layer Content and select a different kind of adjustment layer.

- **Vector shape** This can be easily modified. The vector can be distorted, rotated, scaled, and adjusted with no loss of quality. This shape clips out the background.

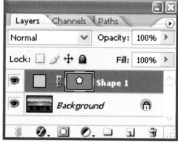

FIGURE 5-4 A shape layer in the Layers palette

Shape layers can be organized much like other layers. Shape layers add practically nothing to the file size.

You can easily convert a shape layer to a regular layer, the same way you convert a text layer, by rasterizing it:

1. In the Layers palette, right-click (CONTROL-click on the Mac) the layer name.

2. Choose Rasterize Layer from the menu. The shape layer is now a regular layer.

Adjustment Layers

You use adjustment layers to make alterations to the tone and color of layers beneath the adjustment layer. An adjustment layer is *nondestructive*. This means that although the adjustment visually affects a layer, it will not alter the pixels in the actual image. This is good news, because every time you alter the pixels in an image you lose some quality.

If you make a change and then change your mind, you can make further adjustments or simply delete the adjustment layer and the original image will be preserved.

The primary uses for adjustment layers are to enhance and correct photography, but they also have many creative uses. It's important to note that when you apply an adjustment layer, *it will affect all the layers underneath it.* The layer will also affect the entire image unless you make a selection before adding the adjustment layer. If you make a selection, only the selected portion will be affected.

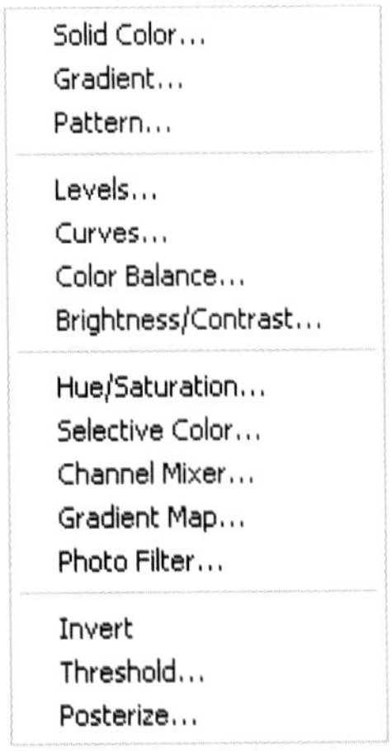

Solid Color...
Gradient...
Pattern...

Levels...
Curves...
Color Balance...
Brightness/Contrast...

Hue/Saturation...
Selective Color...
Channel Mixer...
Gradient Map...
Photo Filter...

Invert
Threshold...
Posterize...

FIGURE 5-5 The adjustment layer options

To create an adjustment layer:

1. Click the Create Adjustment Layer button in the Layers palette, or choose Layer | New Adjustment Layer.

2. You will see 15 possible adjustment layer options, as shown in Figure 5-5. Choose an option, and its dialog box will open.

3. Make the adjustments and click OK.

Note *The adjustment layer dialog boxes are the same dialog boxes you see when you choose commands from the Image menu. Space limits us from looking at them all here, so you can take a look at them yourself. The main dialog boxes you will use are covered in depth in Chapter 12.*

When an adjustment layer is applied to the document, it appears in the Layers palette with an icon showing what kind of adjustment was made.

- **Solid Color** Fills the layer with a solid color
- **Gradient** Fills the layer with a color gradient
- **Pattern** Fills the layer with a repeating pattern
- **Levels** Adjusts the tones in an image
- **Curves** Similar to levels, adjusts the tones, but with more precise control
- **Color Balance** Handles basic color correction and shifting
- **Brightness/Contrast** Brightens an image and adds contrast across the board
- **Hue/Saturation** Controls color shifting and effects
- **Selective Color** Adjusts process colors for printing
- **Channel Mixer** Exercises precise control over the color channels
- **Gradient Map** Replaces the color table in an image with a gradient
- **Photo Filter** Creates photographic colorizing effects that resemble lens filters
- **Invert** Inverts the colors and produces a negative effect

- **Threshold** Converts to solid black and white and sets the shift point
- **Posterize** Reduces the number of colors in each channel

Advanced Layer Features

By now, you should be getting the hang of layers and you should be ready to start experimenting with them. This section introduces some of the more creative features of layers. A lot of the cool collages and images that have caught your attention were probably created using these tools. (Perhaps these images prompted you to learn Photoshop.)

Layer Masks

Layer masks are among the most useful and misunderstood features of the Layers palette. These masks give you amazing control over the way layers interact with each other. Layer masks allow you to blend all or part of an effect or image to underlying layers. You can even adjust the opacity to a section of a layer.

A layer mask can be filled with solid black or white and can contain up to 254 levels of gray. By default, a layer mask is filled with white, as shown in Figure 5-6, which has no effect on the parent layer.

If you were to fill the layer mask with solid black, as shown in Figure 5-7, its parent layer would be completely transparent. The layer mask will alter the transparency of the layer to which it is attached.

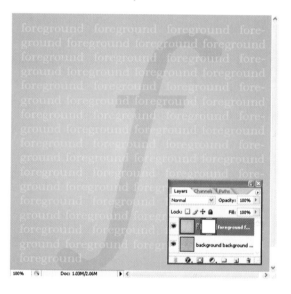

FIGURE 5-6 A layer mask filled with white has no effect.

The transparency is directly related to the amount of gray in the layer mask. For example, if the mask were filled with 50 percent gray, the layer would be 50 percent transparent, as shown in Figure 5-8. When you fill the mask with a solid shade

FIGURE 5-7 A layer mask filled with black makes the parent layer transparent.

FIGURE 5-8 A layer mask with 50 percent gray is 50 percent transparent.

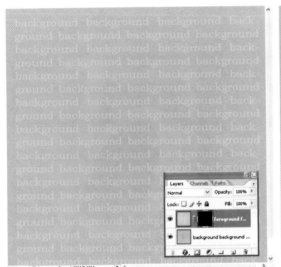

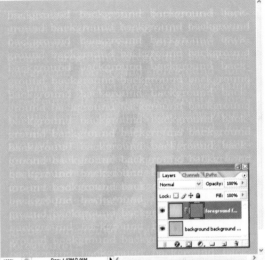

of gray, you are performing the same task performed when you use the Opacity slider.

So why use a layer mask? Because it provides a nondestructive way of compositing layers. If you don't like the effect, you can simply repaint on the mask. Masks let you control where and how much of the transparency is applied. For example, you could fill the mask with a black-to-white gradient, and this would produce a smooth "fading away" of the image. This is a popular use for layer masks.

Another example of using a mask would be to use a black or gray brush to paint away sections of the masked layer, allowing portions of the layer underneath to show through, as shown in Figure 5-9.

The flipside in Figure 5-10 fills the mask with black and uses a white brush to paint in only the areas you want to keep.

To work on the layer mask, click the mask thumbnail in the Layers palette. To go back to the layer, click the layer thumbnail.

Let's walk through some layer masking to give you an opportunity to grasp some of the layer skills. Using layer masks, we will combine images of a satellite dish and a woman (see

FIGURE 5-9 Painting on a mask with black produces transparency.

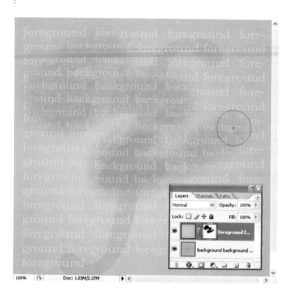

FIGURE 5-10 Painting on the mask with white paints the layer back in.

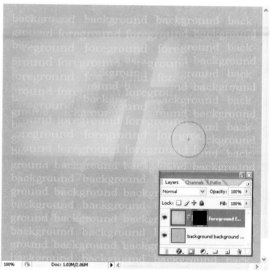

Figure 5-11) to create an advertising poster for a communications company.

1. Begin with two pictures of roughly the same size. In this case, we're combining the two images shown in Figure 5-12.

FIGURE 5-11 Using layer masks

Royalty Free Images from Hemera™

FIGURE 5-12 Attaching a layer mask to the selected layer

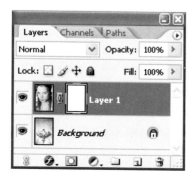

2. Click and drag one image into the other image window. You will see an arrow with a plus sign, indicating that you are adding a new layer to the image.

 Tip

Hold down the SHIFT *key while dragging to center the new image in the window.*

FIGURE 5-13 Smooth blend of images

3. You now have two images in one document. Each picture is on its own layer.

4. In the Layers palette, click the Create New Layer Mask button. A layer mask will now be attached to the selected layer. You can see the mask is filled with white and currently has no effect on the image.

5. Now we'll apply a black-to-white gradient to the layer mask. This will create a smooth blend between the layers. Press the D key to reset the foreground and background colors to black and white.

6. Choose the Gradient tool from the toolbox, and set the options to Foreground To Background and Linear.

7. Starting at the top-left corner of the image, click and hold down the left mouse button and drag diagonally to the bottom-right corner of the image.

8. Release the mouse button and a gradient will be created in the mask, resulting in a smooth blend of images, as shown in Figure 5-13.

Notice that the layer mask is highlighted and you can see the gradient in the mask thumbnail on the Layers palette, as shown in Figure 5-14.

Now we'll paint directly onto a mask with a brush to demonstrate the versatility of masks. We will paint the woman's chin back into the picture. Remember that the

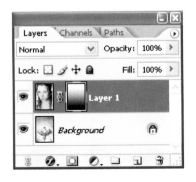

FIGURE 5-14 The gradient depicted in the mask thumbnail

5

darker the gray, the more opaque the image will be. If you notice on the layer mask shown in Figure 5-15, the gray is around 50 percent in the area of the chin. Because we want to bring back the top layer, we will use lighter than 50 percent to paint.

1. Choose a large soft brush—a 100 pixel brush will work. Make the foreground layer white.

2. Make sure the layer mask is selected, and begin to paint around the woman's chin. Notice the pixels are returning, as shown in Figure 5-16.

3. Continue until you have painted all the pixels back in the chin area, as in Figure 5-17.

Let's practice masking out details. We will paint back some of the satellite dish to the right of the woman's chin. This time, we want to make the image semitransparent. Remember that setting the mask layer to black will hide the top layer. We don't want to paint the background in solid,

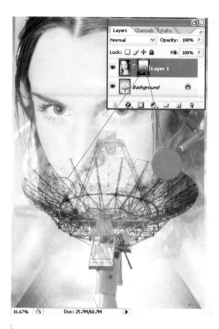

FIGURE 5-15 The gray is around 50 percent on the mask at this point, amounting to 50 percent opacity on the layer.

FIGURE 5-16 Pixels are returning.

FIGURE 5-17 All pixels are back in the chin area.

FIGURE 5-18 Painting out the top part of the layer

FIGURE 5-19 Adding a drop shadow

we just want a hint, so we could choose a gray shade—30 percent gray would work. Another option is to choose black and reduce the opacity of the brush from the top options bar.

FIGURE 5-20 Layer mask on the text layer

1. Choose 30 percent and begin to paint out part of the top layer. Notice that the layers are blending smoothly (see Figure 5-18).

2. Now let's finish our artwork and add some type with the Text tool (see Figure 5-19). You can add a drop shadow if you choose by clicking on the little *f* symbol at the bottom of the Layers palette and choosing Drop Shadow, as shown in Figure 5-20. Accept the default settings.

Now let's blend the bottom part of the top text to transparent. Normally, you would have to rasterize the text layer to apply a gradient to it. But this isn't true when you're using masks.

1. Create a layer mask on the text layer.

2. Using the same gradient technique we just used, create a gradient that goes from the top of the text characters to the bottom, as shown in Figure 5-21.

We have finished our poster. We have a professional-looking design that isn't more complicated than a few layer masks.

Clipping Groups

Clipping groups are an underused and interesting effect. You can compare clipping groups to looking through binoculars—you see only what's available within the confines of the lenses' view area. Much more exists than what you can see through the lenses, but everything else is "clipped" away. With clipping groups, imagine that the binocular lenses are the base layer and the view is the clipped layer.

To create a clipping group, you must start with a layer other than a background. This layer must contain a combination of solid and transparent areas. Shape layers and text layers are ideal. This will become our base layer. Anything we apply to this layer as a clipping group will fit into the shape of the base layer.

FIGURE 5-21 Creating a gradient

 You can combine layer masks with clipping groups for interesting results.

Let's demonstrate this effect.

1. Begin with some text, a background, and a layer that you want to clip to the text, as shown in Figure 5-22.

FIGURE 5-22 Choose a layer (A) to clip to the text (B)

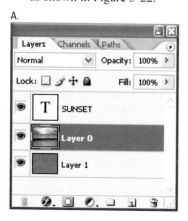

FIGURE 5-23 Preparing to clip the layer

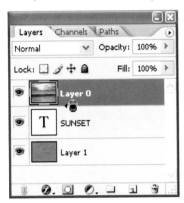

2. In the Layers palette, move the image layer above the text layer. Remember that the base clipping layer must be underneath the layers you want to clip.

3. Here is where it all happens (see Figure 5-23). Place your mouse between the two layers you want to clip and hold down the ALT key (OPTION on the Mac). Your cursor will turn into a little figure 8. This means that the two layers will be converted into a clipping group.

4. Click the mouse, and the clipping group will be created. Notice that the clipped layer is indented, as shown in Figure 5-24.

Figure 5-25 shows what happened to our image after we finished this procedure. Notice that the photo now appears inside the text. Because nothing is finalized yet, you can still ungroup the layers; to do so, repeat step 3, or drag the clipped layer to another location on the Layers palette.

FIGURE 5-24 Clipped layers are indented.

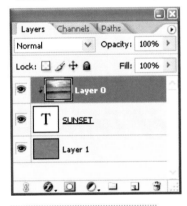

FIGURE 5-25 Image after clipping

FIGURE 5-26 Dressing up the clipping group

Figure 5-26 shows an example of a clipping group dressed up a little. I used a duplicate of the photo for the background and faded it out using a Levels adjustment layer. An unmodified copy was clipped to the text. Finally, a drop shadow was added for effect.

Smart Objects

Photoshop CS2 introduced something totally new: *Smart Objects*. These objects act like containers that hold layers. What makes Smart Objects special is that the files keep their original format, letting us adjust these objects as much as we like without any loss of quality. Several formats are supported:

- **Vector, Illustrator, EPS, PDF**   This format maintains the original vectors from Illustrator.

- **Camera Raw**   You can alter the raw settings at any time (see Chapter 12 for more about Camera Raw).

- **Nested layers**   Layers stored in a Smart Object can be updated at any time.

Using Smart Objects with Layers

Another advantage of using Smart Objects is that you can create instances of objects. For example, you can create several layers and turn them into a Smart Object. You can then duplicate the Smart Object, and when you change the contents of one object, all duplicated objects are updated automatically. You can make the Smart Objects linked or independent by the way they are duplicated.

Let's create and work with a Smart Object:

1. Create a document with a layer, as shown in Figure 5-27.

2. Convert the layer to a Smart Object by opening the palette options menu and choosing Group Into A New Smart Object, or by right-clicking the layer name and choosing the same option.

FIGURE 5-27 A document with a layer

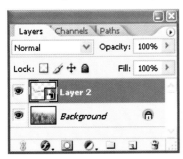

FIGURE 5-28 The layer grouped to a Smart Object

FIGURE 5-29 Duplicated Smart Objects

Figure 5-28 shows how a Smart Object looks in the Layers palette.

3. To duplicate a Smart Object that is linked to the other Smart Objects, drag the Smart Object to the New Layer icon in the Layers palette. (When you edit the contents of one Smart Object, all duplicates will be updated as well.)

4. To copy a Smart Object that is not linked to another Smart Object, right-click in the Layers palette and choose New Smart Object Via Copy. Figure 5-29 shows four duplicate objects: the top one is independent, as you will see in a moment. You can see the four jets in the image; remember, the top one was created via a copy.

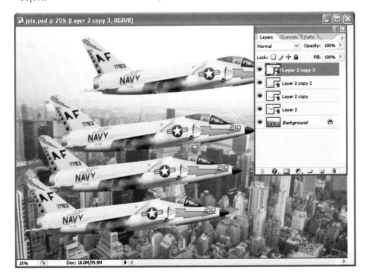

5. To edit the contents of any Smart Object, double-click its icon in the Layers palette; in this case, double-click the first object that was created (in layer 2).

6. You will see a dialog box with instructions. Click OK to open the object in its original format—in this case, a Photoshop layer. A new document opens, as shown in Figure 5-30.

FIGURE 5-30 Editing the contents of a Smart Object

7. Edit the content of the layer. In this case, I changed the orange color to blue.

8. Choose File | Save to save the changes to the layer.

9. Close the window, and the object will be updated in the main document, as shown in Figure 5-31.

FIGURE 5-31 All the instances are updated except the object created via copy.

You can now see that all the duplicated objects were also updated. This is because they are *occurrences* of the original Smart Object. The object that we duplicated via copy is a brand new object and thus is independent and not updated.

Create Smart Objects with Different File Types

You can create different types of Smart Objects. Let's work with a few in a composition:

1. Create a new document.

2. To insert a Camera Raw file and preserve its format, choose File | Place and select the Camera Raw file.

3. To insert an Illustrator image, either select the image and choose File | Place or cut and paste the Illustrator image into the Photoshop document; it will automatically become a Smart Object.

4. To convert multiple layers into a Smart Object, select all the layers and choose Group Into New Smart Object from the palette options menu, as shown in Figure 5-32.

FIGURE 5-32 Grouping multiple layers into a Smart Object

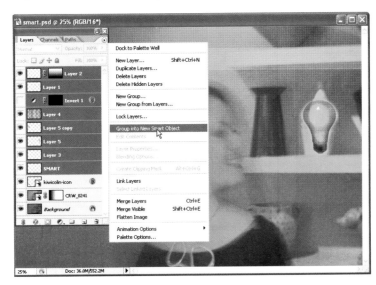

5. To edit the contents of a Smart Object, double-click its icon. In Figure 5-33, you can see that the Smart Object contains multiple layers. When you double-click it to edit it, a new document opens with all the layers intact. You can then edit these layers as you normally would in Photoshop. Save and close the document to update the Smart Object.

FIGURE 5-33 Editing the contents of the Smart Object

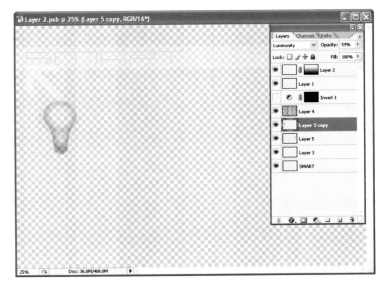

6. Double-click the icon of the Camera Raw Smart Object. The Camera Raw dialog box opens, allowing you to edit the raw contents, as shown in Figure 5-34.

7. Click Done to close the window and update the Smart Object.

Figure 5-35 shows a document that uses different kinds of Smart Objects. Notice that layer masks, blending modes, and opacity control can be applied to Smart Objects.

Update a Vector Image in Illustrator

Vector objects can be added from Adobe Illustrator by either placing the Illustrator image into Photoshop using File | Place or by dragging the object from Illustrator and dropping it into the Photoshop document. These vectors will be converted to Smart Objects. This allows them to be scaled and edited without any quality loss, as they will remain as vectors. Once you have placed a vector Smart Object into Photoshop, it can be updated in Adobe Illustrator. Here's how:

1. Launch the original image in Adobe Illustrator (if the program is installed).

2. Make the changes, save, and quit Illustrator.

3. The vector will be updated.

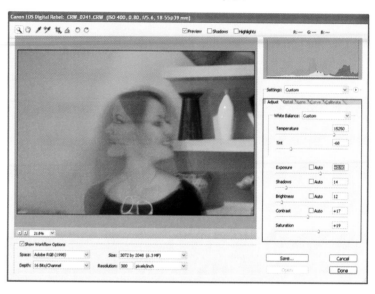

FIGURE 5-34 Editing Camera Raw

FIGURE 5-35 The document showing three types of Smart Objects

Working with Smart Objects and Layers

You can right-click a Smart Object and choose an option from among the several that appear. The following commands are important for you to know:

- **Edit Contents**   This is the same as double-clicking an object to edit in the original format.

- **Export Contents**   Allows you to save the contents of a Smart Object as a document with a default format of PSB, but you can choose other formats if you want.

- **Convert To Layers**   This is the same as rasterizing a vector. Choose this command and everything in the Smart Object will be rasterized and will become a "regular" layer. If the Smart Object includes multiple layers, they will be "flattened" into a single layer.

You can nest Smart Objects within other Smart Objects.

Layer Comps

Photoshop CS2 has a wonderful feature called *layer comps*, which are designed to free the graphic designer from the shackles of creating and saving multiple versions of a file. Designers using Photoshop work in various ways: perhaps you love the way a layer style works with a font, or the arrangement looks good more than one way and you want to show someone two or three different layouts. Experimenting with different layout options is called *comping* (*comp* is short for *composition*).

Before layer comps, to create comps, you had to save the file, make the changes, and save the file again under a different name. Layer comps remember the position, visibility, blending modes, styles, and transparency of every layer in your image. They allow you to save multiple layouts of your image all in the same file. You can save layouts and preview them all with the click of a button. What's more, when you save the file, the layer comps are saved, too.

Let's look at the way this little toy works. Figure 5-36 shows the Layer Comps palette.

When you are satisfied with a layout, but you want to explore a bit further, click the New Comp button in the Layer Comps palette and your layout will be saved. Experiment a little

FIGURE 5-36 The Layer Comps palette

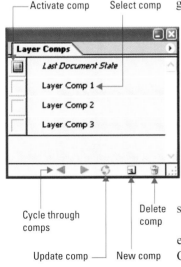

and then save another comp. Experiment still more—perhaps hide a layer and create a new one with a new element—and save that, too. If you want to make some changes to a particular comp, first select it and then click the Update Comp button.

When you want to view the saved layouts, just click the area to the left of the comp's name and the associated layout will be displayed.

 You can export the layer comps as documents by choosing File | Script | Export Layer Comps As...Files, PDF, or WPG.

Layer Blending Modes

If you want real interactivity and powerful creative effects, layer blending modes are the way to go. At the top of the Layers palette (also available in the Layers Styles palette) is a drop-down menu, where you can select various blending modes, as shown in Figure 5-37. These incredibly useful modes affect the way layers interact with each other. The blending modes are also available from the options bar when the Painting and Gradient tools are selected.

Two layers are mainly affected by the blending modes: the *base color* layer, which is the existing image, and the *blend color* layer, which is the layer to which you are applying the blending mode, usually on top of the base color layer. (You can also blend multiple layers together; in this case, they would all become blend layers.) In this section, we'll discuss blending modes.

FIGURE 5-37 Blending modes

Normal
Dissolve

Darken
Multiply
Color Burn
Linear Burn

Lighten
Screen
Color Dodge
Linear Dodge

Overlay
Soft Light
Hard Light
Vivid Light
Linear Light
Pin Light
Hard Mix

Difference
Exclusion

Hue
Saturation
Color
Luminosity

Normal Modes

In normal modes, color and opacity are unaffected.

- **Normal** The standard mode in which images are blended without any special effects.

- **Dissolve** When you lower the opacity, the blend layer dissolves rather than turning transparent.

- **Behind** Paints only on the transparent pixels and ignores opaque pixels. Available only with the painting tools.

- **Clear** Erases opaque pixels and performs just like the Eraser tool. Available only with the painting tools.

Darkening Modes

Darkening modes will cause white to disappear on the blend layer.

- **Darken**   Where the blend layer is darker, it becomes dominant. Where it is lighter, the base image becomes dominant.

- **Multiply**   The white areas on the blend layer appear completely transparent. Only the darker areas affect the base color. This is commonly used for drop shadows, allowing the underlying color to bleed through.

- **Color Burn**   Use to paint deeper shadows onto images by increasing the contrast on the base layer.

- **Linear Burn**   Darkens the base color by decreasing the brightness.

Lightening Modes

The opposite of darkening modes, lightening modes will cause black to disappear on the blend layer.

- **Lighten**   Where the blend layer is lighter, it becomes dominant. Where it is darker, the base image becomes dominant.

- **Screen**   The dark areas on the blend layer appear completely transparent. Only the lighter areas affect the base color.

- **Color Dodge**   Decreases contrast on the base layer.

- **Linear Dodge**   Lightens the base color by increasing the brightness.

Light Modes

Light modes will cause 50 percent gray to disappear. They have no effect on black or white.

- **Overlay**   The shadows and highlights of the base layer are not affected; the colors are blended together.

- **Soft Light**   If the blend color is lighter than 50 percent gray, the colors are dodged; if the blend color is darker than 50 percent gray, the colors are burned.

- **Hard Light**   50 percent gray disappears and white and black are unaffected. Lighter than 50 percent gray screens and darker than 50 percent multiplies.

5

- **Vivid Light**   Same as Hard Light but the result is burned or dodged colors, depending on the percentage of gray.

- **Linear Light**   50 percent gray disappears and white and black are unaffected. Lighter than 50 percent gray increases brightness and darker than 50 percent reduces the brightness.

- **Pin Light**   If the blend color is darker than 50 percent gray, pixels are lighter.

- **Hard Mix**   Reduces everything to eight colors: cyan, magenta, yellow, red, blue, green, black, and white. If the blend layer is lighter than 50 percent gray, the color shifts the base hue to one of the eight colors; if it's less than 50 percent, the blend hue shifts to the closest of the eight colors.

Inverting Modes

Inverting modes are good to get radical and psychedelic effects.

- **Difference**   Inverts the color where the layers overlap. Black is ignored.

- **Exclusion**   Inverts the color where the layers overlap, but with less intensity than Difference.

Color-Based Modes

These are more practical modes. They affect only certain aspects of the image at a time and affect the underlying image.

- **Hue**   Changes the color of an image. When applied, only the color is affected in the underlying image; all the other properties are unaffected.

- **Saturation**   Affects only the amount of color in the underlying image. When you overlay with a strong color, the color itself is ignored and only the strength of the color is applied. If the top color is black, white, or gray, the image underneath will appear without color as a grayscale image.

- **Color**   This is like Hue and Saturation mixed together. This is the best mode for colorizing grayscale pictures.

■ **Luminosity**   This is the opposite of the Color mode. The color will be preserved, but the grayscale values can be changed.

Using Blending Modes for Creative Results

The best way to get familiar with blending modes is to experiment and try different modes on different layers and see how they look. Some images will look better with certain blending than others. Let's look at a few common uses for blending modes.

Making White Disappear

You'll recall that the darkening modes cause white to disappear altogether and leave black intact. These are excellent modes to use when a layer has unwanted white areas around the image. For example, suppose you have a page of black text on a white background and you want to overlay a colored image with it. You would like the white to be invisible so that it looks like the black text is on top of the image. You could select all the white and remove it using several tools, but why bother when you can accomplish exactly the same result using the Multiply blending mode?

To change the blending mode, select a layer and choose a mode from the upper-left drop-down menu in the Layers palette. Figure 5-38 shows the layer converted to Multiply mode; the text looks as if it were typed directly onto the background.

To experiment with different blending modes, choose a layer, select the Move tool, and then press SHIFT- + *(plus sign) to cycle through the modes. To cycle backward, press* SHIFT- – *(minus).*

Making Black Disappear

You can make black disappear in exactly the same way you make white disappear, except use Screen mode instead of Multiply.

Changing Image Color Without Losing Detail

When you change a layer to Color mode, all the image detail is retained from the base layers and the image takes on the color

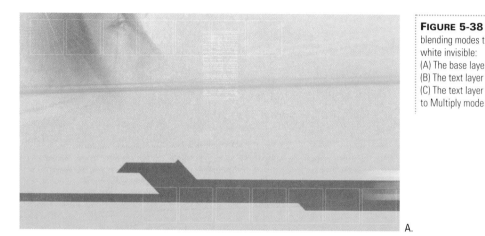

A.

FIGURE 5-38 Using blending modes to make white invisible:
(A) The base layer
(B) The text layer
(C) The text layer changed to Multiply mode

B.

📄 bg2.psd @ 100% (Layer 22, RGB/8#)

(3)The Light Modes - Will cause 50% gray to disappear. No effect on black or white.

- Overlay: The shadows and highlights of the base layer are not effected, the colors are blended together.

- Soft Light: If the blend color is lighter than 50% gray then the colors are dodged, if the blend color is darker than 50% gray then the colors are burned.

- Hard light: 50% gray disappears and white and black are unaffected. Lighter than 50% gray screens and darker than 50% Multiplies.

- Vivid Light: Same as Hard Light but the result is burned or dodged colors depending on the percentage of gray

- Linear Light: 50% gray disappears and white and black are unaffected. Lighter than 50% gray increase brightness and darker than 50% reduces the brightness

- Pin Light: If the blend color is darker than 50% gray, pixels lighter

C.

📄 bg2.psd @ 100% (Layer 22, RGB/8#)

(3)The Light Modes - Will cause 50% gray to disappear. No effect on black or white.

- Overlay: The shadows and highlights of the base layer are not effected, the colors are blended together.

- Soft Light: If the blend color is lighter than 50% gray then the colors are dodged, if the blend color is darker than 50% gray then the colors are burned.

- Hard light: 50% gray disappears and white and black are unaffected. Lighter than 50% gray screens and darker than 50% Multiplies.

- Vivid Light: Same as Hard Light but the result is burned or dodged colors depending on the percentage of gray

- Linear Light: 50% gray disappears and white and black are unaffected. Lighter than 50% gray increase brightness and darker than 50% reduces the brightness

- Pin Light: If the blend color is darker than 50% gray, pixels lighter

A.

B.

C.

FIGURE 5-39 Using color blend mode: (A) The original collage (B) A colored layer revealed (C) Changing to Color mode

of the blending layer. This is a great trick for a fast change to a collage, and it's a popular and useful layering trick that produces stunning results with very little effort.

Notice how we can create three totally different options with only two mouse clicks. Figure 5-39 shows the following three steps:

1. Start with a blue collage.

2. Add a colored layer that is more of a salmon color; this overrides a lot of the detail in the collage.

3. Switch the layer to Color mode; changing to Color mode allows all the detail to show through, while retaining the colors of the new blend layer.

Making Objects Overlay in a Natural Way

When we apply text objects on top of other objects, they tend to look a little unnatural. This is because the base image has highlights and shadows that are not apparent in the text. By changing to Overlay mode, you will allow the shadows and highlights to show through to the blend layer, as shown in Figure 5-40. This makes the text look like it is a part of the object and blends in nicely with its surroundings.

FIGURE 5-40 Blending text into textures: (A) The text before blending (B) The text with Overlay mode applied

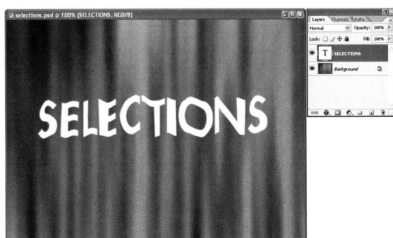

A.

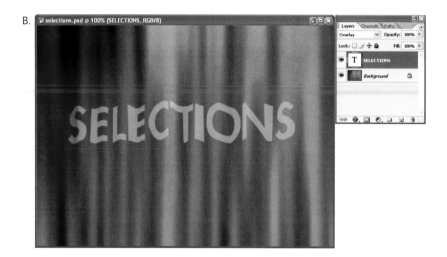

Removing the Layer Color

The Luminosity mode will cause a layer to shed its color and allow the base colors and textures to come through. In Luminosity mode, the image will retain its highlight and shadow information.

In Figure 5-41, I added a face on top of an image and changed it to Luminosity mode. To enhance the organic effect further, I could lower the opacity to 50 percent. You will find that changing the opacity will make a big difference when blending images. Use the opacity with different blending modes to achieve surrealistic results.

FIGURE 5-41 Luminosity mode

Chapter 6

Demystify Channels

How to...

- Understand channels
- Use RGB channels
- Use CMYK channels
- Convert color to grayscale
- Use the Channels palette
- Use alpha channels
- Create spot colors

Channels sound really complicated, and to be honest they can be. Before you say "forget this" and skip to the next chapter, though, let me tell you a couple of things about these little beasts.

You don't have to understand everything about channels to use them. For example, most of us have no idea how they put a movie onto a little plastic disc called a DVD. But that doesn't stop us from slipping *The Matrix* into our DVD players and watching Neo do his thing.

By leveraging the power of channels, you will find that they make everyday tasks easier and more accurate. For example, by using channels, you can make better selections, your line art will look better than ever, and all kinds of cool special effects will be at your fingertips. So have I sold you yet? How about I break channels down into plain English and leave out all the techno mumbo jumbo? Deal? Good; then read on.

Channels Explained

Channels are the raw information that Photoshop uses to produce color. As you know from messing around with a paint box as a child, the paint box doesn't come with all the colors you need, but you can mix colors to create new ones. For example, mixing red and yellow will create orange. You may also remember hearing about *primary colors*, which are yellow, red, and blue. By mixing combinations of these primary colors, you can create a range of new colors. The range that you can create is called the *color gamut*.

In Photoshop, you work with channels using a handy user interface called the Channels palette, which looks little bit like the Layers palette you used in Chapter 4 and is described in its own section a little later in this chapter. Before we get into technicalities of use, though, you need to understand a little bit about the two main kinds of channels that you use in Photoshop: CMYK channels and RGB channels.

Note *Each channel contains 256 levels of color in its 8-bit default mode. For photographic purposes, 16-bit channels can be used; these would have to be scanned from a high-resolution scanner or taken from a digital camera in Raw mode. 16-bit channels contain up to 32,000 levels of color per channel. You cannot make an 8-bit channel true 16-bit simply by choosing the 16-bit mode; the image must be captured in 16 bits of color. We will cover 16-bit mode in Chapter 12. Photoshop CS2 now offers limited support for 32-bit images, called High Dynamic Range (HDR).*

CMYK Channels

FIGURE 6-1 A CMYK image showing the Channels palette and a strip in CMYK colors

In Photoshop, you can think of the channels as the primary colors, and by mixing them together you can create a new gamut of colors. In *CMYK mode*, the colors are similar to their paint-box cousins. CMYK stands for *c*yan (blue), *m*agenta (red), *y*ellow, and blac*k*. Black is added because mixing the other three colors produces a muddy brown rather than a pure black, and there's no way to render a full-color image correctly without using black. In the painting world, artists also use pure black and pure white pigments. In Photoshop, we don't need white because the paper is usually white.

Figure 6-1 shows a color image with the Channels palette open. (For more on the palette, see "The Channels Palette," later in this chapter.) The figure includes a test strip in cyan,

magenta, yellow, and black so that you can see the effect that the channels have on the image.

Because each color has its own channel, you'll see four channels in the Channels palette for a CMYK image. You can see how each channel is separated and how the ink will disperse in Figure 6-2A through D. To look at just one channel, click its name in the Channels palette. If, for example, you click the Cyan channel, the preview displays only the parts of the image that use cyan ink (as shown in Figure 6-2A).

Note *By default, the previews appear in black and white because it's easier for you to see the channel contents in black and white. You can change the channel previews to appear in color by choosing Edit | Preferences | Display & Cursors and checking the box Color Channels In Color.*

Previewing your color channels in the default black and white is a good idea, because when you are preparing the color plates for printing, the plates are in black and white. The appropriate colored ink will be printed in the black areas of each plate (see Figure 6-2D). Notice how the test strip on each channel in the figure is solid black for its respective color.

When printing in CMYK on a printing press, colors are printed as tiny dots at different angles and shapes, which are arranged together in such a way that it fools the eyes into seeing colors that really are not present at all. If you take a loupe (a magnifying device, not unlike a mounted magnifying glass) and look at a *process printed* piece (another name for a four-color [CMYK] print), you will be able to see these tiny dots. Even without using a loupe, you can sometimes see the dots on a low line screen image, such as a newspaper photo. (A *line screen* tells how many lines of dots per inch are present.)

When these colors are arranged and printed in the printing process, the new colors are created. When the piece is printed on a printing press, only four ink colors are used, and they combine to make all the colors you see on a finished printed piece. Because of this, *CMYK mode* should be used *only* if you are preparing files to be printed on a *commercial printing press.*

Tip *When creating CMYK documents, it's sometimes best to work in RGB first and convert to CMYK at the end for the following reasons: CMYK doesn't support all the Photoshop filters; RGB has more colors available; and because CMYK has an extra channel, the file size will also be almost a third larger, which can slow down system performance. You'll learn about RBG colors shortly in the section "RGB Channels."*

A. Cyan channel

B. Magenta channel

C. Yellow channel

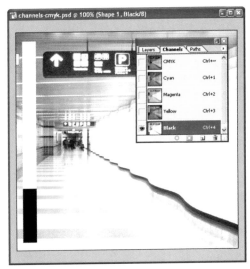

D. Black channel

FIGURE 6-2 An image's color dispersal as represented by each channel

Note *The reason we began with CMYK channels and not RGB channels is simple. CMYK channels are the easiest to understand when relating to the "real world." CMYK colors are subtractive colors, which means that if you take all the colors away, only white will remain. The more color you add, the darker the image will be. That's easy to understand!*

Did you know?

The Prepress Process

When a document is printed on a commercial printing press, the file must pass through a few phases. The first stage is called "ripping," where film or negatives are made from your file. These negatives are not that different from what you get from a normal camera, except the printing negatives are much larger, and each negative caters only to one color. Four individual "film plates" are made, one for each color of cyan, magenta, yellow, and black. The film is then "burned to plates"—chemicals are applied to an aluminum, rubber, or paper sheet, called a plate. The chemicals react to the film and cause indentations on the plate. The plates are then loaded onto the printing press, where the indentations pick up inks and apply them to the pages that are being printed.

Current printing trends are moving to DTP, direct-to-plate, printing. In DTP, the film process is eliminated and the electronic files are sent directly to the plates.

RGB Channels

RGB stands for *red*, *green*, and *blue*. This is the main color space you will use most of the time in Photoshop. Remember what you just learned about mixing color for CMYK? In RGB, everything is the opposite! RGB mode is called *additive color* because the three colors *combined* make white. "How can this be?" you may ask. Think of CMYK as inks and RGB as light. With RGB, we are painting with light. RGB is the standard color space used for monitors, where the three primary colors are used; they are called *monitor primaries*.

 Green is used instead of yellow because cleaner colors can be produced on monitors using green.

You may remember a high school science experiment for which you used different colored markers to mark up a round piece of cardstock. You then spun the card really fast until all the colors blended into pure white. How did this happen? Because the human eye also sees in additive color. White light is a combination of all the colors of the spectrum—just look at a rainbow as it splits the light into individual colors, which were really there all the time, even though we couldn't see them.

Figure 6-3 shows several preview images: Starting at 6-3A, you see an RGB image with a test strip. The *test strip* contains pure colors for each of the three channels, which allows you to see how each color interacts with each different channel.

Figures 6-3B through D show each individual color channel. In RGB channel previews, whenever a solid color is used, the test strip and channel shows as white. For example, look at the red channel image in Figure 6-3B. Imagine that instead of white, we are showing red light; so where there is no red light, it is shown as black, and where there is intense red light, it is shown as white. It makes sense, then, that *no* light would mean *no* color and *a lot* of light would mean *a lot* of color. Study the test strip for each of the channels shown in the figure.

FIGURE 6-3 RGB channels—notice that each color channel shows as white.

A. The composite of all channels

B. Red channel

C. Green channel

D. Blue channel

6

Each channel is also capable of displaying 256 levels of gray (8-bit color).

FIGURE 6-4 Mixing the blue and red channels produces a purple image.

We can mix channel views by first choosing a color channel by clicking its name in the palette and then showing a second channel by clicking the visibility icon—the little eye to the left of the channel thumbnail, as shown in Figure 6-4, just like the icon on the Layers palette. In Figure 6-4, the red and blue channels both show the visibility icon. Notice how the combined channels display as a purple color? Guess what? If you mix blue and red together, you get purple.

Changing Grayscale Mode to RGB Mode

Figure 6-5 shows an image in grayscale. *Grayscale* is the term for an image that has no color present. You may have called it "black and white." Notice that only one channel appears in the Channels palette. That is because no extra color information is needed for a grayscale image. If you wanted to add color to this image, you would first have to convert to RGB mode so that channels would be available in which to store the color. To convert from grayscale to RGB mode, choose Image | Mode | RGB from the main menu.

After you change to RGB mode, the actual image would still look exactly the same, and the information copied would be exactly the same for

FIGURE 6-5 A grayscale image contains only one channel on the palette.

each channel. But we would now be able to *add* some color so that Photoshop could display it.

Converting Color to Grayscale

You can also convert a color image to grayscale by using one of several methods:

- With the image open in Photoshop, press CTRL-SHIFT-U (CMD-SHIFT-U on the Mac).
- From the main menu, choose Image | Adjustments | Desaturate.
- Convert to grayscale mode.
- Create a new document with new channel information.
- Use Channel Mixer to create a custom grayscale conversion.

The first two methods will *equalize* the channels; in other words, the channels will all display the same image even though the palette now includes color channels, as shown in Figure 6-6.

FIGURE 6-6 Grayscale Channels palette settings in RGB mode

The third method, convert to grayscale mode, will just "throw away" all the color information and transfer all the grayscale information into the grayscale channel. If you want to print a single-color image, you will first need to convert your image to grayscale. Then you can apply whatever color you want to the image.

Channels can be used to your advantage when converting to grayscale. Rather than simply convert to grayscale and let Photoshop make all the decisions, you can choose which channel you want to use as your new grayscale image and convert the single channel into a new document. This is a good conversion method, because you get to make some decisions. Here's how it's done:

FIGURE 6-7 The blue channel produces the cleanest preview with the most detail.

1. Open an image that's in a color mode, and click each of the channels until you see one that has better toning and clarity than the rest. For our example, we'll use the blue channel, as shown in Figure 6-7, because it looks best on this image.

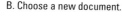

2. Click the arrow at the top right of the Channels palette to open the flyout menu, as shown in Figure 6-8A. Choose Duplicate Channel.

A. The flyout menu from the Channels palette

B. Choose a new document.

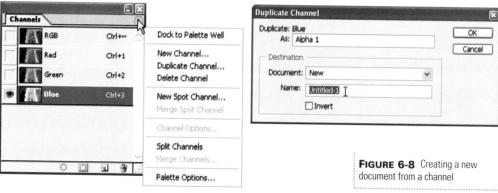

FIGURE 6-8 Creating a new document from a channel

3. The Duplicate Channel dialog box, shown in Figure 6-8B, opens. In the Document field, choose New. This will create a new document from this channel. You can name it whatever you want.

FIGURE 6-9 The new image and its Channel palette

Figure 6-9 shows a new document Channel palette showing only one channel, called Alpha 1. (More in the section "Alpha Channels.") The new channel looks exactly like the old one shown in Figure 6-7, except this image is now in *multi-channel* mode, which is a special mode that lets you add or delete channels as you wish. A multi-channel image with a single channel looks the same as an image in grayscale mode. You should convert the image from multi-channel to grayscale mode: choose Image | Mode | Grayscale from the main menu.

In Figure 6-10, you can see the difference using this method makes compared to just converting to grayscale mode. It's worth the little bit of extra effort. The image in Figure 6-10A is the image we converted from a channel. The image in Figure 6-10B is the result of converting to grayscale. Notice how much better Figure 6-10A looks.

FIGURE 6-10 The image converted from a channel (A) and the same image converted to grayscale (B).

A.

B.

Using Channel Mixer to Create a Custom Grayscale Conversion

This method produces superior results over the other methods because you have complete control over how the conversion occurs. By using Channel Mixer, you can decide how much of each channel will display in the grayscale image. The image will also remain in its original color space, making more levels of gray available for the final grayscale image.

1. On the Layers palette, click the Adjustment Layers button and choose Channel Mixer.

2. Click the Monochrome button.

3. By default, just the red channel (cyan if you are in CMYK mode) is displayed, as indicated by its value of 100 percent. Slide the other channels to the right to include them in the mix; be sure to lower the red channel so that the total mix does not exceed 100 percent.

4. After you have the desired mix, click OK.

 A document can contain up to 56 channels.

The Channels Palette

Now that you have some understanding about channels, let's take a closer look at the Channels palette—particularly its functionality.

The Channels palette behaves pretty much like the Layers palette (as discussed in Chapter 4). Choose Window | Channels from the main menu to open the Channels palette, if it isn't already visible on the workspace.

The icons on the Channels palette are similar to those on the Layers palette, and the two palettes' appearance is almost the same. If you want to display individual channels, click the channel name. To show all the channels, click the topmost channel, which is called a *composite* channel.

Figure 6-11 shows the Channels palette with several channels, including two alpha channels. An *alpha* channel is an extra non-printing channel used to aid us in special tasks. (Alpha channels are discussed in the next section.)

FIGURE 6-11 The Channels palette

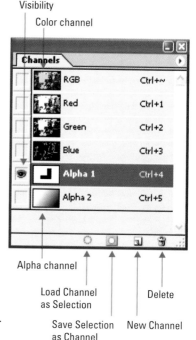

At the bottom of the Channels palette, you will notice four buttons. The functions of these buttons are listed here:

- ■ **Load Channel as Selection**   Loads the contents of a channel into a selection. This button is used mostly in conjunction with an alpha channel (discussed next).

- ■ **Save Selection as Channel**   Creates a channel out of a selection. This is a good way to save a selection for later use. This button is handy when you're masking objects.

- ■ **New Channel**   Creates a new channel.

- ■ **Delete**   Drag an unwanted channel to this trash can to delete it.

You can also load a channel as a selection by pressing CTRL *(CMD on the Mac) and clicking the thumbnail.*

Alpha Channels

Alpha channels are storage channels that are useful for saving specific, selection information and special effects information. They are used for masks or track mattes for animation. As you will have discovered by now, once you turn off a selection (deselect) or close the document, the selection is gone. You can use alpha channels to save and reuse selections, even after you close a document. All the selection information is saved in this alpha channel for later use (see Figure 6-12).

FIGURE 6-12 Create an alpha channel and the dialog box for a new channel opens.

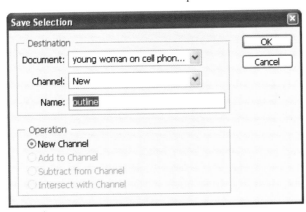

Alpha channels are used mainly for image manipulation and saving selections. They do not print with the file. They are saved with the file and can be turned into selections at any time. But more than that, an alpha channel can store a soft or feathered selection. A feathered selection will create a soft, faded transition as opposed to a hard-edged transition. An alpha channel can contain up to 256 levels of grayscale (in 8-bit color), just like a regular channel.

Because an alpha channel is used for the main purpose of image manipulation, alpha channels will not print or affect the appearance of your printed images.

When you create an alpha channel, it holds a *mask* of your selection. When you load a selection using a channel, black is loaded while white is ignored. Gray is treated as a *soft selection*, meaning that the selection contains some transparency. You can even save and load a selection that has areas using different transparencies on sections of the channel.

Creating Alpha Channels

To create an alpha channel, do one of the following:

- Click the New Channel button.
- In the Channels palette, make a selection, and click the Save Selection As Channel button.
- With a selection active, choose Select | Save Selection. The Save Selection dialog box will open, asking you to name the new channel.

Figure 6-13A shows how a new alpha channel looks in the preview. Notice that the new channel contents in Figure 6-13B are solid black and white, creating a very sharp selection.

FIGURE 6-13 Creating an alpha channel (A), and the alpha channel displayed (B)

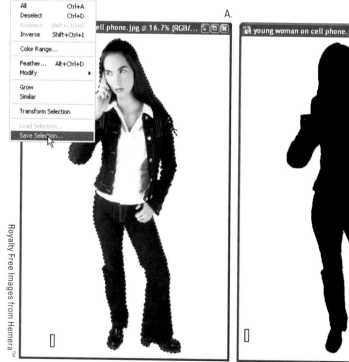
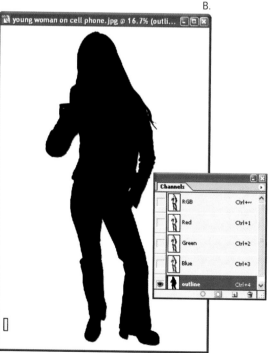

Royalty Free Images from Hemera™

Loading the Contents of an Alpha Channel

Once you have created an alpha channel or opened an image that contains an alpha channel, you can load the channel as a selection in several ways:

- CTRL-click (CMD-click on the Mac) on the channel thumbnail you want to load, as shown in Figure 6-13B.

- While working in the main image window, choose Select | Load Selection, and then choose which channel you want to load from the drop-down menu in the Load Selection dialog box.

- Choose the target channel, and then click the Load Channel As Selection button in the Channels palette.

 For more information on selections and their uses, see Chapter 10.

FIGURE 6-14 The image on a new background after using an alpha channel to load a selection

After you have loaded the alpha channel, you can use the selection for many purposes. For example, you could use a selection as a mask to protect parts of an image while painting and applying regional effects. Another common use would be to lift the image off its background and drop in onto a new one, as shown in Figure 6-14.

Here's how you place an object into a new document using an alpha channel:

1. Open an image that contains an object saved in an alpha channel. This is your *source* document.

2. Open the document that will serve as the background into which you want to place the object. This is your *destination* document.

3. On the source document, load the selection from the channel.

4. Click the layer thumbnail in the Layers palette. Making sure the correct layer is active (if a multi-layered image is used), drag the selected object to the destination document.

5. Release the mouse and position the object to suit your tastes.

Spot Colors

CMYK offers a relatively small gamut of colors. Very bright colors, for example, cannot be reproduced in this format, and color precision is not guaranteed. When you need special colors, you use *spot color*, an extra color that is printed at the same time as the CMYK inks. Unlike CMYK color, spot ink is a solid color.

Note *Generally, a special ink brand called Pantone color is used in the United States. These inks are part of a matching system that helps you choose accurate colors, similar to a paint chip you would pick up from a paint store. Each country has its preferred ink matching system. Check with your printer to determine which system is preferred.*

The color will match exactly the colors you see in a special printed color chip called a Pantone color guide. Typically, you would need to use one or more spot colors in the following situations:

- You need an exact match of a color.
- You want to use metallic inks.
- You want to use fluorescent inks.
- You want to use a spot varnish.
- You want to print a two- or three-color project.

No matter what your need for spot color, the creation process in Photoshop is the same. You will need to leverage the power of spot channels.

Some printers have eight-color printing presses that are capable of printing CMYK plus four spot colors at the same time.

Creating Spot Colors

You can create a spot color using the spot channels in Photoshop. Figure 6-15 shows a color postcard that requires a spot color for the logo. Assume that compuFIX is a large company, the color of the logo is very important, and budget is not an issue (since it's more expensive to print a five-color job).

FIGURE 6-15 For this advertising piece, we want to make the logo a spot color.

FIGURE 6-16 The logo selected

1. Convert the RGB image to CMYK by choosing Image | Mode | CMYK. Choose No when a dialog box asks whether you want to flatten the image.

2. To select the object that we're turning into a spot color, CTRL-click (CMD-click on a Mac) the layer thumbnail that contains the logo. This will load the selection, as shown in Figure 6-16.

3. Open the Channels palette by clicking on its tab in the main window. If the palette is not displayed, choose Window | Channels from the main menu.

4. To turn the selection into a spot channel, click the arrow at the upper-right corner of the palette to reveal the palette options menu and choose New Spot Channel, as shown in Figure 6-17.

5. The New Spot Channel dialog box will open automatically. Click the color swatch in this dialog box to open the Custom Colors dialog.

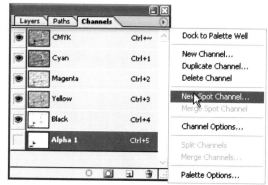

FIGURE 6-17 Creating a new spot channel

6. Click the Custom Color button to launch the options and in the Color Libraries field, choose PANTONE Solid Coated. Two types of paper can be used: plain *uncoated* paper (such as newsprint) and *coated* paper (such as the finished paper used in art books and magazines). Coated papers are coated with chemicals that prevent the paper from absorbing too much ink (blotting). This results in crisper images and cleaner colors. Generally, with a high-quality color job, you will be using coated paper.

7. Choose a Pantone color, as shown in Figure 6-18. Then click OK.

FIGURE 6-18 Choosing a custom color

8. Photoshop will return you to the New Spot Channel dialog box; you'll notice the information that appears in the Name field is the same as the color you chose in step 7 (see Figure 6-19). Make a note of the color and give it to your printer, who will need to know the ink number so the color can be correctly matched.

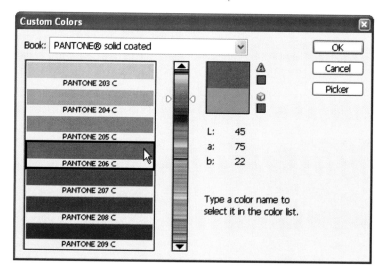

9. Now let's set Solidity. Unless you want the color to be *screened* back (printed semitransparent) choose 100%.

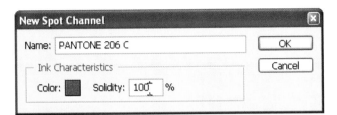

FIGURE 6-19 Setting the solidity

10. Click OK to create your new spot channel (shown in the Channels palette in Figure 6-20). Notice that the name of the channel is the Pantone color name. The logo in the image has also been changed to this color.

FIGURE 6-20 The Channels palette and image showing a spot channel and color

Knocking Out Colors

When we create a spot color, we can either have the printer *overprint the color* or we can create a *knockout*. A knockout "knocks out" all the color behind it. In an overprint, the spot color ink is printed directly over the other inks. This works well for varnishes, metallic inks, and very dark spot colors.

Imagine, for example, that you need to add a bright red spot color over the top of some very dark inks. The red ink would not show up too well—at best it would look dirty. If you are printing with a light color over dark colors, you can create a *knockout*, for which you remove any ink behind the spot color and print directly on the paper. Figure 6-21 shows the difference between printing an overprint and a knockout.

FIGURE 6-21 Printing an overprint and a knockout

Creating a Knockout

Follow these steps to knock out color:

FIGURE 6-22 Selection loaded in the Layers palette

1. In this example, we're going to deal with the logo again, so we choose the logo channel. In the Channels palette, CTRL-click (CMD-click on the Mac) the spot channel thumbnail. This will load the selection and open the Layers palette, as shown in Figure 6-22.

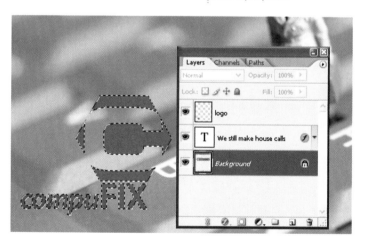

2. Create a new layer, and move it to the top of the layer stack.

3. Choose the new top layer and fill the selection with white. The white will hide the color from the rest of the layers and leave a nice, clean base over which our spot color will print.

What Is Trapping?

When you create a knocked out image, you also need to consider *trapping*. During a printing operation on a printing press, the paper can sometimes slip a little bit. This causes a problem called *misregistration*, which occurs when the paper slips and the ink doesn't quite cover the exact area where it's supposed to cover. The result is that little white gaps can be seen on the edges of the spot color area.

This problem can be corrected by a process called *trapping*. To use trapping, you'll make the knocked out area slightly smaller than the actual ink area. This way, if the paper slips slightly, because you've left a little leeway to work with, the ink still covers the empty space.

To create trappings in Photoshop, you simply contract your selection a little bit, so that a pixel or so of ink leeway is removed from the knocked out area.

To do this, choose Select | Modify | Contract and enter a setting of 1 pixel, as shown in the illustration. To accommodate multiple spot colors, just repeat the steps for each knocked out area.

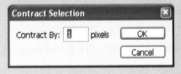

Saving the File

To enable your printer to reproduce the spot color and other colors and images, you must save the file correctly. You can cuse the following file formats:

- **PSD (Photoshop Document)**   Photoshop native file. This will work if you are printing directly from Photoshop or assembling your files in Adobe InDesign.

- **TIFF (Tagged Image File Format)**   The new Photoshop TIFF supports layers, channels, and spot channels. You can print these files directly from Photoshop or InDesign.

■ **DCS 2.0 (Desktop Color Separation)** An Encapsulated PostScript (EPS) file. PostScript is the language most printers use. This format is supported by QuarkXPress and Adobe InDesign. If you save as DCS 2.0, when the pop-up menu appears, choose the ASCII format. Choose a single file with color composite. (Also use an 8-bit preview.) This way, the image will look halfway decent in your page layout software. It will print much better, too.

Chapter 7

Create and Understand Paths

How to…

- Understand raster graphics
- Understand vector graphics
- Create paths
- Use the Pen tool
- Convert a curve to a straight line
- Convert a straight line to a curve
- Use the Freeform Pen tool
- Convert a selection to a path
- Use custom shapes
- Create a path from a shape
- Fill and stroke paths
- Edit paths
- Turn a path into a selection
- Manage and load shapes
- Create custom shapes

Apples and oranges are used as a cliché when trying to compare two totally different things. The truth is, they really are not so different—they are both fruit, they are both round, and they both taste great together in a fine salad. Like apples and oranges, graphics in Photoshop come in two flavors: raster graphics and vector graphics. Both are graphical formats that work together to produce what you see on screen, but they function in totally different ways.

In this chapter, we look at these two types of graphics. By the end of the chapter you will not only know the difference between the two, but you will be able to create graphics using both technologies—a sort of graphics salad, if you will. You'll also jump into the world of paths, which are useful for all kinds of tasks, from drawing to cutting out objects cleanly.

Apples and Oranges: Raster vs. Vector Graphics

Because you probably use them all the time on your computer, you're likely already familiar with raster or bitmap graphics. Most of Photoshop is based on this format. Raster graphics are made up of pixels, tiny squares that each contain one color.

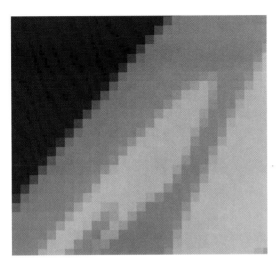

FIGURE 7-1 A close-up of the pixels that make up a raster graphic

When colors are applied to these pixels and they are mixed together on your viewing screen, you no longer see the individual pixels—instead, you see the entire image. In Chapter 6, you read about using a loupe to view the dots of color on a printed color image. Pixels work in a similar way to "blend" colors on your computer screen.

Figure 7-1 shows part of an image zoomed up to 1600 percent. You can see the individual pixels that form the image. To give you an example of how tiny these pixels are, the average 17-inch screen contains 800,000 of them!

Photoshop is essentially a raster-based program. Most of the graphics and just about all the images you output are based on pixels. Vector graphics, on the other hand, are based on math. To those of you who are mathematically challenged: don't worry, because all the math happens behind the scenes, and you don't have to be a scientist to use vectors.

Think of vectors as "joining the dots." A minimum of two dots (called *anchor points*) are necessary for any vector image to happen. When you create two points, Photoshop will draw a line between the points, as shown in Figure 7-2. You will then tell Photoshop whether you want a straight line or a curved line to be drawn. If you move one of the points, Photoshop will adjust the curve to fall between the lines so that they are still connected.

FIGURE 7-2 A vector showing two points joined

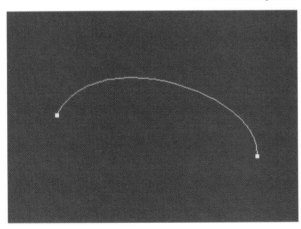

In an illustration program such as Adobe Illustrator, when we draw a circle, the first point marks the center, and the second point marks the radius. The program then knows to draw a circle based on this information. Such programs are based on vector graphics. Vectors have several benefits:

- They can be easily edited at any time
- They are a small file size

- Because they are based on math, you can scale them up and down (resize) without any loss of quality

The features in Photoshop that use vectors are

- Paths
- Text
- Shape layers
- Smart Objects (which can contain vectors; see Chapter 5)

Paths Explained

Paths are made of curves, lines, and points. Think of them as the lines you would draw with your ink pen to connect the dots. The technical name for the curves created by lines are *Bézier curves*, named after their inventor, Pierre Bézier.

A path in Photoshop has four basic components, as shown in Figure 7-3.

FIGURE 7-3 Anatomy of a path

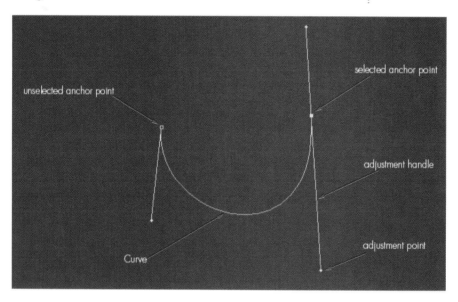

- **Anchor points** These points tell the curves where to begin and end. When selected, the anchor point is solid, or filled. The point will display as unfilled (or hollow) when it's not selected. You can edit only selected points.

- **Adjustment handles**   These join the anchor points and adjustment points, as a visual reference.
- **Adjustment points**   Click these to make changes to the shape of the curves.
- **Curve**   The shape that is being drawn.

Paths do not print and they are not visible in the final image. They appear as reference points to help you draw complex shapes and perform other operations. You can, however, draw shapes with paths and then fill them with color or images, and these colors or images will print and are visible in the final image. You can create a precise outline around an image using paths, which could then be used to "cut out" the image. A path will create the cleanest edge possible in Photoshop, so it lends itself well for such purposes. You can also save the path with the final image, which makes it possible to reuse the path later. You can even use paths as guides to curve text (which is covered in Chapter 8).

Creating Paths: the Pen Tool

Now that you have a basic understanding of what paths are, we are going to examine some techniques for creating them.

The "mother" of the path is the Pen tool. Most paths begin their existence when we create them with the Pen tool. The concepts of the Pen tool are not difficult to grasp, but the execution is another thing altogether. Because the Pen tool requires some practice to master, you should experiment with it before you tackle any important projects. Mastery of the Pen tool will help you work successfully in Photoshop for years to come.

Drawing a Straight Line

Drawing a straight line is fairly straightforward (excuse the pun):

1. Choose the Pen tool from the toolbox.

2. Click anywhere on your canvas.

3. Click at another spot, and a straight line appears between the two clicks. For a perfectly horizontal or vertical line, hold down the SHIFT key as you click to create the line.

4. Click as many times as you want to connect the line to the next point(s) to finish drawing the path.

You can hold down the SHIFT *key as you click to draw vertical lines, horizontal lines, or perfect 45-degree angles.*

Drawing an S Curve

Now let's create an S curve. This is a bit more difficult than a straight line. Figure 7-4 illustrates the process.

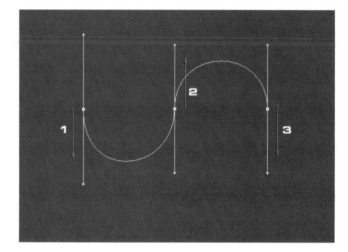

1. Select the Pen tool. Choose the Paths option from the options bar. Click, and then drag down with the Pen tool. Dragging defines the direction of the curve.

2. Click and drag up for the second point. You will see your first curve begin to form into the shape of a *U*.

FIGURE 7-4 Drawing an S curve

3. Click and drag down for the third point, and notice a nice *S* shape.

FIGURE 7-5 Pen types

You will probably have to try this a few times to make your curve look even.

 Turn on Show Grid to assist in drawing paths. To turn on this option, choose View | Show | Grid from the main menu.

Drawing a W Curve

When you draw a sharp curve, as in a *W* shape, you'll use the Convert Point tool. Figure 7-5 shows several pen types, with the Convert Point tool at the bottom of the list in the toolbox.

You can also access this tool by pressing the ALT key (OPTION on the Mac). The Pen tool will switch to the Convert Point tool until you release the key, when the tool will revert back to the active Pen tool.

Now let's draw the W curve, as illustrated in Figure 7-6.

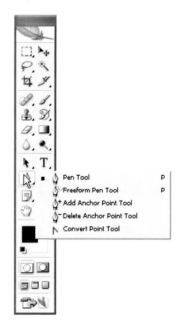

1. Click and drag down with the Pen tool; this defines the direction of the curve.

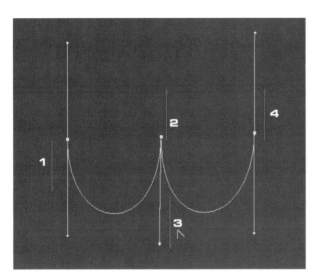

FIGURE 7-6 Creating a W curve

FIGURE 7-7 Converting a curve to a straight line

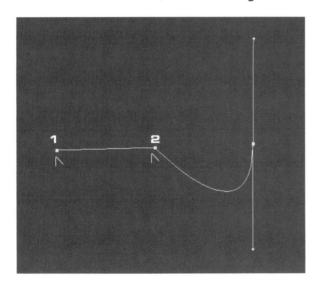

2. Click to set the second point and drag up. This makes a U curve. Hover the mouse over the second anchor point you just created. Press the ALT key (OPTION on the Mac) and you will see the cursor change to the *convert point logo* (a little V shape).

3. Drag in the direction you want the next curve to go—in this case, drag down. You will notice an adjustment handle is created, but no path. You are now "telling" the path to change direction.

4. Click and drag up, and you will see a W curve.

You have now created two types of curves; keep practicing drawing curves with the Pen tool until you become comfortable with its use.

Converting a Curve to a Straight Line

Once you have created a curve, you can change it to a straight line anytime. The technique is illustrated in Figure 7-7. Begin with either an S curve or a W curve that you've already created.

1. Choose the Convert Point tool. (To edit the initial point, the actual tool must be selected; you cannot press the ALT key or OPTION on the Mac.)

2. Click the first point. It will now become a straight point, and the end of the line will still be a bit curved because the second point is still a curve.

3. Click the second point and the curve will become a straight line.

Converting a Straight Line to a Curve

This is the opposite of the preceding instruction. To convert a
line to a curve, you will need a path with a straight line on it.

1. Choose the Convert Point tool.

2. Click the first point, and drag either up or down to
begin a curve.

3. Click the second point and drag again. You will now
have a curve.

4. Don't forget to CTRL-click (CMD-click on the Mac)
or press ESC to finish drawing the curve.

Using the Freeform Pen Tool

This tool is simple to use. Just choose the tool and begin to draw
on the page, just as you would with an ink pen in the real world.
The Freeform Pen tool will add all the anchor points for you
and clean up the path a little bit to reduce the number of points.
The disadvantage of using this tool is that you have no control
over where the points are created. However, you can edit them
just like all the other path tools. (See the sidebar "Add and
Delete Anchor Points.") Figure 7-8 shows the result of using the
Freeform Pen tool.

FIGURE 7-8 Freeform Pen tool
drawing

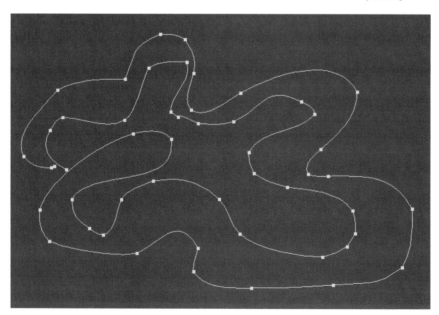

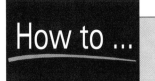

Add and Delete Anchor Points

In Figure 7-5, two pens in the pen group show a plus sign and a minus sign. These are the pens you use respectively to add and delete anchor points.

To delete an anchor point:

1. Choose the Delete Anchor Point tool, or just hover the Pen tool over an existing anchor point. You will see a minus sign.

2. Click to delete the anchor point.

To add an anchor point:

1. Choose the Add Anchor Point tool, or just hover the Pen tool anywhere over part of a curve that doesn't already have an anchor point. You will see a plus sign.

2. Click to add the new anchor point.

7

Creating a Closed Path

So far, all the paths we have discussed are called *open* paths—meaning that a distinct start and end point appears. Think of these paths as being similar to pieces of string—you can curve them or pull them straight, but no matter what the shape, the string has a beginning and an end.

In Photoshop, you can use another type of path, called a *closed* path, an example of which is shown in Figure 7-9. In a closed path, the start and end points are the same, and the path forms a closed loop. Any path can be turned into a closed path.

When you are creating a path, hover the mouse over the start point and a little

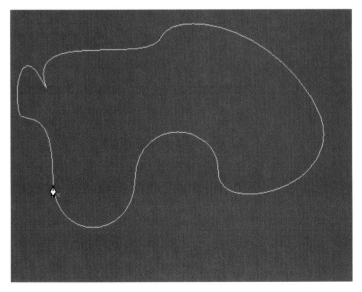

FIGURE 7-9 Creating a closed path

circle will appear, like that shown in Figure 7-10. This circle lets you know that you are at the start point; if you click, you will close the path.

FIGURE 7-10 The start point of a path

FIGURE 7-11 An image showing an active selection

Illustration courtesy of www.photoshopcafe.com

Converting a Selection to a Path

You can now breathe a sigh of relief, because the hardest part is over. Not all path making is difficult. Following is an easy way to create a path. Photoshop has a great feature called *make a path from selection*. All you need is an active selection and you can turn it into a path in a jiffy.

In Figure 7-11, we have loaded one of the layers as a selection. Here's how you can turn it into a path:

1. Load the selection.

2. Choose Window | Paths from the main menu to open the Paths palette, if it's not already visible.

3. Do one of the following:

   ▪ Click the Make Work Path From Selection button, as shown in Figure 7-12.

   ▪ Click the flyout menu at the upper-right corner of the Paths palette and choose Make Work Path. You will see an option asking for a tolerance setting. This determines how tightly you want the path to follow the selection. Choose a smaller number to make a more accurate path, but with more points. Choose a larger number to make a smoother path, but less accurate. The default setting of 2.0 works for most situations, so leave it at that for now.

4. You now have created what is called a *work* path. This is a temporary path used to create quick edits and effects. When you choose another path, the work path will be replaced. To save this path, click the flyout menu, and choose Save Path.

FIGURE 7-12 The Paths palette

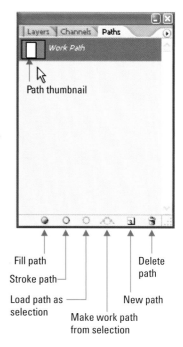

Path thumbnail

Fill path

Stroke path

Load path as selection

Make work path from selection

Delete path

New path

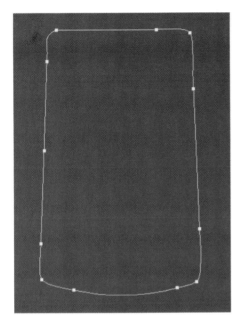

FIGURE 7-13 The path created from the selection

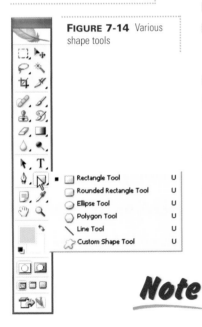

FIGURE 7-14 Various shape tools

The default name is path 1. After you have saved the path, it will stay with the document, even after you turn off your computer and then turn it back on; the path will still be available for the document as long as it's saved as a PSD, TIFF, or EPS format (which is covered in Chapter 1). You can even transfer the path to other documents just by clicking and dragging. Figure 7-13 shows the path created from the selection in Figure 7-12.

Note *You'll learn to convert a path to a selection a little later in this chapter.*

Creating Paths Using Shape Tools

Another quick way to create a path is to use one of the shape tools, set to a path option. Several shape tools are available from the toolbox, as seen in Figure 7-14.

▪ **Rectangle** Rectangles and squares

▪ **Rounded Rectangle** A rectangle with rounded corners; choose the corner radius (how round the corners are) from the tool options bar (see Figure 7-15)

▪ **Ellipse** Circles and ellipses

▪ **Polygon** Everything from triangles to 100-sided polygons; choose the amount of sides from the tool options bar

▪ **Line** Straight lines; choose the line thickness from the options bar

▪ **Custom Shape** Lets you create your own shapes; choose a shape from the drop-down list in the options bar

Note *We will create a custom shape at the end of this chapter.*

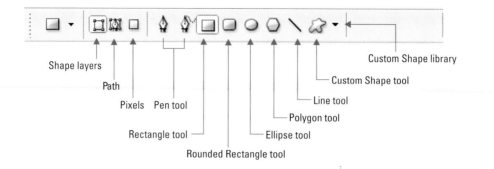

Shape layers
Path
Pixels   Pen tool
Rectangle tool
Rounded Rectangle tool
Ellipse tool
Polygon tool
Line tool
Custom Shape tool
Custom Shape library

FIGURE 7-15 Tool options bar

Creating a Path from a Shape

Here is how to create a path from a custom shape. Figure 7-16
illustrates all the steps required to perform this task.

1. Choose the Custom Shape tool.

2. Choose the Path option from the left of the tool
   options bar.

3. Choose the shape you want to create from the Custom
   Shape Library drop-down menu.

4. Click and drag to draw the shape's path.

5. The shape becomes the work path in the Paths palette.

 Hold down the SHIFT *key as you draw to constrain the shape's proportions.*

Filling and Stroking Paths

Now that you have created a path, you can use it for a number
of things, including adding type to the path (see Chapter 8). For
now, we are going to add a fill and stroke to a path using the
options on the Paths palette.

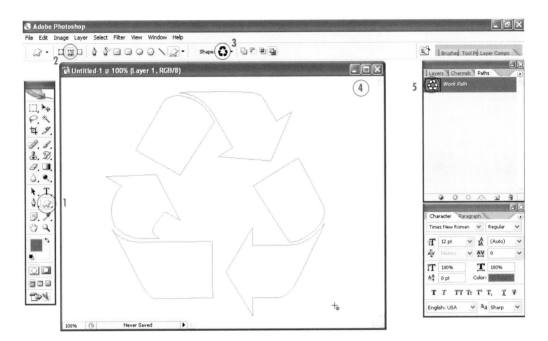

FIGURE 7-16 Creating a path from a custom shape

Filling a Path with Color

This is a simple one-click, one-trick pony. You can fill a path with the current foreground color.

1. Choose the foreground color from the Color Picker in the toolbox; this is the color you will use to fill your path.

2. Click the Fill Path button from the Paths palette, as labeled in Figure 7-12. This button will always fill the path with the current foreground color.

Stroking a Path

Contrary to popular understanding, stroking is not just something you do with a puppy or kitten. Inside the mind of the Adobe engineers, stroking means adding an outline, so for us Photoshop users, outlines are called *strokes*. Stroking is similar to the fill task, except Photoshop uses the currently selected brush to draw the stroke. Of course, it goes without saying that you will need an active path, but I will say it anyway.

1. Choose the Brush tool from the toolbox.

2. Choose Window | Brushes to open the Brushes palette, and choose a brush.

3. Set your foreground color to your desired color.

4. Click the Stroke Path button on the Paths palette, as shown at left, and the path will now show an outline around it.

Figure 7-17 shows an example of an icon with both a color fill and a color stroke applied.

FIGURE 7-17 A path filled with foreground and stroke color

Editing Paths

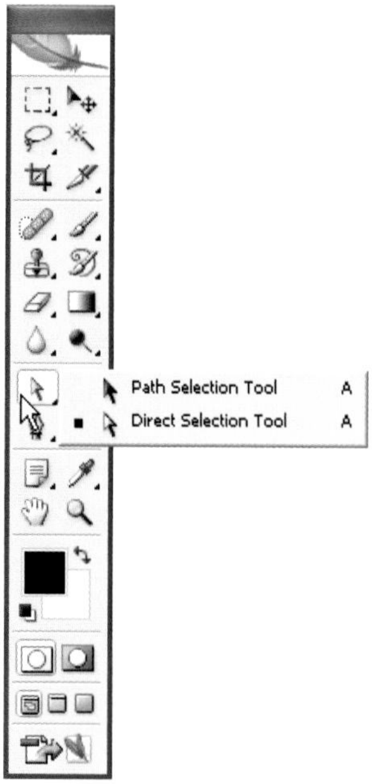

Whatever method you use to create your path is up to you; how you create paths depends on your current needs. No matter what method you use, once paths appear in the Paths palette, they are all treated exactly the same. You can edit and manipulate all the paths in exactly the same way.

You can use two main tools for editing paths after they are created, as shown in Figure 7-18.

- **Path Selection tool** Click anywhere on a path with this tool, and the entire path is selected. Use this tool when you want to move, copy, or delete paths.

- **Direct Selection tool** Use this tool to select individual anchor points. With this tool, you can reshape your paths, move anchor points, reshape curves, and control adjustment handles.

Selecting and Moving the Entire Path

When an anchor point is selected, it appears as a solid point; when it is not selected, it appears as a hollow point. This is the same when you use a selection tool to choose a path or point.

FIGURE 7-18 The path selection tools

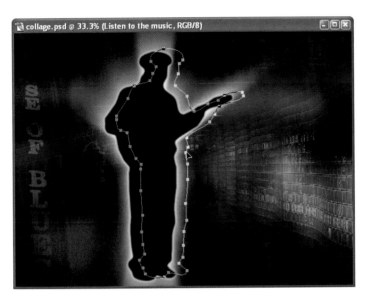

FIGURE 7-19 The Path Selection tool selects and moves the entire path.

To select the path, choose the Path Selection tool and click anywhere on the path. Notice in Figure 7-19 that all the anchor points are selected (they're all solid). You can use this tool to copy, delete, or move a path to a new location. To move the entire path, just drag it with the mouse.

Editing Individual Anchor Points

Choose the Direct Selection tool to select either single points or groups of anchor points. When you click a path with this tool, the path is activated, but no anchor points are selected. Figure 7-20 shows an active path with no anchor points selected.

To select a group of anchor points, click and drag the Direct Selection tool around a group of anchor points; they will become active and ready for editing.

To select a single anchor point, click it with the Direct Selection tool; the point will become filled and the adjustment handles will become visible. You can now edit the path.

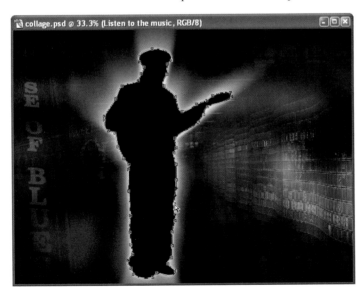

FIGURE 7-20 An active path with unselected anchor points

Editing a Path

To edit a path:

1. Choose the Direct Selection tool from the toolbox.

2. Click the path to activate it.

3. Click an individual anchor point or a group of points.

4. Either drag the anchor point, as shown in Figure 7-21, or click and drag the adjustment handles to edit the path.

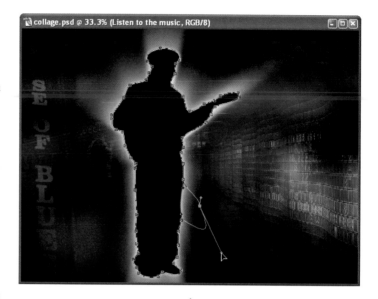

FIGURE 7-21 Modifying the path

 By default, both sides of the adjustment handles move together. To move just one side of a handle, hold down the ALT key (OPTION key on the Mac) while you drag.

Converting a Path to a Selection

Because a path can present the cleanest edge out of any tool in Photoshop, it would make sense to be able to turn a path into a selection and take advantage of that sharp edge to cut out images or mask them for editing.

Some stock photography, such as Photo Objects from Hemera, as shown in Figure 7-22, come with paths included to make it easy to lift an image off its background. Of course, you can always make your own path, too.

Here's how to create your own path:

1. Open the Paths palette by choosing Window | Paths, if it is not already visible.

2. Click the path's thumbnail to make the path active.

3. You can now use one of three ways to make a selection from a path.

FIGURE 7-22
An image with a path

FIGURE 7-23
The image with a
selection from a path

- Click the Path To Selection button from the Paths palette.

- Click the palette options menu and choose Make Selection.

- CTRL-click (CMD-click on the Mac) the path's thumbnail to load it as a selection.

Use whatever method is the most comfortable for you. Figure 7-23 shows the image with the active selection.

Working with Paths and Shapes

When you are drawing with the Pen tool or any of the other shape tools, three types of options are available. Figure 7-24 shows the options on the tool options bar. Select one of these options before you begin to draw:

- **Shape Layer** Creates a shape layer, which is a vector mask. See Chapter 5 for more on shape layers.

- **Path** Creates an editable path.

- **Fill Pixels** Creates a solid area of color using the current foreground color. This is not editable, and it is not a vector;

rather, it is treated just like a paint brush in a raster format. (See the beginning of this chapter for vector and raster details.)

FIGURE 7-24 Custom shape styles

Fill Pixels

Paths

Shape Layer

Managing and Loading Shapes

In Chapter 5, we discussed shape layers, which are useful for creating shapes that can be applied and modified quickly. At the heart of shape layers are custom shapes, which are stored in a library.

When you open the custom shapes library for the first time, you will notice that only a handful of shapes are available for use. Figure 7-25 shows a preview of the default shapes. More shapes ship with Photoshop, and you can access them with just a few clicks. If you can't find what you are looking for in the library, it's also easy to create your own shapes and save them to the library. In this section, we will look at managing and creating shapes.

FIGURE 7-25 The default set of shapes

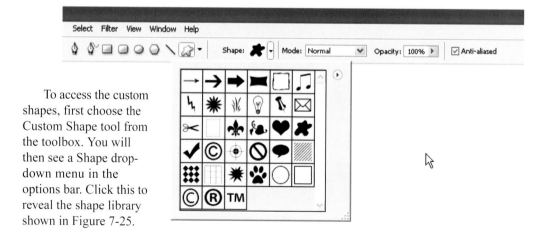

To access the custom shapes, first choose the Custom Shape tool from the toolbox. You will then see a Shape drop-down menu in the options bar. Click this to reveal the shape library shown in Figure 7-25.

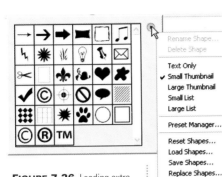

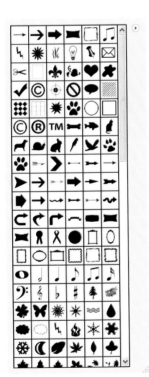

FIGURE 7-26 Loading extra shapes into the library

Loading Shapes

Here's how to load the extra shapes that ship with Photoshop:

1. Choose the Custom Shape tool.

2. Open the library from the Shape menu on the tool options bar.

3. Click the little arrow at the upper right to open the palette options menu, as shown in Figure 7-26.

4. In the bottommost list, choose one of the categories, or choose All to load all available shapes.

5. An option box appears, asking whether you want to replace the current shapes. Click OK to replace the shapes in the library, or click Append to add the shapes to the current library without removing the existing shapes.

Figure 7-27 shows the library with all the shapes loaded and all ready for use.

Loading Shapes from an External Source

You can also load shapes from another source (for example, perhaps you have downloaded some shapes from the Internet). Here's how:

1. Choose the Custom Shape tool.

2. Open the library from the tool options bar's Shape drop-down menu.

3. Click the arrow at the upper right to open the palette options menu, as shown in Figure 7-26.

4. Choose Load Shapes.

5. Navigate to the location in which your shapes are saved. Your shapes will have a .CSH file extension.

6. Click OK.

FIGURE 7-27 The library with extra shapes loaded

Creating Custom Shapes

In the final section of this chapter, we will create a custom shape. Before you start, you'll need a path to work with.

1. Either open an image that has a path, or create one (perhaps create a path from a selection).

2. Click the path thumbnail in the Paths palette. Refer to Figure 7-22 to see a path selection.

3. Choose Edit | Define Custom Shape.

FIGURE 7-28 Creating a custom shape

4. You will see a dialog box like the one in Figure 7-28, showing a thumbnail preview of the shape and requiring that you type in a name.

5. Type a name into the box.

6. Click OK.

That's all there is to it. When you open the custom shapes library, your new shape will appear (see Figure 7-29). You can apply this shape to any image in any size as a path, shape layer, or fill pixels.

FIGURE 7-29 Our new shape in the library

Chapter 8

Create and Manipulate Text

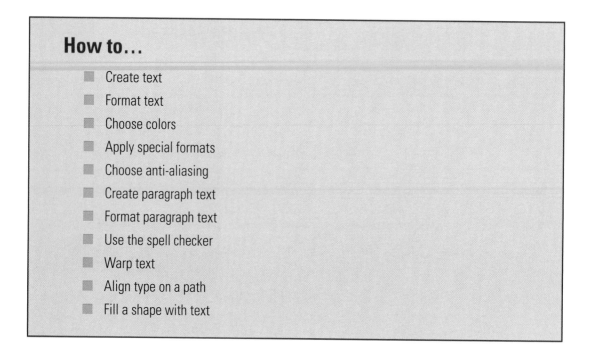

How to...

- Create text
- Format text
- Choose colors
- Apply special formats
- Choose anti-aliasing
- Create paragraph text
- Format paragraph text
- Use the spell checker
- Warp text
- Align type on a path
- Fill a shape with text

Although Photoshop is primarily an image-editing program, Adobe realized that more and more people need to use text with the program. As a result, many text options are included in Photoshop, some simple and some complex. We can now create everything from fancy and wild type effects to readable paragraph text.

In this chapter, you will learn how to use all the type tools to make your p's and q's behave themselves, just like they should.

Creating Text

To create text in Photoshop, choose the Type tool from the toolbox, as shown in Figure 8-1. Then, when your mouse hovers over the document window, the mouse cursor will show as an *I-beam* pointer, just as it does in a word processor program.

Click anywhere in the document window and type in some characters. The characters are displayed in the main document window.

FIGURE 8-1 The Type tool selected from the toolbox

You don't need to create a new layer to add text; when you begin to type, a new text layer will be created automatically.

Once you have finished typing the text, you will notice that the I-beam is still active. You need to tell Photoshop when you have finished typing in the text, which is called *applying the text*. If you press ENTER (RETURN on a Mac) as you type, the text will wrap to a new line. To apply the text to Photoshop, do one of the following:

- Click the checkmark at the far right of the tool options bar.
- Click any tool other than the Type tool in the toolbox.

If you click and hold your mouse over the Type tool in the toolbox, you will notice that several Type tool options appear:

- **Horizontal Type tool** The standard type tool, which causes text to appear horizontally across the screen.
- **Vertical Type tool** The type runs vertically and text is stacked in a column; this is perfect for Asian characters.
- **Horizontal Type Mask tool** This tool creates a mask selection in the shape of the type, aligned horizontally across the screen. It's useful for special effects and for filling the text selection with another image or other elements.
- **Vertical Type Mask tool** Creates the text as a selection mask rather than pixels, and displays the text vertically.

To use any of these tools, click in the document, choose your formatting from the toolbox, and begin typing.

 When using the Type Mask tools, you will type normally; the text will appear in a pinkish color.

Make your formatting changes and then apply the type by clicking the checkmark in the options bar or by clicking another tool in the toolbox. As soon as you apply the type, the pink color will disappear and you will be left with just a selection. After the selection is active, you can no longer make any formatting changes, so it's important that you make these changes before applying the type.

Tip *When creating text with either the Type or the Type Mask tools, you can switch from the type I-beam to a transform box by holding down the* CTRL *key (*CMD *on the Mac). You can then use the transform box to reshape the text by dragging any transform handle, or you can reposition the text by clicking and dragging inside the transform box.*

Moving Text

After you have applied text to your document, it can be easily repositioned by choosing the Move tool and dragging the text to a different position on the page.

You may want to move the text while you're still in the process of typing it (for example, perhaps your text is running off the page). To reposition the text while you're typing, hold down CTRL (CMD on a Mac) and drag your text to a new location. As soon as you release the key command, the pointer will turn back into the I-beam and you can continue typing your text.

Formatting Text

What use is text if you can't format it? For instance, if you were creating an invitation, you would want to use a nice script font, or you'd want to use a solid headline style for a newsletter. Photoshop allows you to edit many attributes of your text. You can change the font size, style, color, alignment, and even the scaling.

Applying Fonts and Styles

Before you can format any text, you must first highlight it. To highlight text, choose the Type tool, click and hold down the mouse button at the beginning of the text, and then drag the cursor through all the text that you want to format. Only highlighted text will be affected by the formatting. (You are probably already familiar with this method from word processing programs.) Once you have highlighted the text, you can change it by choosing another font or style from one of two places.

■ The Character palette, shown in Figure 8-2, is best for advanced formatting.

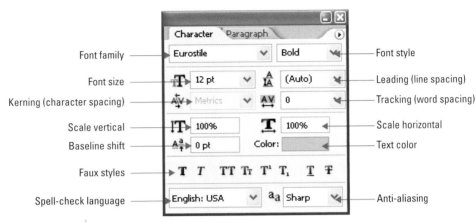

Font family
Font size
Kerning (character spacing)
Scale vertical
Baseline shift
Faux styles
Spell-check language

Font style
Leading (line spacing)
Tracking (word spacing)
Scale horizontal
Text color
Anti-aliasing

8

FIGURE 8-2 The Character palette

■ The tool options bar also has the basic formatting options, as shown in Figure 8-3.

FIGURE 8-3 The type options on the tool options bar

When you choose the Type tool, the basic formatting options will automatically be shown in the options bar. They will perform identically to the formatting options in the Character palette.

To launch the Character palette, press the toggle button on the tool options bar, shown left.

Font Sizes

You can specify a font size or choose one from a list. To choose a size, click the Font Size field and a list will appear with the most common sizes, in points. You can also type the size directly into the Font Size field in the palette. The beauty of typing directly into the field is that you can make the text any size that you want, even sizes that aren't specified in the list.

Font Families

To select a new font, click in the font window of the Character palette. You will see a menu like the one shown in Figure 8-4, which contains a list of all the installed fonts that are available for use in Photoshop. The fonts are displayed with a WYSIWYG sample to the right of the font name so you can see how each font looks. Choose the font you want from the menu.

 You can turn off the font preview or change its size by choosing Edit | Preferences | Type (Photoshop | Preferences | Type on the Mac). Deselect Font Preview Size to turn off the sample, or choose a preview size from the menu.

Font Styles

After you have chosen a font, you may want to apply italics, boldface, or another font *style*, which are simply variations of a font. The Font Style field is to the right of the font, and you can choose from the drop-down menu of the styles for your chosen font. Here are some of the common styles:

- **Bold**   Boldfaced style
- **Italic**   Italic style
- **Oblique**   Another name for Italic
- **Condensed**   Thinner type style
- **Expanded**   Wider type style
- **Black**   Similar to bold
- **Heavy**   Very bold

Bold
Italic
Oblique - Another name for Italic
Condensed - Thin type style
Expanded - Wide type style
Black - Similar to bold
Heavy- Very bold

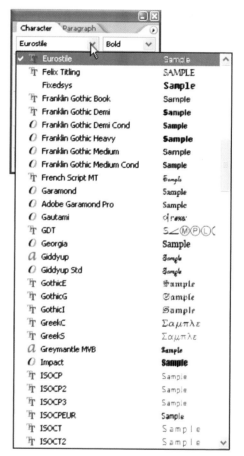

FIGURE 8-4 The font menu

Faux Styles

Sometimes a font style that you have in mind does not appear in the list. This is because you don't have that particular font installed, or it's just not available. In either case, Photoshop will allow you to "fake it." These styles are called faux styles, and you can create them by clicking the little buttons (see Figure 8-2) on the Characters palette to apply a simulated style to the text.

Regular

Bold

Italic

ALL CAPS

Sᴍᴀʟʟ Cᴀᴘs

Superscript

S_{ubscript}

<u>Underline</u>

~~Strikethrough~~

- **Bold**   Thicker text
- **Italic**   Skewed text
- **All Caps**   Displays each character in capital letters
- **Small Caps**   Displays each letter a little smaller than the regular caps
- **Superscript**   Raises smaller text to the top of the text line, such as the squared sign in math: 2^2
- **Subscript**   Lowers the small text, such as the molecular structure in chemical notations: H_{20}
- **Underline**   A line appears along the baseline of the text
- **Strikethrough**   A line appears through the text itself

8

Color

What a cruel and ruthless world it would be if our favorite image-editing program allowed us to produce text only in black. As luck would have it, Photoshop's designers have included the ability to colorize text right in the Character palette and options bar.

Whenever you see a colored rectangle in a Photoshop tool, it's probably a link to a Color Picker; in the case of the Character palette, the word *Color* appears next to this rectangle. The text Color Pickers work just like the other Color Pickers in Photoshop: click it, and a window will appear with lots of colors. Choose a color and click OK.

To change the color of your text, click the Type tool and highlight the text you want to colorize. You can even highlight a character and make it a different color from the rest of the text to create a rainbow of text colors. (This is not recommended for most design purposes, however.)

Using Advanced Character Formatting

You might want to tweak a bit more than the font, color, and size, and for that, you again use the Character palette. (In fact, all of the options we are about to discuss are available from the Character palette.)

Figure 8-5 shows an example of the effect of each of these adjustments. These formatting options are applied just like the standard formatting options (unless specified otherwise).

- **Kerning** Adjusts the space between pairs of characters. To increase or reduce the kerning, insert the I-beam cursor between two characters and press the LEFT or RIGHT ARROW keys on your keyboard while holding down the ALT (OPTION on the Mac) key, or you can enter a setting directly into the Kerning text field in the Character palette. Pay special attention to the spacing between capital and lowercase characters, as they often need a little kerning.

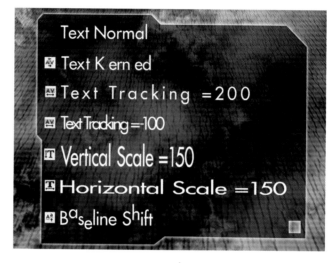

FIGURE 8-5 Special formatting compared

- **Tracking** Adjusts the overall spacing that appears between characters in a word or series of words.

- **Leading** Adjusts the space between lines of text. The default setting is Auto (two points larger than character size), and this works for most cases. To change the leading, highlight the lines of text that you want to alter, and then enter a setting into the Leading field in the Character palette. (Leading isn't shown in Figure 8-5 because it doesn't have an effect on single lines of text—it affects two or more lines only.)

- **Scale Horizontal** Allows you to stretch or compress the text horizontally. Use this feature sparingly, because text was designed to look best at the default proportions. If you are trying to fill space, you are much better off adjusting the tracking instead.

- **Scale Vertical** Same as Scale Horizontal, but works on the vertical instead. Similar warning goes here: consider leading first.

- **Baseline Shift** Allows you to move either entire words or individual characters up or down in proportion to the rest of the text. Select the character(s) you want to move and enter a setting into the field. A positive setting will move the text up and a negative setting (prefaced by the minus sign) will move the text down.

Using Anti-Aliasing

Anti-aliasing refers to how smooth Photoshop will display the text. Without anti-aliasing, the text would appear a bit jagged. The anti-aliasing process blends the text pixels into the background, making a softer transition. There are five levels of anti-aliasing:

FIGURE 8-6 Examples of anti-aliasing

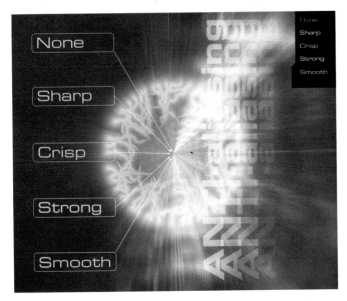

- None
- Sharp
- Crisp
- Strong
- Smooth

8

Figure 8-6 shows examples of how each level affects text. Notice that the effects are more evident on the smaller text. I use the Sharp setting, because it offers a small amount of font smoothing without getting blurry. Sharp was introduced for web use to accommodate the need for extremely sharp text at very small sizes.

 The sharper anti-aliasing settings look best at smaller sizes, and the smoother settings look better at larger sizes.

Formatting Paragraph Text

You can define the formatting aspects of an area for multiple lines of text. The lines will break automatically and the text will wrap to fill the space you allocate. You can choose options for justification, indentation, and paragraph spacing. Photoshop will hyphenate long words for more even-looking lines in the paragraph. Photoshop has advanced in leaps and bounds regarding text handling and can really hold its own.

Creating Paragraph Text

Let's create a paragraph of text.

1. Choose the Type tool so you can define the text area.

2. Click and hold the mouse in the top-left corner of the desired text area, and drag to the bottom-right text area. Then release the mouse to create a text area. You will see a box with dashed borders, similar to the one shown in Figure 8-7.

3. From the Character palette, choose the font, size, and color you want. As you type, notice that the text wraps to the next line when it reaches the edge of the box. (If you don't like typing so much, you can cut and paste text from another source.) After you have entered several lines of text, it should look something like Figure 8-8.

4. Click the checkmark at the top right of the options bar to apply the text.

Adjusting the Text Box

You can resize your text box by clicking and dragging on any of the eight anchor points. The text will wrap automatically to fill the new size.

In Figure 8-8, the text area is horizontal, while the illustration of a piece of paper is angled on the screen. It would look nice to have the text appear at the same angle as the paper. You can rotate the text box and all the text inside will rotate with it.

To rotate the text box, hover the mouse on one of the outside corners until you see a double-sided, curved arrow. Then click and drag. The text box will rotate with the arrow. The result is shown in Figure 8-9.

FIGURE 8-7 Creating the text area

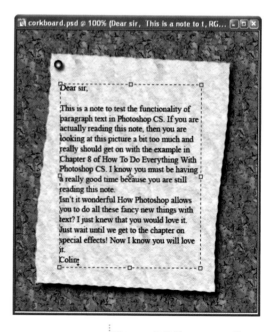

FIGURE 8-8 The text area with text added

Click the checkmark on the options bar or click any tool in the toolbox other than the Type tool to apply the text—in the same way we applied the basic text at the beginning of this chapter.

Formatting Paragraph Text

Do you remember how we formatted characters in the "Formatting Text" section? You can format the individual characters in the paragraph in the same way. Here, we'll use a few of the Paragraph palette's formatting tools, as shown in Figure 8-10.

Indenting Paragraphs' First Lines

Paragraphs are often indented on the first lines, which makes it easier to see where the paragraphs begin and causes the text to look better. Here's how this is done:

1. Choose the Type tool and highlight all the text by clicking and dragging through it. You are now ready to begin formatting the text.

2. Click the Paragraph tab to open the Paragraph palette, as shown in Figure 8-11.

3. Enter a figure into the Indent First Line field. Indents are measured in points. For the text shown in Figure 8-11, I entered 25 points. See how the first lines of all the paragraphs are now indented?

FIGURE 8-9 Rotating paragraph text

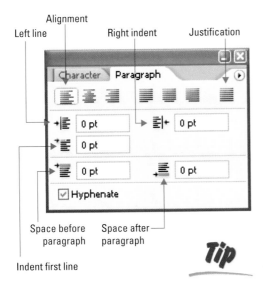

FIGURE 8-10 The Paragraph palette

Tip *To select all the text in the box, click anywhere in the box and press* CTRL-A (CMD-A *on a Mac*).

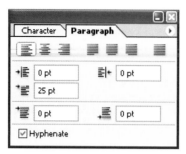

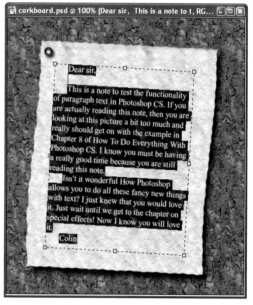

Adding Spacing Between Paragraphs

Let's add a bit of space between each of the paragraphs. Breathing space will separate the paragraphs of text and make the page look more balanced; as a result, it will be more inviting to read.

1. Highlight the text.

2. Open the Paragraph palette.

3. In the Space After Paragraph text field, enter a setting of 5 points, as shown in Figure 8-12.

FIGURE 8-11 Indenting the first line of paragraphs

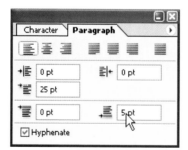

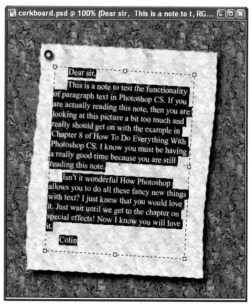

To wrap up the image, highlight the text again and choose a font that looks interesting and that suits the image with which you are working. In Figure 8-13, I used the Papyrus font because it has a nice feel to it and looks

FIGURE 8-12 Adding spacing between the paragraphs

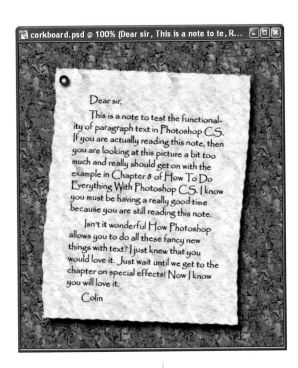

The finished text with a little bit of fine-tuning" in the image -->

FIGURE 8-13 The finished text with a little bit of fine-tuning

good on the paper. As a final touch, I also increased the leading a little bit because the lines looked too close together.

Additional Options for Attractive Paragraph Text

If you click the flyout menu in the Paragraph palette, you will see two options:

- **Adobe Single-Line Composer** This option causes the lines to break based on a single line of text.

- **Adobe Every Line Composer** This option produces better looking paragraphs because it examines the entire paragraph of text and causes the line breaks to appear where they will provide the most attractive blocks of text.

 Choose Roman Hanging Punctuation from the Paragraph flyout menu to cause the punctuation to appear outside the text block. This produces cleaner looking paragraphs of text.

Spell Checking

Even the best of us are prone to a few typos every now and then. It can be frustrating to spend a lot of time designing a really nice piece with spectacular type effects and dazzling colors, only to be embarrassed by a nasty spelling error.

The good news is that Photoshop has its own built-in spell checker, and it's easy to use.

1. Highlight the text you want to check (if you want to check just a section). Otherwise, skip this step to check the entire document.

2. Choose Edit | Check Spelling.

3. The spell checker will do its stuff. After a little whizzing and whirring, if you're lucky, in a few moments a dialog box will pop up saying "Spell check complete," meaning that no spelling errors were found. You can click OK and go your merry way.

4. If you aren't so fortunate, you will see the Check Spelling dialog box shown in Figure 8-14. The suspect word will be displayed along with a list of suggested spellings.

5. If the word was spelled incorrectly, choose the correct word from the list or enter the correct spelling in the Change To text box. Then click Change. If more than one instance of the word is included in the document, click Change All.

FIGURE 8-14 Check Spelling dialog box

6. If your word was spelled correctly and the spell checker's dictionary didn't recognize it, you can do one of two things:

■ Click Add to add it to the dictionary. The next time you run the spell checker, it will remember the new word.

■ Click Ignore to ignore the instance of the word and continue running the spell check. You can also click Ignore All if more than one instance of the word appears.

7. Continue checking every word the spell checker identifies.

Photoshop can check spelling in multiple languages. To check in a different language, change the language option in the Character palette before running the spell checker.

Setting Alignment

Now that we have all this fancy text in our document, let's learn about alignment. Figure 8-15 shows all the alignment options in the Paragraph palette. To apply these, highlight the text and choose one of the options by clicking its button.

Justified last line left

Right aligned

Justified last line center

Centered

Justified last line right

Left aligned

Full justified

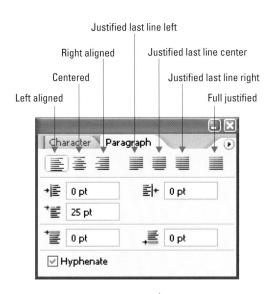

FIGURE 8-15 The alignment options

- **Left** All the text is aligned to the left and the right edge is ragged.
- **Centered** All the text is centered.
- **Right** Opposite of left; text is aligned to the right.
- **Full Justified** The text is aligned left and right to form a box shape, and the last line is stretched to fit the box. (This option can leave some large gaps in the text.)
- **Justified Last Line Right** Same as Full Justified, except the last line is aligned to the right; makes for less gaps.
- **Justified Last Line Centered** Same as above, but the last line is centered.
- **Justified Last Line Left** Justified with the last line left-aligned. This is the most appropriate option for most justified text.

8

FIGURE 8-16 Examples of alignment

This is paragraph text that has been right aligned This is paragraph text that has been right aligned This is paragraph text that has been right aligned This is paragraph text that has been right aligned This is paragraph text that has been right aligned This is paragraph text that has been right aligned This is paragraph text that has been right aligned

This is paragraph text that has been center aligned This is paragraph text that has been center aligned This is paragraph text that has been center aligned This is paragraph text that has been center aligned This is paragraph text that has been center aligned This is paragraph text that has been center aligned

This is paragraph text that has been left aligned This is paragraph text that has been left aligned This is paragraph text that has been left aligned This is paragraph text that has been left aligned This is paragraph text that has been left aligned This is paragraph text that has been left aligned

This is paragraph text that has been Full Justified This is paragraph text that has been Full Justified This is paragraph text that has been Full Justified This is paragraph text that has been Full Justified This is paragraph text that has been Full Justified This is paragraph text that has been Full J u s t i f i e d

This is paragraph text that has been Justified Right This is paragraph text that has been Justified Right This is paragraph text that has been Justified Right This is paragraph text that has been Justified Right This is paragraph text that has been Justified Right This is paragraph text that has been Justified Right

This is paragraph text that has been Justified Centered This is paragraph text that has been Justified Centered This is paragraph text that has been Justified Centered This is paragraph text that has been Justified Centered This is paragraph text that has been Justified Centered

This is paragraph text that has been Justified Left This is paragraph text that has been Justified Left This is paragraph text that has been Justified Left This is paragraph text that has been Justified Left This is paragraph text that has been Justified Left This is paragraph text that has been Justified Left

Usually, the justified options look nice for wide columns of text to make them look formal and unified. The aligned paragraphs are better on narrower columns because they have more flexibility in line breaks and avoid the gaps between words. Single aligned text is also more casual in application.

Using Warp Text

If you are familiar with Word Art from Microsoft, you will already have an idea of the functionality of Warp Text. This is a fun and useful tool used to create interesting curves and waves that your text will follow. The best way to learn about this tool is to experiment. Let's walk through the basic functionality. The Warp Text button (the T with the curve under it) in the tool options bar is shown here.

Applying Warp Text

Whenever you want to warp your text, follow these steps:

1. Select the text you want to warp.

2. Click the Warp Text button in the toolbox.

3. You will see the Warp Text dialog box, shown in Figure 8-17. Click the Style drop-down menu.

4. Choose the style that is the closest to the shape you want. For this example, we'll choose Arc.

5. Adjust the Bend percentage to increase or reverse the effect.

6. Move the Horizontal and Vertical Distortion sliders to bend the text through space. Figure 8-17 shows some text in the shape of an arc, with a negative horizontal distortion applied. When you apply a negative amount in the distortion, the text appears to move away from you.

Figure 8-18 shows a positive amount of distortion. Notice how it has the opposite effect and the text now appears to be coming toward you. We have also used the Flag shape for the style, which makes the text appear to "twist." Experiment with the different shapes and settings and you will get the hang of this tool really quickly. Try applying the Warp Text option to paragraphs of text for some very interesting results.

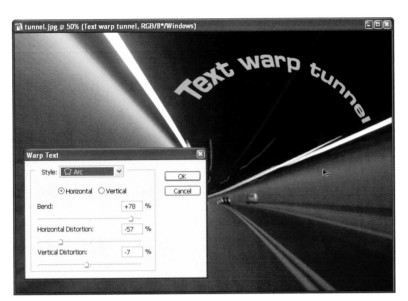

You are bound to have a lot of fun with this tool. You can create some really funky text shapes with minimal effort. Hopefully, you can tear yourself away from all the fun soon, because we are about to look at another exciting feature of Photoshop, the Type On a Path tool.

FIGURE 8-17 Arc text with negative horizontal distortion

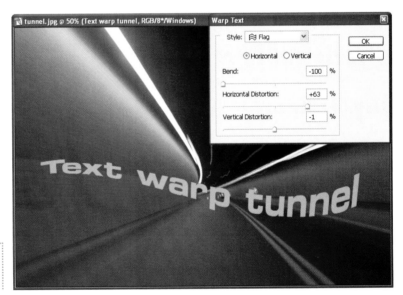

FIGURE 8-18 Flag text with positive horizontal distortion

Typing on a Path

You can align type in Photoshop to make the type follow the curvature of a path. In Chapter 7, you learned all about paths and how to create and manipulate them. You are about to learn how to make text flow with your paths. As you have also learned, two types of paths can be specified: open paths and closed paths. We will examine how to add text to both.

Typing on an Open Path

An *open* path has distinct start and finish points. It looks like a wave or a squiggle. These types of paths lend themselves very well as guides for text.

When you are drawing with the Pen tool, be sure that you select the path option, as shown next. This will ensure that a clean path is created.

Let's jump headfirst into creating our first type on a path effect:

1. Create a path with the Pen tool, as in Figure 8-19. (Refer to Chapter 7 for details on using the Pen tool.)

2. Choose the Type tool and select the formatting you want: font, color, size, and so on.

3. As you move your cursor over the path, you will notice that it changes to an I-beam with a curve through it, as shown in Figure 8-20. This tells you that you are now in the "hot zone," and the Type tool is detecting the presence of a path. Move the curser to the approximate position where you want the text to begin.

Image: photos.com

FIGURE 8-19 Using the Pen tool, create an open path.

FIGURE 8-20 The cursor detecting a path

4. Click where you want to begin typing. As you type, you will notice something very cool: the text follows all the contours of the path. Type in some words, as we did in Figure 8-21.

5. Click the checkmark on the options bar or click another tool to apply the text.

Editing Type on an Open Path

You have learned how to create type on a path; you are now going to learn how to make changes to the text and to the path. You can format the text on a path by doing the following:

1. Before you can make formatting changes to the text, you must first select it. To select the text, choose the Type tool, and then click and drag through all the characters you want to format. The text should now be highlighted.

2. Make the formatting changes just like you would with normal text. Change the size, font, color, or any other attribute, including the tracking and kerning.

You can adjust the curve even with the text attached. The text will reflow to follow any changes you make on the curve. This is a great way to smooth out any little kinks in the way the text flows on the path.

If you want to reposition the text along the path, take these steps:

1. Choose the Path Selection tool from the toolbox.

2. Hover the tool near the end of the path until you see a small arrow. This arrow tells you that you are about to move the start/finish point of the text.

FIGURE 8-21 The text follows the path.

3. Click and drag the type along the path, and release the mouse button when you are happy with the new position.

To get better results with text on a path, keep these things in mind:

- Adjust the tracking to get a nice flow. Generally, curved text should use wider than normal tracking because the insides of the curves bring the characters closer together than normal.

- Adjust the individual kerning on certain characters to fine-tune the way they flow together.

- Avoid sharp bends in the paths.

Figure 8-22 shows our effect with a few of these tweaks.

Typing on a Closed Path

Typing on a closed path is similar to typing on an open path, except a closed path is a loop, so it has no definitive start or end points. An excellent example of this is a circle. You can use custom shapes with the Paths option chosen from the options bar or create a closed path with the Pen tool.

Let's flow some text around a circle. This is a common use for text on a path for logo design, for example.

1. Choose the Circular Shape tool.

2. In the options bar, choose the Paths option.

3. Draw a circle that is the same size and position as the object you want to flow the text around. Figure 8-23 shows an image with the circular path attached.

FIGURE 8-22 The finished text with some tweaks

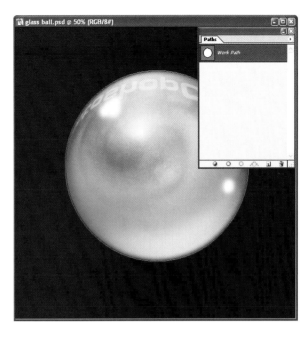

FIGURE 8-23 The circular path created on the image

When drawing with the Circular Shape tool, hold down the SHIFT *key and the shape will be constrained to an even circle rather than an ellipse. Hold down the* SPACEBAR *while creating a shape to reposition the shape on the canvas while drawing.*

4. Click the mouse anywhere on the circular path; this will become your starting point to add text. Figure 8-24 shows the cursor ready for some text.

5. Begin typing your characters; you will notice that they flow nicely around the circle.

FIGURE 8-24 Ready to add some text

6. To adjust the font and size, format the text in exactly the same way you did in the previous section.

Figure 8-25 shows a sphere with the text wrapped around it.

Caution *If your text is too large, some of the characters will not show when you create type on a path. To select all the text on the path (even text that doesn't appear on screen), click with the Type tool and press* CTRL-A *(*CMD-A *on the Mac); otherwise, all the text will not be selected. After you've selected all the text, reduce the size of the font to make it fit on the path.*

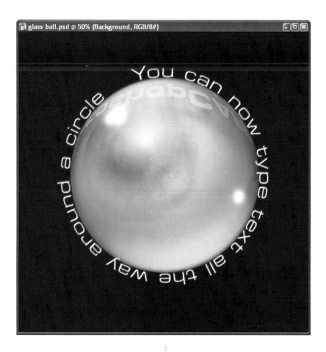

FIGURE 8-25 Text wrapped around the outside of a circle

Typing on the Inside of the Path

While creating the type on the circle, you might have asked, "What if I want the text to go the other way, on the *inside* of the path?" You will be happy to know that this is easy to accomplish.

1. Choose the Type tool and hover the mouse at the beginning of the text area until you see the arrow appear.

2. Click and drag the mouse to the inside of the circle. The text will follow to the inside, as shown in Figure 8-26.

3. You can also change the text back to the outside anytime by dragging it back to the outside of the circle or shape.

FIGURE 8-26 Type on the inside of the circle

Filling a Shape with Type

We have looked at some neat features of the Type On a Path tool. Now let's look at another feature of this unique tool. You can fill shapes with text and, in effect, have the text flow in the shape of the path. Figure 8-27 shows an advertisement I designed to mock the wet weather in a gloomy city, and to ask how to find the sunny weather of San Jose, California.

To fill a shape with type, follow these steps:

1. Create a path using the Custom Shape tool. Choose an arrow shape and path from the options bar.

2. Draw the shape on your page.

3. Hover the mouse cursor inside the shape. You should see an I-beam with brackets around it. This is the Type On a Path tool.

Do you know the way to San Jose?

4. Click the mouse and begin to enter text (or paste it from another application). The text will fill the inside area of the shape, and the shape will act as a container for the text.

5. Click the checkmark or another tool to apply the effect. Text can be formatted like any other text.

FIGURE 8-27 Type on a path

Chapter 9

Save Time with Automation

How to...

- Use tool presets
- Use actions
- Create your own actions
- Modify actions
- Load presets
- Create droplets
- Create a picture package
- Create a contact sheet
- Create a web gallery
- Produce a PDF presentation

Imagine that you must lay out and design a 50-page catalog. You need to extract images from a CD, resize them, and then insert them onto the pages. You also must insert a box, stock number, and heading on each page. In the midst of all this planning, you realize it's lunchtime. So you prepare one page, click a button, and let your computer keep working while you take a break. When you return, you see that all 50 pages are done. Science fiction? No; it's reality. Your lunch tasted great, and while you were eating, the graphics for your brochure were finished by Photoshop. After a little tweaking, the catalog will be delivered to the client on time.

Productivity and automation are two of Photoshop's greatest strengths, and the information you'll learn in this chapter could make this book pay for itself many times over.

Creating and Using Tool Presets

You know the process by now: You choose a tool, select a color, select a size, apply, and do it all over again. The problem is, every time you need to go back to a setting, you must go through the entire process again. Not so with tool presets. You can choose all your settings, save them, and recall them for later use. Think of them as style sheets for all things Photoshop.

The tool presets work with all the tools in the toolbox, including the nested tools. The tool presets will remember all the options you set for any selected tool, including color, line width, font, style—and more.

Tool Preset Picker

Figure 9-1 shows the Tool Preset picker, which can be accessed by choosing Window | Tool Presets. At the bottom of the palette, you'll notice a checkbox called Current Tool Only. When you check this box, only the options for the selected tool will appear on the palette. I keep this option turned on all the time; it is a great clutter reducer, as you can see in the palette on the right.

Tool preset

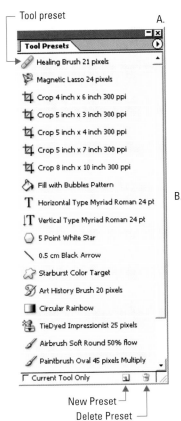

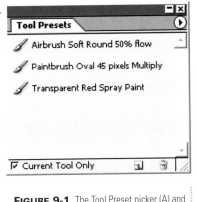

New Preset
Delete Preset

FIGURE 9-1 The Tool Preset picker (A) and the palette showing tools for the Current Tool Only selected (B)

 The Tool Preset picker can also be accessed by clicking the far left icon in the options bar. This icon is always the Tool Preset icon, no matter what tool is selected.

Creating Presets

Creating presets is a simple process:

1. From the toolbox, choose the tool you want to use for a preset.

2. Choose all the settings for the tool as you normally would.

3. Choose Window | Tool Presets to open the Tool Presets palette, and click the New Preset button.

4. In the New Tool Preset dialog box, enter a memorable name for the preset, as shown in the following illustration:

The new preset name will appear in the Tool Presets palette.

With a few tools, additional options are available via a checkbox located in the New Tool Preset dialog box. They're shown here:

Tool	Checkbox Option
Brush tool	Include Color
Gradient tool	Include Gradient
Pen tool	Include Color
Shape tool	Include Color

Using Presets

Using the presets you create is even simpler than creating them:

1. Choose a tool from the toolbox.

2. Choose Window | Tool Presets, if the Tool Presets palette isn't already visible, and highlight the preset you want.

3. Use the tool with all the preset settings.

Working with Actions

The main automation tools in Photoshop are called *actions*. You can have Photoshop take care of repetitive tasks automatically by using actions. An action is the same as a macro, which is similar in concept to pressing the Record button while you work. Actions record all your tasks—simple as that. The Actions palette, shown in Figure 9-2, records each click of the mouse. It will take note of all the settings and tools you used to achieve a particular task.

When you have finished the task, click the Stop button and the recording stops. Photoshop will remember all this information

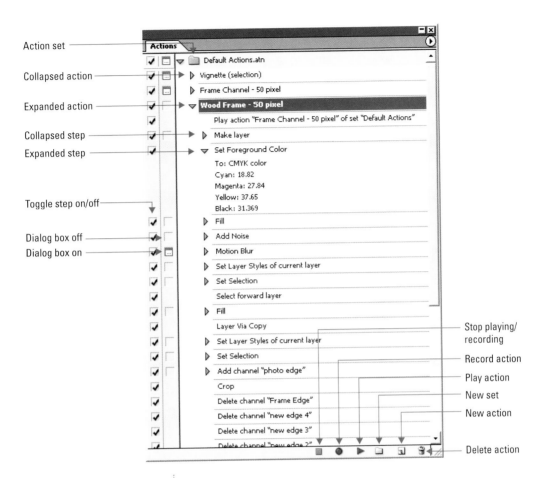

Action set

Collapsed action

Expanded action

Collapsed step

Expanded step

Toggle step on/off

Dialog box off

Dialog box on

Stop playing/ recording

Record action

Play action

New set

New action

Delete action

FIGURE 9-2 The Actions palette

in an action file, a text file that's assigned an *.atn* extension. At any time, you can open another image, click Play, and Photoshop will *run* the action. As the action runs, everything that you recorded will take place on the current image.

Actions can be saved to a disk, shared with friends or coworkers, and distributed to other users via the Internet. Sites such as http://www.actionfx.com and http://www.actionxchange .com have sprung up to accommodate the demand for these actions to Photoshop users around the world.

All the functionality of actions are stored in the Actions palette, which has two parts:

■ **The transport controls**   Where you record, stop, play, create, and delete actions. This set of controls performs similarly to the controls on a tape recorder, VCR, or DVD player.

■ **The Actions window**   Displays the following information:

  ■ **Action sets**   These collapsible folders contain groups of actions. Actions can be saved only as sets, or groups. Individual actions must be included in a set for the Save Action function to work.

  ■ **Actions**   Can be expanded to see the actual settings used in each step.

  ■ **A toggle step box**   Uncheck to skip certain steps of an action, if desired.

  ■ **A toggle box for dialogs**   Allows you to pause the action with an open dialog box so that you can make the adjustments manually. This is useful for effects such as sharpening and blurs.

Playing Actions

When you want to apply an action to an image, you call this *playing* or *running* an action (see Figure 9-3).

FIGURE 9-3 Image before action is run

Picture courtesy of Ablestock.com

Here's how you run an action on an image:

1. If the Actions palette is not open, press F9 (OPTION-F9 on the Mac, so as not interfere with Expose), or choose Window | Actions to open it.

2. Choose an action from the Actions palette by clicking its name.

3. Click the Play button at the bottom of the palette.

4. Some preset actions display a dialog box containing information the creator of the action wants you to read. If this appears, read the message and then click OK.

5. Photoshop will run the action on its own. The action will complete and you will see the result (see Figure 9-4).

FIGURE 9-4 Image after applying an action

Button Mode

You can also display the Actions palette by using *button mode*. In button mode, all the palette clutter is reduced, and you will see only a list of buttons labeled with the names of the actions, as shown in Figure 9-5. To run an action, you simply click its button.

You cannot record actions in button mode.

Here's how to switch to button mode:

1. Open the Actions palette (see Figure 9-2).

2. Choose the top-right arrow to open the flyout menu, and choose Button Mode.

3. To switch back to normal mode, repeat steps 1 and 2.

Creating Your Own Actions

Although preset actions are available, as you'll soon discover, the real benefit of actions is that you can create your own. You may need to perform a unique task many times—such as reducing the size of a picture or adding a custom frame to a series of images. You can save a lot of time by performing this task once and saving it as an action.

Here's how to create an action:

1. Open the Actions palette and the image you want to work on.

2. Choose a set or click on the Create New Set button in the Actions palette.

3. Click the Create New Action icon, and the New Action dialog box appears.

4. Choose a name and recording options, as shown in Figure 9-6. This is where you can assign a keyboard shortcut to your action by choosing a function key and modifiers.

5. Click the Record button.

6. Perform all the steps you want to include in the action.

7. Click the Stop icon.

Your action is completed and ready for use.

Adding Pauses and Comments

Actions can record almost anything. However, you can't use actions to record manual work, such as painting, airbrushing, or other types of touch-up work.

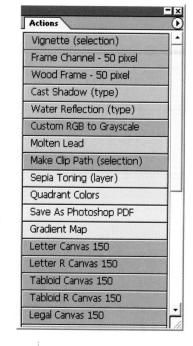

FIGURE 9-5 The Actions palette in button mode

FIGURE 9-6 Creating a new action

To enable you to accomplish these tasks during an action, you can record some stops, or pauses, into your actions. These will pause the action so you can perform the manual work; then you can continue the action.

Here's how to add a pause while recording an action:

1. Begin recording the action.

2. When you come to a point at which you need to insert the stop, click the flyout menu and choose Insert Stop.

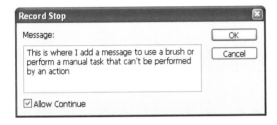

3. You will see the Record Stop dialog box, as shown in Figure 9-7.

4. Enter the message you want to display, and click the Allow Continue checkbox so that the action can continue after the task has been performed.

5. Click OK and continue recording the action as usual.

When the action is played back, your message will be displayed in a message box. You can then perform the task and click Continue. The action will continue playing until the end, or until another stop or pause is reached.

 You can add as many stops or pauses as you want into an action.

Using Modal Steps

Modal steps is a fancy name for making adjustments to dialog boxes as you are running actions. No two images are the same, and the settings that look great on one image may look less than ideal on another. For example, you may have created an action for scanning that sharpens and color corrects each image. You can cause the action to pause and wait for your settings each time a dialog box is used. This way, you can choose the best settings for your particular image.

To call up a dialog box during playback:

1. Click the toggle box to the left of the step for which you want to call up the dialog box (refer to Figure 9-2).

2. Play the action.

3. When the action reaches the modal step, the dialog box will open.

4. Make your adjustments to the settings, as shown in Figure 9-8.

5. Click OK in the dialog box.

6. The action will continue until the next pause or until the end.

Modifying Actions

After an action has been recorded, you can make modifications to it. You can add, delete, or modify steps. You cannot modify actions while the palette is in button mode, however.

To add a step:

1. In the Actions palette, click the action to expand it.

2. In the expanded action, click the point at which you want to add the step.

3. Click the Record icon.

4. Record the new step. When you're done, click the Stop icon.

To delete a step:

1. In the Actions palette, click the action to expand it.

2. Drag the step you want to delete to the Delete Action icon (which looks like a garbage can) at the bottom of the Actions palette.

To replace an action step:

1. Open an image.

2. Expand the Actions palette.

3. Double-click the step you want to modify or replace.

4. Make the changes.

5. Click OK.

FIGURE 9-8 Making manual adjustments during an action

Picture courtesy of Ablestock.com

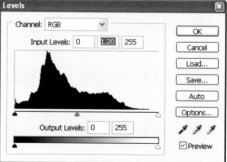

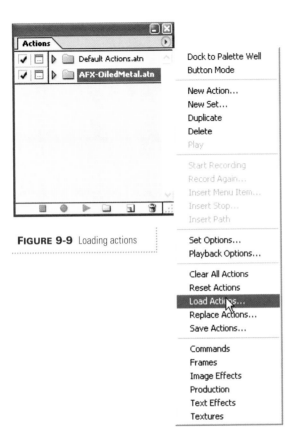

FIGURE 9-9 Loading actions

Loading and Saving Actions

Photoshop comes with quite a few actions already included. You can also purchase actions on CD, share them with friends, and download them from the Internet. Whichever method you use to obtain actions, they must be loaded into Photoshop before you can use them. You can always identify an action file, because it uses an *.atn* filename extension.

Loading New Actions

To load actions into Photoshop:

1. Open the Actions palette.

2. Click the flyout menu in the upper-right corner.

3. Choose Load Actions, as shown in Figure 9-9.

4. Navigate to the saved actions.

5. Click Load.

A quick way to add an action is to double-click its icon. It will be added to Photoshop and the program will launch, if it's not already running.

In Photoshop, actions are cross-platform—that is, they work on both Macs and PCs. Just make sure you add the .atn extension to the filename if you're moving an action from the Macintosh to a PC.

You can now play back the actions. Choose either actions that ship with Photoshop or third-party actions, as shown in Figure 9-10, from web sites such as actionfx.com.

FIGURE 9-10 A third-party action

Saving Actions

When you have invested some time creating all your new actions, you'll want to save them for later use.

To save your actions:

1. Open the Actions palette.

2. Choose an action set. As mentioned earlier in the chapter, individual actions cannot be saved; they must be part of a set. If you want to save an individual action, you must first create a set and then drag the action into the set.

3. On the flyout menu in the Actions palette, choose Save Actions.

4. Navigate to the location where you want to save the action, and then click Save.

Processing Multiple Images at Once

You can apply the same action to a group of images by using *batch processing*. The easiest way to do this is to create a new folder and copy the images to the folder that you want to process. Copying like this is a good idea, because if something goes wrong, your original images are still intact. The batch processing option will work on folders, too, so you can apply processing to all the files within the folder.

To run an action on several files at once:

1. Choose File | Automate | Batch.

2. Under Play, choose the set and action that you want to run.

3. Under Source, choose one of four options:

   - **Folder**   Click Choose to select the folder of files to be affected
   - **Import**   Select individual images
   - **Opened Files**   Select files that are currently open in Photoshop
   - **Bridge**   Select images in Bridge

4. Choose from the following options:

   - **Override Action "Open" Command**   If the action includes a step that tells it to open an image, check this box; otherwise, leave it unchecked.

- **Include All Subfolders** Any folders nested under the target folder will also be processed if you select this option.

- **Suppress File Open Options Dialogs** Checking this option will ignore any error or warning messages on the files. You can choose to check the warning manually. For a truly automated experience, check this box.

- **Suppress Color Profile Warnings** Choosing this option will display a warning if the color profiles are not matched. Check the box to prevent these warning dialog boxes from displaying, or monitor them manually and click OK on each one yourself.

5. Choose the destination folder where the files will be saved. You'll see two options here:

- **Save And Close** The files in the existing folder will be overwritten by the processed files.

- **Folder** The processed images will be placed in their own folder and the originals will remain intact. Options will become available for naming. Choose the desired options from the menus that appear, and enter a serial number; this number will represent the first image. All additional images will be named sequentially from the starting number you set.

6. Click OK.

You can also run all the batch actions from Adobe Bridge.

Now go make some coffee. When you return, open the destination folder and you'll see that all your files are processed.

Applying an Action to a Folder of Images

Let's walk through the process of applying an action to a folder of images. We'll change several images from color to grayscale and save the copies in a new folder.

1. Prepare a folder and place all the images that you would like to process into this folder. If you don't already have an action ready, record one now.

2. Choose File | Automate | Batch.

3. In the dialog box that appears, choose an action set and action from the Play options area, as shown in Figure 9-11A.

4. In the Source field, choose Folder.

5. Click Choose, and then select the folder from the browser window, as shown in Figure 9-11B.

6. Choose the playback options to run the action without interruptions, as seen in Figure 9-11C.

7. In the Destination field of the dialog box, choose Folder.

8. Click the Choose button and the browser window will pop up.

9. Select a folder or create a new folder by clicking Make New Folder and naming it, as shown in Figure 9-12A.

10. If you create a new folder, name the new images. The default settings are fine for most cases, as shown in Figure 9-12B; or you can type in your own names.

11. In the Errors field at the bottom of the dialog, choose an error option. You can choose one of two options:

   ■ **Stop For Errors**   If the file contains an error, the action will stop processing the rest of the folder.

   ■ **Log Errors To File**   If you choose this option, the action will play until the end and any error messages will be saved in a file. Click the Save As button and choose a filename for the error log. The log will be saved as a text file.

A.

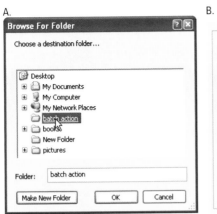

B.

FIGURE 9-12 Choosing a folder for the processed images: (A) Create a new folder on your hard drive. (B) Set the file's Save options

FIGURE 9-13 The processed images in a new folder

12. At the upper right of the dialog box, click OK, and the action will run.

13. If any steps are marked for your interaction, the action will pause for your input and then continue when you click Continue. Otherwise, Photoshop will process all the images for you in one batch.

Open your destination folder, and you'll see that all your images are processed, as shown in Figure 9-13.

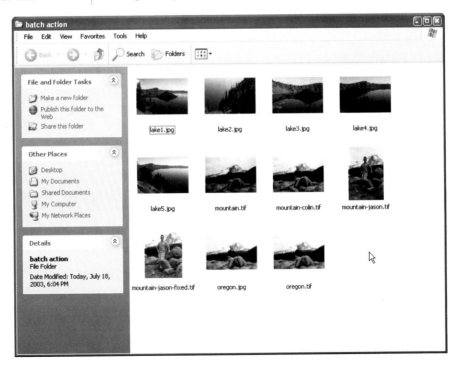

Using Droplets

A *droplet* is like an "action in a box." The droplet will appear as a small icon that you can add to your Desktop or in a folder. When you drag and drop one or more files on the icon, Photoshop will launch and run the selected action on the file(s). This is a handy tool for people who must complete identical tasks on files on a regular basis.

Here is how you create a droplet:

1. Choose File | Automate | Create Droplet. You'll see the dialog box shown in Figure 9-14.

FIGURE 9-14 The Create Droplet dialog box

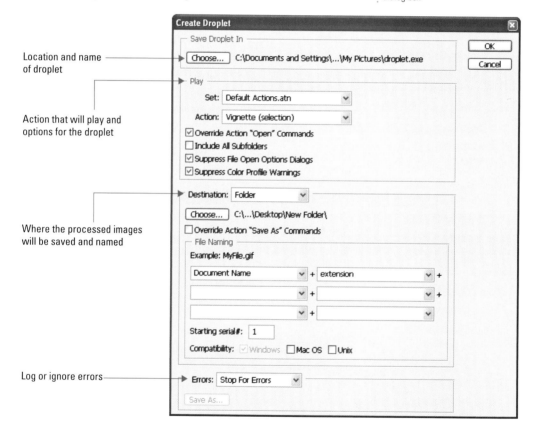

Location and name of droplet

Action that will play and options for the droplet

Where the processed images will be saved and named

Log or ignore errors

2. Click Choose. Type in a name for your droplet, and select the location where it will be stored.

3. In the Play options area, choose the Set and Action to play from the droplet. In this area, you can also choose

Suppress Color Profile Warnings so that the action won't require your interactivity.

4. Choose a Destination folder for the processed files.

5. Choose an Errors option: Stop For Errors, or Log Errors To File. If you log the errors, they will be saved as a text file.

6. Click OK, and your droplet will be created.

When you go to the folder in which you created the droplet, you'll see an icon similar to that shown in Figure 9-15. To use the droplet, simply drag and drop your files onto the icon. You don't even need to open the files.

FIGURE 9-15 A droplet icon

droplet.exe

Creating a Picture Package

Do you remember when you received your high school photos? They came on a sheet with several different sizes for you to cut apart. In Photoshop, you can create a similar image grouping called a *picture package*. Photoshop can arrange your images onto sheets for you. You can then print the images and trim the photos. This enables you to cram many images on a sheet of paper, without having to do any math, and thus saving a lot of paper.

Here is how to create your own picture package:

1. Choose File | Automate | Picture Package. You'll see the Picture Package dialog box shown in Figure 9-16.

2. In the Source Images section, choose either File or Folder to process either a single image or a group of images.

3. In the Document area, choose the Page Size you want.

4. Choose a Layout; you can choose from many preset options, or choose Custom to create your own layout.

5. Choose the Resolution.

6. Choose Flatten All Layers unless you need to retain layers for some reason.

7. For most instances of photo printing, the mode should stay on RGB.

9

Choose either an
image or a folder

Locate the file

Output size

Choose a layout

Choose a resolution

Choose this option if
you want to print text
on an image

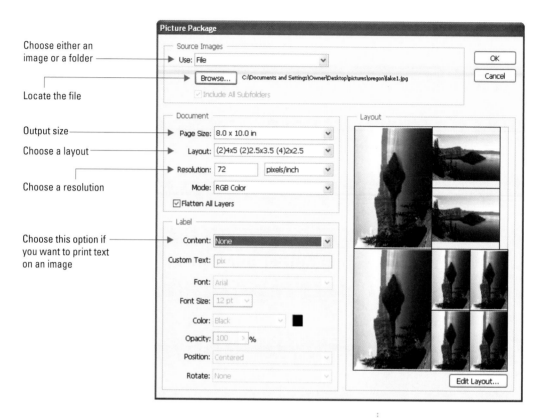

8. In the Label area, choose whether or not you want to
include labels to your pictures. If you want to add labels,
type in the information here and select the formatting
you want.

9. You'll see a preview in the layout window, as shown in
Figure 9-16. If it all looks good, click OK, and Photoshop
will process the images. You will see a lot going on.
Grab a cup of tea and admire all the work that you
don't have to do manually.

FIGURE 9-16 Picture package
options

You can now print and trim the images. Send copies to your
friends and family and show them what a Photoshop master
you are!

Using Contact Sheet II

The *contact sheet* is widely used in the world of photography.
When you order a set of prints, you sometimes have the option

of also receiving a contact sheet, which arranges all the photographs into thumbnails so you can see a small print of each photo on a single page.

Contact sheets are incredibly useful when saving files to a CD. Whether you're dealing with your artwork or pictures from a digital camera, or you're creating contact sheets and inserting them in jewel cases, contact sheets offer a quick and visual way to review the contents of a CD.

Photoshop can create multiple pages full of images, and it will produce as many pages as needed to index all the images in a chosen folder.

Here is how to create a contact sheet:

FIGURE 9-17 Contact Sheet II dialog box

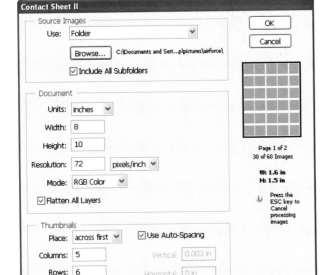

1. Choose File | Automate | Contact Sheet II. You'll see the Contact Sheet II dialog box shown in Figure 9-17.

2. In the Source Images section, choose the folder of images you want to include on the contact sheet.

3. In the Document area, select the document size and resolution.

4. For most purposes, the default setting on RGB Mode and Flatten All Layers works best.

5. Choose Thumbnail options; Default should work for most needs, but you can change as many options here as you want.

6. The preview on the right shows you how many images and pages will be processed.

7. If you want to use the filenames as captions for the images, click the appropriate checkbox and choose formatting options.

8. Click OK when you're satisfied with your settings.

The images will be processed, and you will see a page similar to that shown in Figure 9-18. If you chose the option to do so, a filename will appear under each thumbnail. Print out this page and place it inside your jewel case along with the archived CD, or you can organize the pages into a little booklet or ring binder to help you locate images later.

Creating a Web Gallery

If you want to post a collection of images to an Internet site, you need to resize and optimize each image and then create thumbnails. Then you would create a web page for all the thumbnails, and then create a page for each of the images. Depending on the number of images you want to display, this process could take hours, or even days.

Using Web Gallery makes this job a snap. In just a few minutes, you can process dozens of images and build great looking web galleries.

FIGURE 9-18 The finished contact sheet

Here is how to take a folder of images and turn them into a web site:

1. Choose File | Automate | Web Photo Gallery. You will see the Web Photo Gallery dialog box, as shown in Figure 9-19.

2. In the Site area, choose the style you want to use for the gallery. You can see how it will look in the preview.

3. In the Source Images area, choose the folder where your photos are located.

Choose a preset layout

Your e-mail address

The folder where the images are

Process subfolders

Where you want the web
gallery located

Set the options

Preview

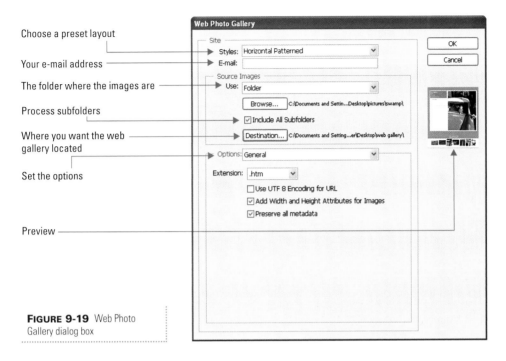

FIGURE 9-19 Web Photo
Gallery dialog box

4. Check the Include All Subfolders box if you want to
include images in subfolders of the folder you selected.

5. Click the Destination button to specify where on your
hard drive (or elsewhere) you want the web page to
be saved.

6. Set Options if you want to change any of the default
settings.

7. Click OK when you're happy with your settings.

After a little processing time, you'll see the finished web
page pop up in your browser, as shown in Figure 9-20. Click
the thumbnails or arrows to browse all the images one by one.

If you go to the destination folder, you will see all the files
that were created for the web gallery, as shown in Figure 9-21.
To view them on the Web, simply upload them to your web site.

To view the web gallery shown in Figure 9-21, point your
web browser to http://www.photoshopcafe.com/la/. Photoshop
can now create a gallery of images in Macromedia Flash format.
Try some of the new Flash Gallery options—they're very
impressive.

9

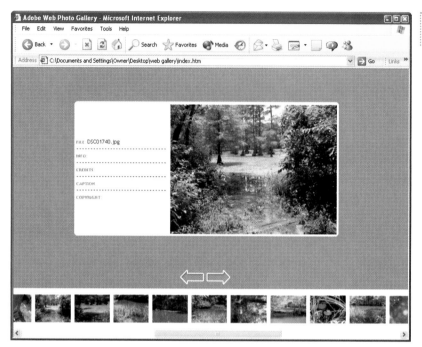

FIGURE 9-20 The finished web page

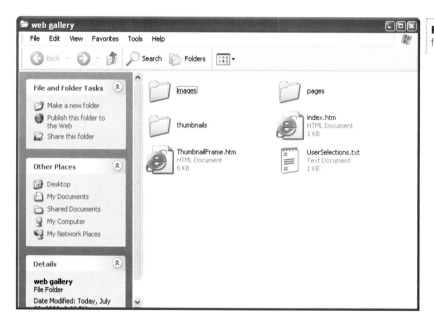

FIGURE 9-21 The files in the web gallery

FIGURE 9-22 PDF Presentation
dialog box

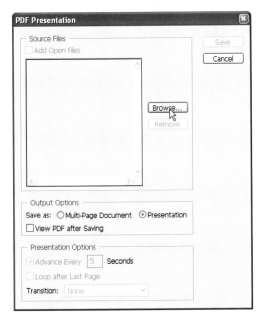

FIGURE 9-22 PDF Presentation
dialog box

Creating a PDF Presentation

Slide show anyone? With PDF presentations, you can create full-screen slide shows of your images, complete with transition effects.

Here's how to create a slide show presentation:

1. Choose File | Automate | PDF Presentation. You will see the PDF Presentation dialog box, as shown in Figure 9-22.

2. If you have images already open, click Add Open Files; otherwise, skip this step.

3. Click Browse to locate the images you want to add to the presentation.

4. Choose the files you want to add to the presentation by CTRL-clicking them (CMD-clicking on a Mac), as shown in Figure 9-23.

5. Click the Open button.

9

FIGURE 9-23 Adding images

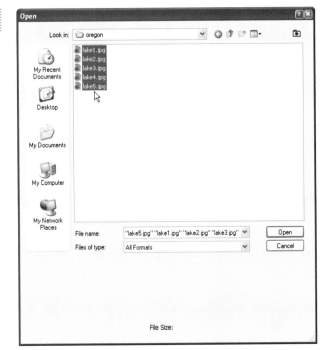

6. Choose Presentation to indicate a self-running presentation.

7. In the Output Options section of the PDF Presentation dialog box, check the View PDF After Saving option to have the presentation run automatically when Photoshop has finished creating it.

8. In the Presentation Options section, choose a delay time between slides (see Figure 9-24). Click Advance Every _ Seconds and choose the number of seconds you want each slide to be displayed.

9. Choose Loop After Last Page to run a continuous presentation. Looped presentations start again from the top after the last slide is shown.

FIGURE 9-24 Choose delay time between slides.

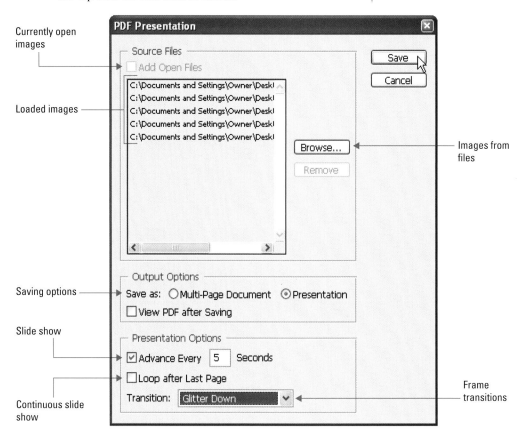

10. Choose a Transition effect for the images.

11. Click Save.

12. Choose the Output Options.

- Choose Multi-Page Document to output a typical PDF file.

- Choose Presentation to create a self-running slide show.

The presentation will take up the full screen and will automatically display all the images according to the transition effect that will display between images, as shown in Figure 9-25.

FIGURE 9-25 The PDF presentation showing a transition effect in progress

To advance the images backward and forward manually, click the left or right mouse button, respectively.

When you have finished the slide show or you want to stop the presentation, press the ESC key on your keyboard. A message will appear to inform you that special features have been created by Photoshop.

 You can use PDF Presentation to showcase Layer Comps. Choose File | Scripts | Layer Comps to PDF.

Part III

The Fun Stuff

Chapter 10 Make Selections

How to...

- Understand selections
- Use selection tools
- Use the Marquee tools
- Feather selections
- Use freeform selection tools
- Select images with the Magic Wand tool
- Use the Color Range tool
- Refine the selection
- Transform selections
- Use Quick Mask
- Create a photographic edge with Quick Mask
- Remove matting

Making selections in Photoshop is similar to taking a pair of magic scissors to a photo and cutting out a particular piece you want to work with, even though the piece is still a part of the original photo. In Photoshop, you use selection tools to select only portions of an image with which you want to work. Other, nonselected, parts of the image are unaffected.

Understanding Selections

You can identify a selection by what are known as the *marching ants*, the animated dashed lines that appear around the selected portion of an image. When you make a selection, only the selected area will be affected by any editing or adjustments you make to the image. For example, Figure 10-1 shows a selection surrounding an image of a cat. If we paint the cat selection with a paintbrush, only the selected portion of the image is affected, while the unselected portions are protected.

cat.jpg @ 25% (RGB/8#)

Have you ever seen anyone paint a car? The first thing they do is tear off huge chunks of masking tape and stick them on all the areas that they want to protect from the paint. Once all these areas are masked, the painter will spray paint over the car. When the masking tape is peeled off, the protected surfaces are free from the offending pigments.

When you make a selection using one of the selection tools in Photoshop, you are in effect protecting all the unselected portions of the image from "overspray." An example of this is shown in the image in Figure 10-2, where I selected the cat object and then made a radical color adjustment. Notice that only the selected area has been affected and the unselected areas are unaffected.

FIGURE 10-1 An image with a selection; only the selected area will be affected.

cat.jpg @ 25% (Color Balance 1, Layer Mask/8)

Feathered Selection

By default, all the selections have "hard" edges. If you need a softer edged selection, you can use *feathering*. You specify the amount of the feather in pixels, which sets how soft the selection will be—a larger feather amount produces a softer selection. Figure 10-3 shows the difference between feathered and non-feathered edges.

You can apply feathering in two ways:

- Choose a selection tool, and the options bar will allow you to enter a feather radius. This setting will apply to all future selections made with this tool. As a result, be sure that you set the feather amount before making a selection.

- You can feather an existing selection by choosing Select | Feather and then entering a feather radius.

FIGURE 10-2 A selected area with a color adjustment applied

 *When setting a feather radius from the options bar, make sure you return the setting to 0 before making the next selection, or the feather will be applied to that selection also.*

Using Selection Tools

Several selection tools are available within Photoshop. Each tool is designed for a specific selection task. In this section, you will learn how to use each tool and how to decide which tool is the best choice for your specific need.

Marquee Tools

The simplest and most commonly used of the selection tools are the Marquee tools, shown in Figure 10-4.

- **Rectangular** Creates a rectangular selection. Hold down the SHIFT key to constrain the selection to a perfect square.

- **Elliptical** Creates an elliptical selection. Hold down the SHIFT key to constrain the selection to a perfect circle.

- **Single Row** Creates a single-pixel-high horizontal selection. To use this tool, click anywhere in the image area and you will see a dashed horizontal line. Drag the mouse to the desired location.

- **Single Column** Creates a single-pixel-wide vertical selection. Used similarly to the Single Row tool.

After you select a tool, click and drag the mouse over the desired area to draw the selection.

Making Simple Selections

Execution of each of the Marquee tools is similar. Click and hold down the mouse button and drag over the image with the mouse to make the selection. All the pixels inside the dragged area will be selected. Figure 10-5 shows an elliptical selection in action.

FIGURE 10-3 An image showing the difference between a hard edge and one with a 25-pixel feather

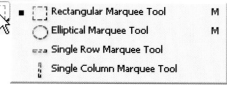

FIGURE 10-4 The Marquee tools

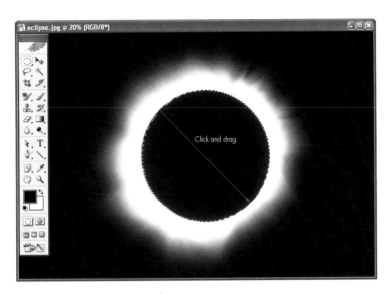

Here are several tips to help you make accurate selections:

- To draw from the center, hold down the ALT key (OPTION on a Mac) while dragging.

- To constrain the proportions, hold down the SHIFT key as you drag.

- To move a selection while drawing, hold down the SPACEBAR after you begin dragging.

FIGURE 10-5 Drawing a selection with the elliptical Marquee tool

FIGURE 10-6 Color applied to an inverted selection

Inverting a Selection

You can also use selection tools to select an area, and then alter the entire image except for the selected area. This is called *inverting* the selection. The Inverse command swaps the selected and unselected areas. Choose Select | Inverse to swap the selected areas, or use the shortcut: SHIFT-CTRL-I (SHIFT-CMD-I on a Mac). Figure 10-6 shows a color adjustment applied to an inverted selection. In this case, the circle was the selected area.

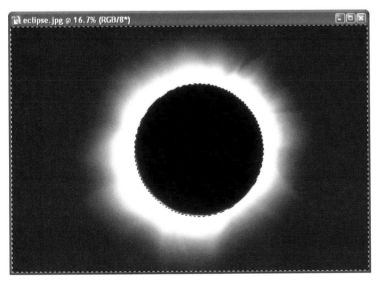

Choosing Selection Options

By default, whenever you make a new selection, it will replace the existing selection. However, you can make more than one selection at a time using several

10

options. Figure 10-7 shows the results of the various selection options, which are available from the options bar whenever you choose a selection tool.

- **New Selection** The default setting, which replaces the existing selection

- **Add To Selection** Adds the new area to the previous selection (or SHIFT key)

- **Subtract From Selection** Cuts the new selection from the existing selection (or ALT [OPTION] key)

- **Intersect With Selection** Replaces the existing selection with the overlapping area of the new selection (or SHIFT-ALT [SHIFT-OPTION] keys)

By using one or more of these options, you can create some pretty complex selection shapes.

A. 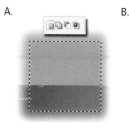 B.

C.  D.

FIGURE 10-7 Results of various selection options
(A) New Selection
(B) Add To Selection
(C) Subtract From Selection
(D) Intersect With Selection

Freeform Selection Tools

So far, we have looked at selection tools that help you create selections based on predefined shapes. Another set of tools gives you much more freedom in your selections: the three Lasso tools. Figure 10-8 shows the tools in the toolbox.

FIGURE 10-8 The Lasso tools

Lasso Tool

The Lasso tool is at the top of the freeform selection tools. You can choose this tool and drag it around an image as you would a pencil on a piece of paper. Figure 10-9A shows a selection made with the Lasso tool.

When you have finished dragging the mouse around the selection, release the button and a closed selection will be created. All the options from the options bar are available with this tool, and with a bit of practice, you can create some very accurate selections. Figure 10-9B shows the selected portion of the image copied to a new layer. A radial blur was then applied to the background.

A.

B.

FIGURE 10-9 A selection created with the Lasso tool (A) and an effect used with the selection (B)

Tips for Using the Freeform Selection Tools

You can use the various options from the options bar, but this can be a bit slow. Here are a couple of keyboard shortcuts to save some time:

■ To add to the selection, press and hold the SHIFT key.

■ To subtract from the selection, press and hold the ALT key (OPTION key on the Mac).

FIGURE 10-10 A selection made with the Polygonal Lasso tool

Polygonal Lasso

The Polygonal Lasso tool differs from the Lasso tool in that it draws only straight lines and you cannot drag around your selection. Figure 10-10 shows an image with a selection created using this tool.

Here's how the tool works:

1. Click anywhere in the image.

2. As you move the mouse, you will notice that a line follows the curser, with one end attached to the click point.

3. Click again and the two points will be connected.

4. Repeat step 2 to click all the way around the image.

5. When you have finished making your selection, click the start point and the selection will be created.

The Magnetic Lasso

This tool is designed to help you select objects in an image, in case you want to trace the outline of an image. The Magnetic Lasso tool detects the edge of an image and automatically adds temporary anchor points called *fastening points*. (See Chapter 7 for more information on anchor points.) The tool will detect changes in color and snap to the color's edges. Figure 10-11 shows the Magnetic Lasso tool in use.

Here's how to use the Magnetic Lasso tool:

FIGURE 10-11 Drawing with the Magnetic Lasso tool

1. Choose the settings from the options bar:

   - **Width** Determines how far, in pixels, the tool will search for edges.

   - **Edge Contrast** This is the sensitivity setting. Use a higher number to ignore more subtle transitions.

   - **Frequency** How often fastening points are added. A higher number will add more fastening points.

2. Drag the mouse around the image. Watch as the tool begins to hug the edges and add fastening points.

3. You can force a fastening point by clicking the mouse. This is useful for areas of sharp transitions of shape or subtle changes in color.

4. Continue tracing all the way around the image until you click the start point.

When you click the start point, all the fastening points will disappear and a selection will be made like the one shown in Figure 10-12.

FIGURE 10-12 A selection made with the Magnetic Lasso tool

The Magic Wand

Imagine having a tool that could detect a certain color in an image and make selections based on the color. For example, suppose your image shows a pumpkin growing in a green field. You can use the Magic Wand tool to make a selection of just the orange pumpkin part of the image. This Magic Wand will not turn a pumpkin into a carriage, but it can turn a pumpkin into a selection.

This tool is useful for images with a large area of solid color, where the selected object is a different color from the background.

Using the tool is simple: just choose the desired settings, click the color you want to select, and the Magic Wand will do its work. The secret to success with this tool is in the settings:

- **Tolerance**   This is the sensitivity setting. A low number will cause the Magic Wand to be very fussy and ignore subtle differences in color. A higher number will cause the tool to look for colors in the general range of the selected color. Experiment with this setting when making selections. The default setting is 32, which is a good starting point for most projects.

10

- **Anti-aliasing**　Choose this option to create smoother edges on the selections.

- **Contiguous**　Choose this option to limit the selection to adjacent areas of similar color. Deselect it to cause the tool to look at the entire image.

- **Use All Layers**　By default, the Magic Wand tool will make selections based on the active layer only. By using all layers, it will look at the entire image.

FIGURE 10-13　An image with a selection by the Magic Wand tool

When you make a selection with the Magic Wand, some areas get missed in the selection because the color may have gradated to a hue outside of the chosen range—for example, see the bottom of the image in Figure 10-13. Here, the blue sky was chosen as the active color, but parts of the bottom portion weren't selected because of the other hues that appear there.

Refining the Selection

You can try the following to refine the selection further:

- *Areas are missed.*　Press the SHIFT key and click in the missed area. This will cause the Magic Wand to add to the selection.

- *Subtle color differences are missed.*　Choose Select | Similar.

- *You want the selection to fill more of the area.* Choose Select | Grow.

- *Too much of the image is selected.*　Lower the tolerance setting, and then, holding down the ALT key (OPTION on a Mac), click inside the area you want to remove from the selection.

How to ...   Use Magic Wand Hidden Settings

When using the Magic Wand tool, a hidden setting can affect the way the tool is used. If you click the Eyedropper tool, a Sample Size drop-down menu will appear in the options bar with three settings, which also affect the way the Magic Wand tool selects pixels:

- **Point Sample**   Sensitivity is at the pixel level. Samples the exact pixel that is directly under the cursor.

- **3 × 3 Average**   Takes the average reading for 3 pixels either direction.

- **5 × 5 Average**   Takes an average reading for 5 pixels either direction.

The Magic Wand is tied to the Eyedropper tool's settings. If you are having a problem with your selections, try changing this tool's settings: switch to the Eyedropper tool, choose a different setting, and switch back to the Magic Wand tool.

FIGURE 10-14 The object removed from its background and added to a new background

Cleaning up the Edges

Once you have made the selection, you can remove the object from the current background and add it to another, as shown in Figure 10-14. Notice the subtle original background color that shows around the edges of the selection? You can remove those by choosing Layer | Matting | Defringe and entering a setting in pixels (see the end of this chapter for more on matting). This setting will determine how many pixels the filter will cut into the image to remove the hint of the original background.

extreme roller blading.jpg @ 50% (Layer 1, RGB/8*)

10

Color Range

This tool is similar to the Magic Wand tool, but it offers more options and you have more control over the areas that are selected. When you choose the Color Range tool, a dialog box opens, where you can set options for finer control over your selection.

Choosing a Color

Figure 10-15 shows an image that we would like to select. It would take some time to trace all the outlines with the Lasso tools. It would also be difficult to select this image with the Magic Wand tool because of the various shapes and tones. You can see that the subject color is different from the background color. Because of this, the Color Range tool is the best choice for selecting this image.

Here's how to use this tool:

1. Open the image in Photoshop.

2. Choose Select | Color Range.

3. In the Color Range dialog box, shown in Figure 10-16, choose the Eyedropper tool and click anywhere inside the part of the image that you would like to select.

4. Increase the Fuzziness slider to refine the selection. The selected areas will be shown as white and the unselected will show as black. Getting the fuzziness just right is a balancing act and therefore will be different for each image. You will need to experiment. Figure 10-17 shows a good selection.

5. Click OK to apply the selection.

Refining the Selection

You may refine the selection further by adding colors to the selected area:

1. For a larger and more precise preview, you can make a choice from the Selection Preview

FIGURE 10-15 The original image—it could take a while to mask this image with the Lasso tools.

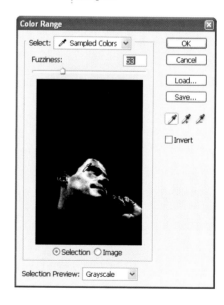

FIGURE 10-16 The Color Range dialog box

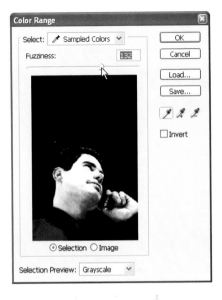

drop-down menu. In Figure 10-18, Grayscale is selected for the preview. This will display a preview in the main image window.

2. Choose the Eyedropper tool with the plus sign next to it. This is the Add To Selection tool.

3. Click another color in the portion of the image you want to select. (Note that you will probably have to tweak the fuzziness whenever you add a color.)

4. Figure 10-19 shows a much stronger contrast between the selected object and the background. This is the kind of selection that you want.

5. To apply the changes, click OK.

Figure 10-20 shows the image with the ants marching around the selected objects.

FIGURE 10-17 Adjusting the fuzziness

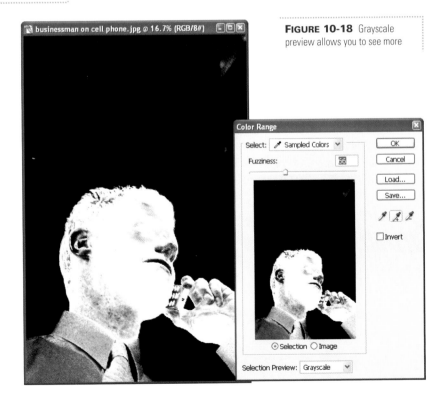

FIGURE 10-18 Grayscale preview allows you to see more

As shown in Figure 10-20, you may find that a few stray pixels appear along with the selection; this is a good time to use the other selection tools, such as the Lasso and Marquee tools, to add to the selection and correct this. You can also use these tools to subtract from the selection to clean up any stray pixels in the background.

With experience, you will develop an eye for the type of images that lend themselves to the Color Range tool selection method.

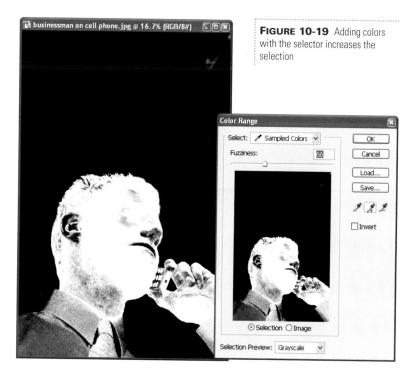

FIGURE 10-19 Adding colors with the selector increases the selection

Transforming Selections

When you make selections, you can adjust them beyond the ability of the selection tools alone. Let's look at the different ways that we can modify our selections.

Modifying Selections

Four options are available under the Select | Modify menu. The results of these options are shown in the images in Figure 10-21.

- **Border**   Creates a border from the selection. Enter a width in pixels.

FIGURE 10-20 The final selected image

- **Smooth**   Simplifies the selection.
- **Expand**   Increases the size of the selection.
- **Contract**   Decreases the size of the selection.

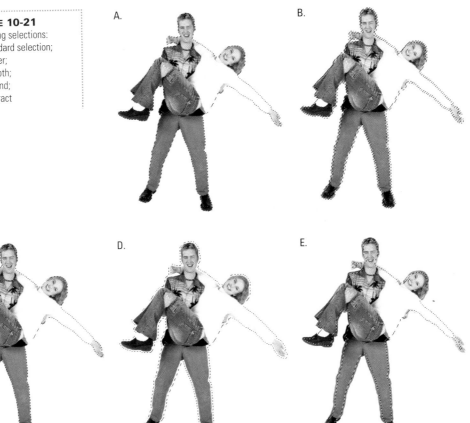

FIGURE 10-21
Modifying selections:
(A) Standard selection;
(B) Border;
(C) Smooth;
(D) Expand;
(E) Contract

Transform Selection

Another set of options is available to transform selections. These tools affect the shape of the selection. To activate these tools, choose Select | Transform Selection. You will see a bounding box and eight adjustment handles. To make modifications, drag the handles. Figure 10-22 shows these options in use.

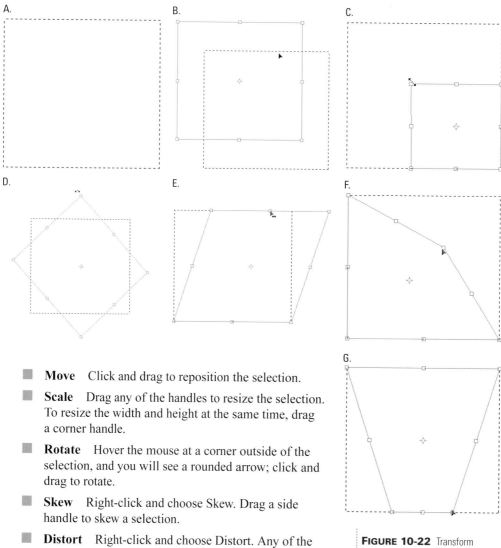

- **Move** Click and drag to reposition the selection.

- **Scale** Drag any of the handles to resize the selection. To resize the width and height at the same time, drag a corner handle.

- **Rotate** Hover the mouse at a corner outside of the selection, and you will see a rounded arrow; click and drag to rotate.

- **Skew** Right-click and choose Skew. Drag a side handle to skew a selection.

- **Distort** Right-click and choose Distort. Any of the handles will move independently.

- **Perspective** Right-click and choose Perspective. When you adjust one corner, the opposite corner will adjust to match.

FIGURE 10-22 Transform selections: (A) Normal; (B) Move; (C) Scale; (D) Rotate; (E) Skew; (F) Distort; (G) Perspective

Press ENTER to apply the transformations, and the marching ants will reflect the changes.

Applying Quick Mask

Quick Mask is a unique tool; you can use it to create a temporary mask of a selection. You can then paint with all the painting tools and even use filters. It will look like a red brush turned down to 50 percent opacity. The magic happens when you switch off the Quick Mask tool. All the areas that were painted will become selections.

It works like this:

1. Click the Quick Mask tool in the toolbox, as shown in Figure 10-23 (or you can press the Q key).

2. Paint with the Brush tool wherever you choose.

3. Instead of the paint color, you will see a red mask appear, like that shown in Figure 10-24.

4. Use the Eraser tool to finesse your selection boundaries and also filters if you wish.

FIGURE 10-23 Choosing the Quick Mask tool

10

dirt road.jpg @ 100% (Quick Mask/8)

FIGURE 10-24 Painting in Quick Mask mode

5. When you have finished painting, press the Q key again or switch back to normal mode from the toolbox.

6. You will see that all the painted areas are selected, as shown in Figure 10-25.

FIGURE 10-25 Returning to normal mode reveals the selection.

You can change the color of the mask in Quick Mask by double-clicking the tool in the toolbox. Choose a new color from the Color Picker and adjust the opacity.

Creating a Photographic Edge with Quick Mask

One use for this type of selection would be to create a high-energy photo edge. Figure 10-26 shows how such an edge might look.

It's easy to reproduce this effect if you follow these steps:

1. Choose the Quick Mask tool.

2. Choose a Brush tool.

3. Paint the image area.

FIGURE 10-26 Picture edge from Quick Mask

4. Return to normal mode.

5. Inverse the selection: choose Select | Inverse.

6. Copy the selection to a new layer by pressing CTRL-J (CMD-J on the Mac).

7. Fill the background with white.

Eliminating Matting

When you have finished removing objects from their backgrounds, you may notice some *halos*—also known as *matting*. Figure 10-27A shows an example of this problem before, and Figure 10-27B shows after matting was removed. Notice the tiny white edges around the leftmost selection that give it an obvious cut-out look.

Photoshop has three tools to help you deal with this problem. These are found by choosing Layer | Matting:

- **Defringe**   Enter a number in pixels. The chosen number of pixels will be deleted around the entire image. Use this option for a multi-colored halo.

■ **Remove Black Matte**   Removes a dark halo.

■ **Remove White Matte**   Removes a white halo, as shown in Figure 10-27.

FIGURE 10-27 Removing the matting from a cutout: (A) Image with a white edge halo; (B) After removing halo

A.

B.

Chapter 11

Make Images Pop with Special Effects

How to...

- Use filters
- Simulate movement
- Create a pencil sketch effect
- Create a pixelized effect
- Combine filters using the Filter Gallery
- Use the Liquify filter
- Change facial expressions
- Choose third-party plug-ins
- Use layer effects
- Use, create, and save styles
- Work with Vanishing Point

In this chapter, we get to play with all the cool toys. You have probably seen Photoshop images that use bevels, sheens, shadows, and other special effects. Perhaps this type of image inspired you to learn how to use Photoshop. When it was first released in 1990, Photoshop had only humble uses, primarily color selection. Now, just about all major motion pictures incorporate the use of effects in Photoshop, including all the *Star Wars* movies.

If you see a great-looking poster or magazine, Photoshop was probably involved in its creation; in fact, Photoshop is everywhere, and almost everyone in the design and entertainment industry uses it. The reason is the program's flexibility and the way that Photoshop can manipulate images with the use of native and third-party filters. Layer styles add another dimension to images; it's amazing how easy it is to transform a dull image into something interesting with just a click or two.

Filters

You can use filters in Photoshop to modify images—to change the texture, shape, form, or color of images. Filters can sharpen

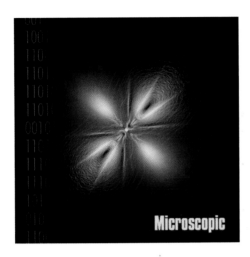

FIGURE 11-1 "Microscopic" image created with filters

or blur an image, or they can be used for complex manipulation, such as lighting effects and distortion. You can filter images beyond recognition or just make subtle changes.

Figure 11-1 shows an image that was created with nothing but filters. I started with a blank canvas and added a Lens Flare and Radial Blur filter. The layer was duplicated and rotated, and the same effect was applied several times.

Two types of filters can be used in Photoshop. The first group, which I call *production filters,* are used to enhance your images (such as sharpening a photo); what I call *creative filters* are used to produce special effects that can mimic reality or mock it (such as blurring or distorting a photo).

The Filter Menu

You access the filters in Photoshop by choosing them from the Filter menu, shown in Figure 11-2.

From the menu, 13 main groups of filters are available; each of these groups contains several filters. These main groups are listed here:

FIGURE 11-2 The Filter menu

Filter	View	Window	Help

Last Filter	Ctrl+F
Extract...	Alt+Ctrl+X
Filter Gallery...	
Liquify...	Shift+Ctrl+X
Pattern Maker...	Alt+Shift+Ctrl+X
Vanishing Point...	Alt+Ctrl+V

Artistic ▶
Blur ▶
Brush Strokes ▶
Distort ▶
Noise ▶
Pixelate ▶
Render ▶
Sharpen ▶
Sketch ▶
Stylize ▶
Texture ▶
Video ▶
Other ▶

Digimarc ▶

- **Artistic**   (Creative) These filters mimic traditional art such as watercolor and pastel work.

- **Blur**   (Production/Creative) These filters blur pixels in various ways.

- **Brush Strokes**   (Creative) These filters give the images brushed appearances.

- **Distort**   (Production/Creative) These filters allow you to bend and warp images.

- **Noise**   (Production/Creative) These filters either introduce or reduce film grain.

- **Pixelate**   (Creative) These filters introduce uniform patterns that give the image a pixelized look.

- **Render**   (Creative) These filters introduce new objects or create a 3-D effect.

- **Sharpen**   (Production) These filters sharpen the edges of pixels and sharpen the image.

- **Sketch**   (Creative) These filters work from the current foreground and background color swatch.

11

- **Stylize**   (Creative) These filters allow for special effects mainly dealing with the edges of images.

- **Texture**   (Creative) These filters add various real-world textures to images.

- **Video**   (Production) These filters are used for video production work.

- **Other**   (Production/Creative) These filters are used to perform assorted tasks. Figure 11-3 shows a gallery of images.

FIGURE 11-3 Examples of filter use

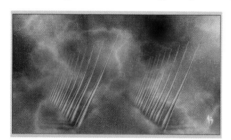

A. Major use of the Difference Clouds filter

B. Blurs and wave filters

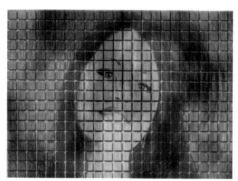

C. Brush filters and blurs

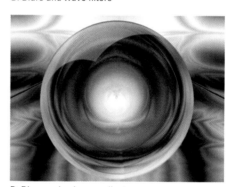

D. Blurs and polar coordinates

E. Fibers, motion blur, and displacement

F. Background uses noise and lighting effects

 *Many of the filters in Photoshop will not work in CMYK mode, so it's advisable that you work in RGB mode if you need to do extensive filter work.*

Using Filters

Because Photoshop comes with so many filters, we won't be able to walk through the use of each one. We'll cover a few of the important ones in this section, however. As for the others, you'll find that once you begin to use the filters, a little experimentation will go a long way. Spend some time playing around with the filters, and you'll find out what each one does. Try combining two or more filters to achieve interesting results. For a good resource on filters and special effects, check out the videos by your author, Colin Smith (http://www.photoshopCD .com). You'll also find a number of free tutorials at http:// www.photoshopcafe.com.

In this section, we walk through a few easy-to-produce special effects using some of the filters that ship with Photoshop.

FIGURE 11-4 The original image

Using Radial Blur to Zoom into an Image

This effect is great for adding movement and excitement to an image. The zooming effect is similar to a photographer snapping a picture while zooming into an image. This effect is difficult to achieve with a camera, but it's easy to do with Photoshop.

1. Begin with an image in RGB mode, as shown in Figure 11-4.

2. Choose Filter | Blur | Radial Blur.

3. In the Radial Blur dialog box, choose the Zoom Blur Method, and set the Amount slider to a small amount, such as 16, as shown in Figure 11-5.

4. Click OK.

FIGURE 11-5 Radial blur added

You should now see something like the image shown in Figure 11-6. If the effect is too intense, try again with a lower Amount setting.

The Good Quality setting works well and is much faster to render than the Best setting.

Using Motion Blur to Simulate Movement

This effect will add the streaks that you see in an image behind an object that appears to be moving with speed. This is a great effect to use with sports photos, because it adds some extra action to the image.

FIGURE 11-6 The result

FIGURE 11-7 Original photo with a copy of the subject on a new layer

1. Begin with a new image in RGB mode.

2. Duplicate the background layer.

3. Extract the image from the background on the new layer (see Chapter 10). The Layers palette should now look something like that shown in Figure 11-7.

4. Hide the top layer.

5. Choose the bottom layer.

6. Choose Filter | Blur | Motion Blur.

7. In the Motion Blur dialog box, choose the Angle and Distance, as shown in Figure 11-8A. The effect of your choice is shown in Figure 11-8B.

8. Show the top layer again.

9. Position the top layer near the beginning of the motion trail, as shown in Figure 11-9.

Photo courtesy of Hemera Images

A.
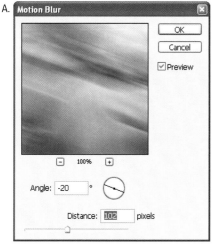

FIGURE 11-9 Final result

B.

FIGURE 11-8 Adding Motion Blur (A), and the effect (B)

FIGURE 11-10 Original photograph

Tip *If you want to blur only the subject and not the background, duplicate the extracted layer (step 2), and then blur the duplicated layer instead of the background.*

Adding a Pencil Sketch Effect

This effect is so popular that I wish I had a dollar for every time someone has asked me to explain it. Using the effect, you can make a photograph look just like a pencil sketch. This is easy to do, and the result can be stunning.

1. Start with a photograph in RGB mode, as shown in Figure 11-10.

2. Duplicate the layer with the image on it (Background).

3. Desaturate the image by choosing Image | Adjustments | Desaturate.

4. Duplicate the desaturated layer by pressing CTRL-J (CMD-J on the Mac).

5. Invert the layer by choosing Image | Adjustments | Invert, or press CTRL-I (CMD-I on the Mac).

11

6. Change the Layer Blending mode to Color Dodge, as shown in Figure 11-11. The image should now be a white screen, because we have just cancelled out the image.

7. Choose Filter | Blur | Gaussian Blur, and adjust the amount until you are satisfied with the result.

8. Click OK.

You should now see something like the image shown in Figure 11-12.

Note you can hide the first desaturated layer to make the image look like a colored pencil effect.

Adding a Pixelized Effect

In a digital age in which everything is nice and perfect, sometimes you might want to add some imperfections to an image. We have learned how to avoid pixelation in this book, but at times you may want to break the rules for the sake of special effects. We are going to take an image and pixelize it; this will add a "digitized" feel to the image.

1. We begin with an interesting image in RGB mode, as shown in Figure 11-13.

2. Choose Filter | Pixelate | Mosaic.

3. In the Mosaic dialog box, choose a setting that will show the pixels at the size you want. You can use the plus (+) and minus (–) buttons in the thumbnail preview to zoom in or out of the image. Figure 11-14 shows the Cell Size set at 24.

4. The image will now appear pixelized. To make the effect look as though it is pixelized on purpose—and not just a bad scan—use the History brush to remove the effect from the foreground objects. This gives the image a pixelized depth-of-field effect, as shown in Figure 11-15.

FIGURE 11-11 The Layers palette so far

FIGURE 11-12 The final pencil sketch effect

FIGURE 11-13 Original image

FIGURE 11-14 Cell Size setting in the Mosaic dialog box

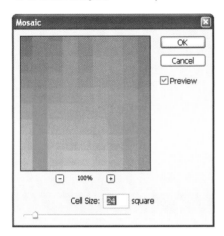

FIGURE 11-15
The final image (notice that the hand and lightbulb are not pixelized)

Combining Filters Using the Filter Gallery

Now let's use a filter for art lovers. You can create the illusion of a hand-painted or pastel image from any photograph. Here, we'll use the Filter Gallery to combine filters. The Filter Gallery lets you experiment with various filters in tandem without damaging your original image. When you start applying a lot of filters, you can quickly lose image integrity if you are not careful.

FIGURE 11-16 Original image

Figure 11-16 shows an image that we are going to turn into an art effect.

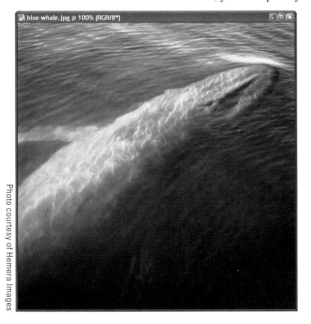

Photo courtesy of Hemera Images

1. Choose Filter | Artistic | Dry Brush. The Filter Gallery will open.

2. Choose the settings shown in Figure 11-17A.

3. Click the New icon at the bottom of the rightmost window.

4. In the box shown at the top center of the Filter Gallery settings area (which shows Dry Brush in Figure 11-17), click the down arrow and choose Smudge Stick.

5. Adjust the settings so that they're similar to those shown in Figure 11-17B.

FIGURE 11-17 Filter Gallery settings (A) Dry Brush filter (B) Smudge Stick filter combined

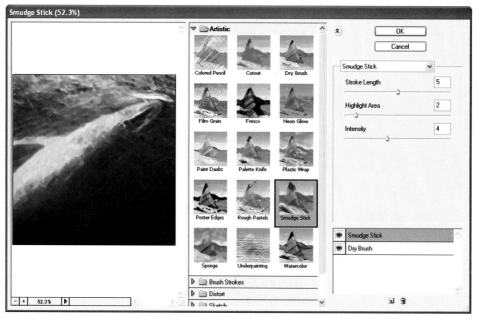

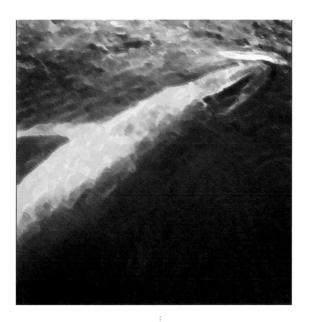

FIGURE 11-18 Final "hand-painted" image

FIGURE 11-19 Original image inside the Liquify window

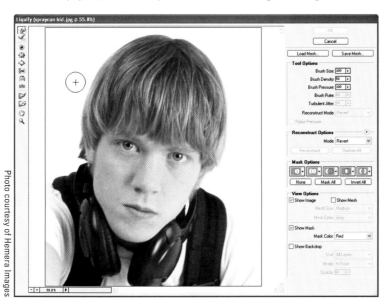

6. You can add as many filter layers as you wish to build up your effect. Click OK when you're done.

Your image will now look like it was painted by hand, as shown in Figure 11-18.

The Liquify Filter

Perhaps the most fun tool in Photoshop is the Liquify filter, and no chapter on special effects would be complete without discussing this tool. Liquify allows you to mold your image like putty so that you can change facial expressions and do some downright weird things to your images. Figure 11-19 shows the Liquify interface.

Along the left side of the Liquify filter window are all the tools available with the filter. The area at the right of the window shows tool options and masking tools, which are used in combination with selection tools or masks in the original image and with the Freeze tool in Liquify. The image preview appears in the center of the window.

Changing Facial Expressions with the Liquify Tool

We can easily change the expression on our subject's face by using the Liquify tool. For instance, we could turn the corners of his mouth up to express happiness or down for sadness. In this case, we'll give the boy an angry/sulky look.

We'll exaggerate the effects to create a caricature. (For realism, you can use more subtle movements.)

1. Open the image in Photoshop.

2. Choose Filter | Liquify.

3. Choose the Push tool.

4. Push the boy's forehead down with a large brush size, as shown in Figure 11-20.

5. Push the ends of the eyes upward to enhance the emotion.

FIGURE 11-20 The Push tool in action

Using the Freeze Tool

When you use the tools in the Liquify window, all the pixels around the brush will be affected. If you want to protect portions of the image, you can apply the Freeze tool. This will protect and "freeze" portions of the image so that they aren't distorted with the rest of the image.

1. Choose the Freeze tool from the tools on the left of the Liquify window.

2. Paint around the boy's chin to preserve the shape of his face, as shown in Figure 11-21A.

3. Use the Push tool to alter the mouth, as shown in Figure 11-21B.

A.

B.

FIGURE 11-21 Adding a Freeze mask (A), and transforming with the frozen region protected (B)

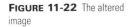

FIGURE 11-22 The altered image

4. Make any other final adjustments until you are happy with the effect.

5. Click OK.

The boy now looks very upset in Figure 11-22.

Third-Party Plug-ins

One of the reasons for the success of Photoshop is the way the program is built: The core part of Photoshop controls all the functionality and file handling, and extensibility is handled by plug-ins, which are available from other software makers. Each plug-in filter is built on its own and is used with Photoshop via a little file called an 8-bit filter (.8bf). To add a new filter, you simply drop it into the Filters directory of Photoshop and it's ready for use.

Several companies make plug-in filters that you can purchase to extend the functionality of Photoshop. Some of the most popular are listed here:

- **Alien Skin Software (http://www.alienskin.com)** Eye Candy, Xenofex, Image Doctor, Splat!

- **Extensis (http://www.extensis.com)** Mask Pro, pxl SmartScale, Phototools, PhotoFrame

- **Auto FX (http://www.autofx.com)** DreamSuite, Mystical Lighting, Mystical Tint Tone and Color, Photo/Graphic Edges, AutoEye

- **Corel (http://www.corel.com)** KPT (Kai's Power Tools) Collection (the original Photoshop plug-ins developed by Kai Kruse), KnockOut

- **Andromeda (http://www.andromeda.com)** ScatterLight Lenses, Shadow Filter, RedEyePro, Cutline Filter, EtchTone Filter

- **nik multimedia (http://www.nikmultimedia.com)** Color Efex Pro, Sharpener, Dfine

- **Kodak (http://www.kodak.com)** GEM, ROC, SHO

- **The Plugin Site (http://www.thepluginsite.com)** Check out this site for more resources.

11

Layer Effects

Layer effects can be used to add dimension and special effects to your layers with one simple click. These effects can be easily applied and customized. You are not limited to a single effect, because all the various effects can be mixed and matched to achieve a huge array of effects. Once you have achieved an effect, it can be saved to a library and recalled in a single click as a layer style. Even a beginner can achieve stunning results using layer effects.

A.

 Layer effects will not work on backgrounds or flattened images. You must start with an active layer to apply the effect. See Chapters 4 and 5 for more on layers.

Let's apply a layer effect:

1. Choose a layer by clicking it in the Layers palette.

2. Click the *f* button at the bottom of the Layers palette.

3. Choose an effect from the drop-down menu, as shown in Figure 11-23A.

4. In the Layer Style dialog box, make adjustments, as shown in Figure 11-23B.

5. Click OK to apply the effect.

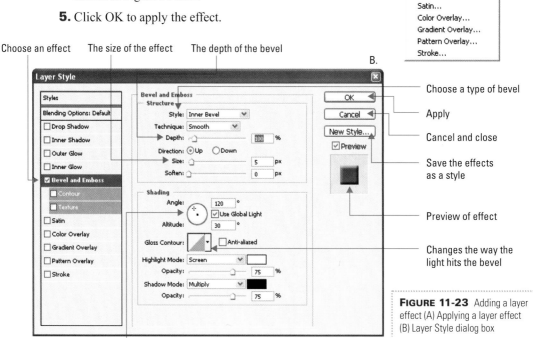

FIGURE 11-23 Adding a layer effect (A) Applying a layer effect (B) Layer Style dialog box

Using Different Effects

You can add more than one effect to an image via the Layer Style dialog box. Here's how:

1. In the Styles column at the left side of the Layer Style dialog box (Figure 11-23B), check the box next to the name of the effect that you want to use.

2. Make adjustments to the effect.

3. Click the name, and the options will change to the chosen effect.

Here is a quick rundown of what each effect does. The illustrations show the original image for a visual example of the layer effects.

- **Drop Shadow**   Adds a soft shadow under the layer that makes the layer appear to "float" in the air.

- **Inner Shadow**   Adds a soft shadow that makes the layer appear cut into the page.

- **Outer Glow**   Adds a soft glow around the layer.

- **Inner Glow**   Adds a glow on the inside of the layer.

- **Bevel and Emboss**   Adds a 3-D look to layers.

- **Satin**   Applies a sheen to the surface of the layer.

- **Color Overlay**   Changes the color of a layer object to a solid color of your choice.

- **Gradient Overlay**   Same as Color Overlay except a gradient is used.

- **Pattern Overlay**   Applies a pattern texture to your layer.

- **Stroke**   Adds a colored outline to your layer.

Copying Effects to Layers

After you have created an effect on a layer, you can easily copy the exact settings to another layer or another document. Two simple methods can be used for duplicating effects to other layers. Here's the first one:

1. Position your mouse pointer over the word *Effects* on the Layers palette. Press and hold the ALT key (OPTION on the Mac).

2. Drag the mouse to the layer to which you want to apply the effect, as shown in Figure 11-24.

3. Release the mouse and the effect will be duplicated to the other layer.

Here's a second method to duplicate effects onto other layers. This method works best on multiple layers at once. It's a great method to use when you're experimenting with web buttons and other items that you need to create over and over again:

1. In the Layers palette, right-click the word *Effects* on the layer with the effect you want to copy.

2. From the context menu, choose Copy Layer Style.

3. Select all the layers to which you want to add the layer effects.

4. Right-click again.

5. From the context menu, choose Paste Layer Style. The effect will now be replicated to all the selected layers.

FIGURE 11-24 Copying a layer effect to another layer

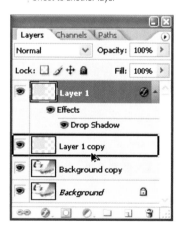

Managing Layer Effects

When you use two or more effects at once, you'll see a list of effects under the layers in the Layers palette. To turn off individual effects, click the eye icon to the left of the effect name in the palette, and that effect will be toggled off; only the visible effects will show in the layer effect. To show the individual effect again, click the eye icon again.

Layer Styles

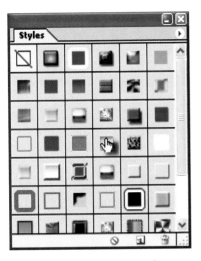

When you use two or more effects together, it is called a *layer style*. Layer styles can be saved for later use, which is nice, because it means you will not have to re-create each effect every time you want to use it. You save the styles in a library called the Styles palette (Figure 11-25), which comes with a collection of *presets*. You can download extra sets from the Photoshop Program CD or from the Web, or you can purchase collections from third parties.

The premade effects can be applied to your layers in a single click. This can be done in one of two ways:

- Highlight the layer and click a style from the Styles palette.

- Drag and drop a style from the Styles palette onto the layer.

FIGURE 11-25 Applying a layer style

FIGURE 11-26 Choosing a colored gradient

Creating Styles

When it comes to creating styles, there is no substitute for experimentation, because the possibilities are endless. To give you a head start, let's look at the components that make up a beveled gold layer style that we'll create.

1. Create a new layer.

2. Choose a gradient effect from the layer style menu.

3. In the dialog box that opens, create a new golden gradient (see Figure 11-26). Make sure you change the Angle setting.

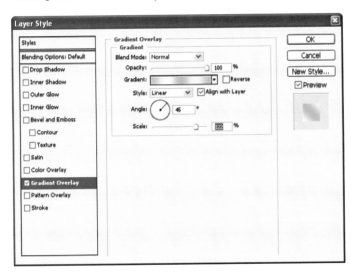

4. Click Bevel and Emboss, and use similar settings to those shown in Figure 11-27. Pay attention to the Gloss Contour.

5. Apply a bevel contour, as shown in Figure 11-28.

FIGURE 11-28 Adding a bevel contour for shape

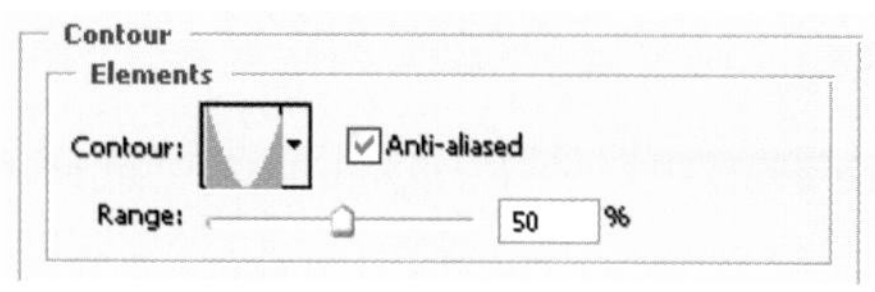

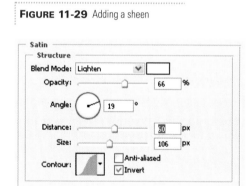

6. Choose Satin, and set the Color to White and the Blend Mode to Lighten, as shown in Figure 11-29.

FIGURE 11-29 Adding a sheen

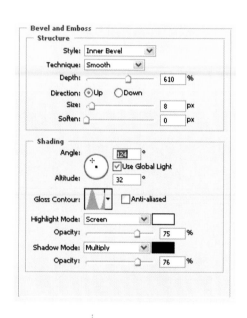

FIGURE 11-27 Adding the bevel for the depth

FIGURE 11-30 Adding a drop shadow

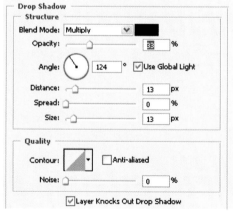

7. Click on Drop Shadow, and change the Softness, Distance, and Opacity as we did in Figure 11-30.

Figure 11-31 shows the layer style applied to some different layers.

FIGURE 11-31 The end result

Saving Styles

Now that you know how to create and use layer styles, you might like to know how to add them to the library and save them for future use.

1. Open the Styles palette.

2. Select the layer with the style in the Layers palette.

3. Hover the mouse over the Styles palette. The cursor will turn into a paintbucket.

4. Click the mouse, and the New Style dialog box will open.

5. Enter a name in the dialog box, and then click OK. The style is added to the library.

Saving the Styles to Disk or to the Internet

You can also save the styles to disk and upload them to the Internet or put them in a safe place for later use:

1. Click the arrow in the upper-right corner of the Styles palette.

2. Choose Save Styles from the options menu.

3. Choose a location to which you want to save.

4. Click OK, and the styles are now saved.

To load styles, repeat these steps, except choose Load Styles in step 2.

Vanishing Point

Photoshop CS2 introduces a very exciting application called Vanishing Point. This tool allows you to define planes in three-dimensional space and then paste, clone, paint, and select from different planes. Photoshop does all the calculations and modifies the perspective automatically. You can now work on flat photos as if they were 3-D. This is an amazing tool.

 Your image must be in RGB mode for this filter to work.

Let's begin by placing a logo on a 3-D surface:

1. Begin with your open image and a layer that contains the logo that you want to place (or use a layer from a different document), as shown in Figure 11-32.

2. Make a selection around the logo. Select its layer, and choose Edit | Copy.

3. Hide the logo layer.

4. Create a new layer. (This is optional if you want the perspective logo on its own layer.)

5. Choose Filter | Vanishing Point.

6. Create a plane in 3-D space. Choose the Create Plane tool and click in each corner to define the perspective plane of the sign, as shown in Figure 11-33. Look for straight edges to make a rectangle in 3-D space.

FIGURE 11-32 The original image and the logo

FIGURE 11-33 Creating the plane

FIGURE 11-34 The plane with the blue grid

FIGURE 11-35 The layer pasted into Vanishing Point

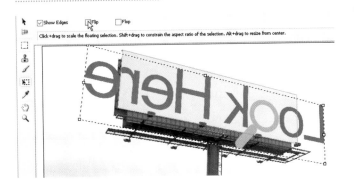

FIGURE 11-36 Flipping and scaling

7. Press the X key to zoom in while selecting your corner points.

8. When you click the third corner, the tool will change to a polygon; click the fourth corner to complete the plane. If all is well, the grid will appear in blue, as shown in Figure 11-34. If the grid is red, the plane is flawed and will need to be adjusted using the Edit Plane tool (the top tool).

9. Press CTRL-V (CMD-V on the Mac) to paste the logo into Vanishing Point. It will appear in the top-left corner, as shown in Figure 11-35.

10. If the object appears flipped, click the Flip box shown in Figure 11-36.

11. Select the Marquee tool, as shown in Figure 11-35.

12. Drag the logo over the plane, and it will snap to 3-D space.

13. Position the logo and choose the Transform tool, as shown in Figure 11-37.

11

14. Drag the corners of
the selection with the
Transform tool to scale
your object to size.

15. Click OK to apply the
transformation, and
return to the main
Photoshop window.

Figure 11-38 shows the logo
placed on the sign in perfect
perspective, almost effortlessly.

FIGURE 11-37 Positioning the
layer

FIGURE 11-38 The final image

Advanced Vanishing Point

Let's look at a few more of the more advanced features of
Vanishing Point.

1. Open an image and choose Filter | Vanishing Point.

2. Create a new plane as we did in the previous tutorial.
Figure 11-39 shows the new plane on the side of the
building.

FIGURE 11-39
Creating a plane

3. Drag out adjacent planes by holding down the CTRL key (CMD on the Mac) and dragging the center handle.

4. Drag the plane all the way to the end of the object, as shown in Figure 11-40. (This can be repeated for any number of planes.)

FIGURE 11-40
Creating an adjacent plane

5. Choose the Marquee tool and notice that this selection also conforms to the perspective of the plane.

FIGURE 11-41 Making a selection

6. Make a selection around an object— in this case, a window, as shown in Figure 11-41.

11

7. Hold down the ALT key (OPTION on the Mac) and drag a copy of the selected object all the way around the corner. Notice that the object changes perspective to match the new plane.

8. Click the Flip box to make the shadow go the right way, as shown in Figure 11-42.

FIGURE 11-42 Copying selection around a corner

9. Hold down the ALT key (OPTION on the Mac) and drag out as many copies as you like. Keep the selection active on the last copy, as you can see in Figure 11-43.

FIGURE 11-43 Duplicating objects

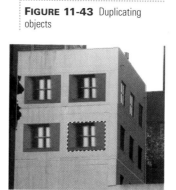

10. To make the color and the edges blend into the base object, choose the Heal option, as shown in Figure 11-44.

FIGURE 11-44 Using the Heal option

Cloning from Different Planes

You are not limited to copying objects with the Marquee tool or limited to working on adjacent surfaces. You can also clone images from different planes. Here's how:

FIGURE 11-45 Creating a disjointed plane

1. Create a plane around a different object in the photo. In the case of Figure 11-45, we have made a plane on a billboard.

2. Choose the Clone Stamp tool.

3. Hold down ALT (OPTION on the Mac) and click the billboard to define the sample area.

4. Choose the plane on the side of the building and begin to drag with the Clone Stamp tool.

5. Notice in Figure 11-46 that we are now cloning onto a totally different angle, and Vanishing Point makes it all in perfect perspective.

FIGURE 11-46 Cloning from one plane to another

Part IV

The Real World

Chapter 12

Enhance Your Photographs

How to...

- Fix less-than-perfect photos
- Make tonal adjustments
- Understand the histogram
- Use brightness/contrast
- Make shadow/highlight corrections
- Use curves and variations
- Set color balance and change hue saturation
- Adjust color with curves
- Automatically crop and straighten photos
- Use the Healing brush and Patch tool
- Use the Clone Stamp tool
- Remove red eye

Whether you have scanned pictures, pulled them off CDs, or imported them from a digital camera, the following principles will apply to most of the photos you work with in Photoshop. We'll look at ways to get the best out of every photograph and then move on to ways to manipulate photos and create works of art.

You don't always get the exact shot you want when you're shooting with a camera. Sometimes the image is too dark or blurry, or perhaps unwanted objects are included in the picture. Bear in mind that the human eye can see a larger dynamic range than the sensor in your camera. Reproducing something that you see onto a printed page can be very difficult indeed, and even the best photographers can use a little help to bring their creative vision to life. Even if the picture is perfectly shot, you may still need to make changes to the subject—perhaps your beautiful model had a battle with acne the night before the shoot and you want to perform a cosmetic touch-up. No matter what your needs, you'll probably find the answer in the pages of this chapter. For more in-depth coverage of this subject, please check out my book *Photoshop CS for Digital Photographers* (Charles River Media, 2004).

In this chapter, we'll repair some of the most common problems often encountered in photography: brightness and color adjustments, sharpening issues, cropping to contain the essence of an image, and correcting damage to photographs.

Tonal Adjustments

A color image has two parts: the grayscale tones (luminosity) that give the image its definition and detail, and the information that makes the image appear in color. *Tone* or *luminosity* refers to the grayscale information in an image. It's probably easiest to think of the image tone as a black-and-white photo. Generally, if a photo is too dark or too bright, the problem is in the tonal area of the image, and no amount of color correction can fix the problem. In Photoshop, you can fix tonal problems without too much difficulty using the tonal correction tools.

FIGURE 12-1 A histogram and its parent image

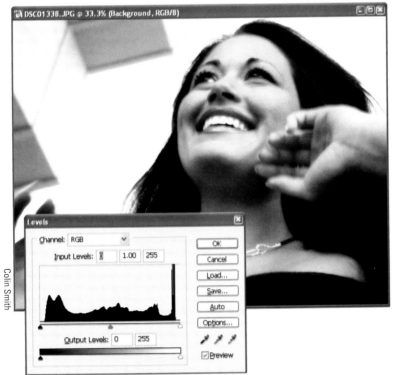

Colin Smith

The Histogram

The histogram in Photoshop provides a visual cue to the tonal properties of an image. The histogram is important because it lets you see at a glance how the tones are spread over the image, and it alerts you to any potential problems in the image tone. The histogram shows a graph of the tonal range and dispersion of an image—it shows you where the pixels are concentrated and how dark or light they are.

Histograms are located in three places: in the Levels dialog box shown in Figure 12-1, in the Histogram palette shown in Figure 12-2, and in the

Camera Raw window (see "Camera Raw" and Figure 12-33 later in this chapter). Figure 12-1 shows an image with its corresponding input and output levels in the Levels dialog box. To open the palette shown in Figure 12-2, choose Window | Histogram.

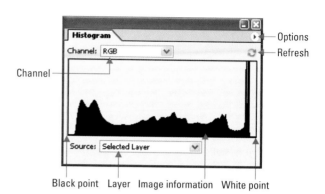

FIGURE 12-2 The Histogram palette

In the Histogram palette, the "mountainous" region represents the pixels in your image. The histogram displays the tones left to right, with black on the left and white on the right. All the tones in between represent shades of gray in an image, from dark to light.

The more the graph peaks at a certain point, the more pixels are located in that tone of gray. As you can see in Figure 12-2, with the currently selected image a lot of pixels range in the very light region, and the next most concentrated area is in the dark gray region. The valleys in the histogram indicate less pixel concentration in the image. No information appears at the far left and right in the histogram. This means that no pixels are present for those particular shades (this is a low-contrast image).

You should be aware of the following settings on the histogram:

- **Channel**   Allows you either to view the color image (default) or view a separate histogram for each color channel. This is useful for identifying problem areas in your image.

- **Layer**   Allows you to view a histogram on a multi-layered image. Choose between viewing a histogram for the entire image or for each layer.

- **Refresh**   If you see a little triangle under this button, click it to see the latest version of the image. Photoshop uses a technology called *screen cache* (which stores some information to memory) to speed up the screen performance. The result is that sometimes the histogram is not up-to-the-minute. It takes only a second to update the view, and the added performance is worth the extra effort.

- **Options**   This drop-down menu contains several advanced viewing options for the histogram:

  - **Compact**   Displays the histogram in a small palette; it stays out of your way while you work.

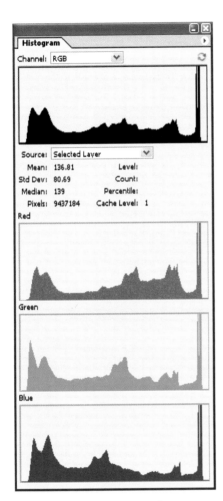

FIGURE 12-3 The Histogram palette in All Channels view with Statistics and Channel In Color turned on

- **Expanded**   Shows a larger view so that you can see more detail.
- **All Channels View**   Opens a histogram for each channel; allows you to compare the various channels' histograms at once. It's informative but uses a lot of screen space. Figure 12-3 shows the histogram in All Channels view.
- **Statistics**   Displays information about the image. Click and drag your mouse inside the histogram to get readings on the selected portion of the histogram.
- **Channel In Color**   Displays the channels' histograms in their respective colors, as shown in Figure 12-3.

Four tools are used in Photoshop to change the tone of images. We'll start with the simplest and quickest and work our way up to the more complex tools.

Brightness/Contrast Tool

The Brightness/Contrast tool is simple and quick to use. However, when using the tool, you have no control over the finer aspects of tonal correction, so if you lighten an image using this tool, everything is lightened across the entire image—it works similarly to the brightness/contrast controls on your monitor.

Figure 12-4 shows an image in desperate need of help. This image is very dark and lacking in punch. We'll use the Brightness/Contrast tool to improve the image.

1. Choose Image | Adjust | Brightness/Contrast. You will see the Brightness/Contrast dialog box with two slider controls, as shown in Figure 12-5:

   - **Brightness**   Controls the lightness or darkness of the image.
   - **Contrast**   Controls the strength of shadows and highlights. Viewing a low-contrast image can be like looking through a foggy window; increasing contrast is like cleaning the window. Be careful not to overdo it and lose shadow and highlight detail.

FIGURE 12-4 The original image

FIGURE 12-5 Adjusting the brightness

2. Move the Brightness slider up until you are happy with how light the image appears.

3. When you lighten an entire image, the shadows are also lightened; this causes a loss of contrast and makes the image appear washed out. Enter the second control: the Contrast slider (Figure 12-6) compensates for this loss by allowing us to restore contrast. Slide the Contrast slider up until you are happy with the way the image appears.

FIGURE 12-6 Adjusting the contrast

As you can see, you can get some pretty decent results without breaking too much of a sweat.

Shadow/Highlight Correction Tool

The next tool is Photoshop's latest tone-correction tool that was added especially for photographers. The Shadow/Highlight Correction tool performs in a similar way to the Brightness/Contrast tool, but it gives you much more control over details. This tool allows you to open up plugged shadows in overly dark images and restore highlight detail in overly bright images. The advantage of this tool is that you can choose the range of shadows and highlights to be affected.

FIGURE 12-7 Original image

Figure 12-7 shows a photograph I took on a rainy night with no flash. I avoided flash because it would reflect on the metal and ruin the image. Because flash wasn't used, the image is a bit dark. When I shot this image, I knew I could bring it home to Photoshop and make it as bright as I wanted. Let's review how to adjust shadows and highlights for a photo like this one.

1. Choose Image | Adjustments | Shadow/Highlights.

2. In the Shadow/Highlight dialog box, select the Show More Options checkbox at the bottom of the dialog if it is not already selected. You will now see the entire dialog box.

3. Let's first make adjustments using the Shadows and Highlights sliders. Each offers three settings:

   - **Amount**   Controls the intensity of the effect.

   - **Tonal Width**   Adjusts how far into the midtones you want to affect with the adjustment. With the Shadows slider all the way to the left, you adjust the very darkest shadows; as you move the slider to the right, you affect more of the lighter shadows and midtones. The opposite is true for the Highlights slider.

   - **Radius**   Affects how the adjustment will interact with the surrounding pixels. Experiment for the best setting.

12

4. Slide the Shadows and Highlights sliders until you are happy with the results.

5. Adjust the Color Correction slider a little; this controls the saturation. Choose a smaller amount to tone back the colors to a realistic level.

6. Slide the Midtone Contrast slider higher to tweak the midtones (see Figure 12-8).

FIGURE 12-8 Final adjustments

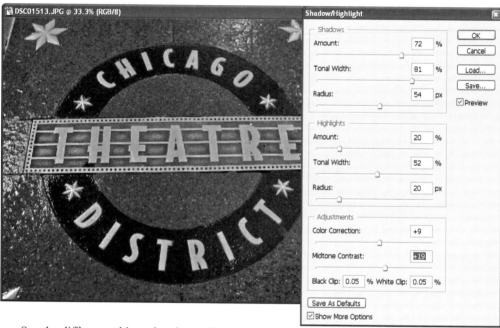

See the difference this tool makes to the picture? It transformed a photo taken at night without a flash into an image that looks as if it were taken in daylight.

FIGURE 12-9 The Levels dialog box

Levels Tool

The Levels tool is deceptively easy to use; the Levels dialog box contains a histogram with sliders, as shown in Figure 12-9. You can slide any of the histogram's three triangles to alter the tonal qualities of the image. The left slider

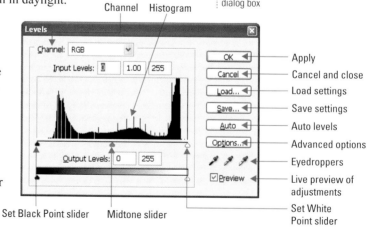

(black) controls the shadows, the middle (gray) slider controls the midtones, and the right slider controls the highlights.

Highlights

One of the most common problems in photos is lack of light, which causes the image to appear too dark (underexposed). This can be remedied while shooting by using a slower shutter speed or larger aperture, thus letting more light into the camera's sensor or film. Of course, if you are working on an image in Photoshop, it's a bit late to wind back the clock and change your shutter speed. Fortunately, the Levels tool comes to the rescue.

FIGURE 12-10 Dull image lacking in highlights

The image in Figure 12-10 looks dull and lacking in brightness. Choose Image | Adjustments | Levels, and you will see that the histogram doesn't show any information on the right end. This means that all the pixels are concentrated in the midtones and shadows portions of the image. The lack of histogram peaks on the right means that no highlights are present in the image.

Colin Smith

FIGURE 12-11 Brightening up the image

By sliding the Highlights slider to the left and causing it to touch the area where the histogram information begins, we have brightened up the image (see Figure 12-11).

Fixing Shadows

Another common problem with images is a lack of contrast, when all the pixel information is concentrated in the midtones and highlights. This results in a faded appearance that lacks visual punch. Figure 12-12 shows a washed-out image. If you look at the histogram, you can see that information in the shadow area (the leftmost area) is lacking.

This is easy to fix. Choose Image | Adjustments | Levels. Drag the Shadows slider (the black triangle in Figure 12-9) toward the right, and notice the contrast change in the image as the shadows are darkened, as shown in Figure 12-13. In this case, we moved the slider a little to the right, close to the Midtone area, and increased the highlights a little by moving the Highlights slider to the left.

FIGURE 12-12 Image lacking contrast

Colin Smith

FIGURE 12-13 Darkening the shadows

Fixing Midtones

At times, the shadows and highlights in an image are correct, but the image still doesn't look its best. The problem, in the case of Figure 12-14, is in the midtones. The shadows are nice and dark and the highlights are nice and bright, but the midtones are dark and don't show much detail.

Choose Image | Adjustments | Levels. Slide the Midtone slider (the gray triangle) to the left. As you move the slider, you will see the image midtones brighten up. If you slide to the right, the midtones will get darker.

In Figure 12-15, we have moved the slider to the left and the midtones are improved. Notice that details, such as the curtain, are now showing; these details were lost in the shadows before we made the adjustments.

FIGURE 12-14 Midtones are too dark

FIGURE 12-15 Lightening the midtones

Auto Levels

In the Levels dialog box, click the Auto button, and the brightest point in the image will be set to white and the darkest point will be shifted to black. All the tones in between will compensate automatically. This setting works well for some images and not so well for others. It's usually best to set the levels manually so you can control the results. If you are in a rush, you could try the Auto setting—if the result is not what you want, you can simply undo the change and make the adjustments manually.

You can also access the auto controls by choosing Image | Adjustments, and then choosing Auto Levels or Auto Contract.

Curves Tool

Curves are the most advanced way to correct image tones in Photoshop. They allow you the most precise control—and also the most potential for messing up your image if you don't know what you're doing. The price that comes with the precision is the price of learning.

Figure 12-16 shows the Curves dialog box.

The following three areas are of most concern:

- **Input**   The horizontal gradient runs from dark to light (left to right). The gradient represents the gray tones in the open image. The input reflects the shades before any changes are made; think of the horizontal gradient as the base of the histogram.

12

■ **Output**   The vertical gradient shows the output of the tone after changes are made. This runs from dark to light (bottom to top).

■ **Curve**   Click and drag this line to alter the way the tones are mapped on an image.

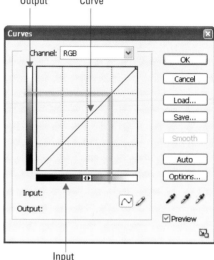

FIGURE 12-16 The Curves dialog box

In Figure 12-16, you will notice that the curve is in its default (RGB) state—bottom left to top right, diagonally. Choose a point on the input and follow it up to the curve (the green line in the figure). See where it intersects with the curve? Follow it to the left and you will see the output shade as displayed in the Output gradient bar. Follow any point in the default curve and you will see that all the shades are equal, Input to Output.

In Figure 12-17, we have dragged the curve upward, which brightens the image. Follow the green line, and you can see how much lighter the output is from the input. That change will be made to the image.

Use Curves

Let's use the Curves dialog box to manipulate an image:

1. Open an image.

2. Choose Image | Adjust | Curves.

3. Click anywhere on the curve to add an adjustment point.

4. Drag the point with your mouse to adjust the curve.

5. Move the point up or down vertically to lighten or darken the selected tone.

6. Move the point left or right to select a different tone to adjust.

7. To remove an adjustment point, drag it out of the window.

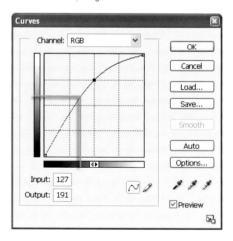

FIGURE 12-17 Brightening an image with curves

 You can add up to 16 adjustment points per curve.

Increase Contrast in an Image with Curves

An image lacking good dark shadows and strong highlights is lacking contrast. This gives a picture a faded appearance.

Colin Smith

Figure 12-18 is a perfect example of an image that is lacking in contrast.

Let's use curves to fix the image. What we are about to do is called the classic *S curve*. This curve will increase contrast in an image.

1. Choose Image | Adjustments | Curves.

2. Click the curve about a quarter of the way from the left. This is the shadow/ midtone region.

3. Drag the curve point down and notice that the shadows in the image get darker, as shown in Figure 12-19.

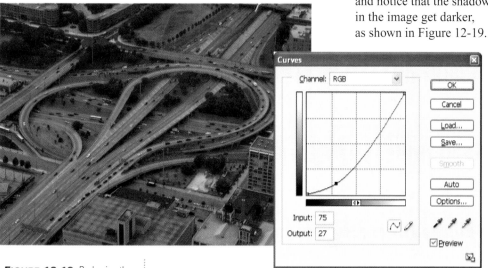

4. Now we will increase the highlights. Click about three quarters of the way along the curve.

5. Drag up, as shown in Figure 12-20. The highlights have now brightened. The overall result is an image with more contrast.

Targeting a Specific Tone with Curves

The best thing about curves is that they give you the ability to target a particular object in an image and bring out its details. When you begin to experiment, you will be surprised at how much detail you can squeeze out of an image. Areas that look totally black or white could in fact be harboring valuable image details.

The decoration on the front of the building shown in Figure 12-21 looks interesting, but the detail is lost because the camera's metering is exposed for the bright sky. Let's bring out the detail in this image using the targeted method. (This method doesn't really target objects as much as it targets particular tones in an image.) We can then darken or lighten the tones to achieve the best results.

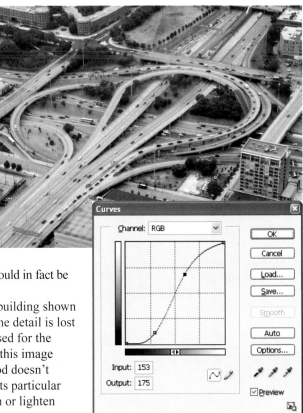

FIGURE 12-20 Increasing the highlights

1. Open the Curves dialog box—choose Image | Adjustments | Curves.

2. You will notice that the cursor turns to an eyedropper tool when it is inside the picture. Hold down the mouse button, and you will see a circle on the curve, as shown in Figure 12-21.

3. This circle indicates the tonal region that the Eyedropper tool is over. Move the eyedropper until it is over a tone area that you want to adjust.

4. CTRL-click the image (CMD-click on the Mac) to add a point to the curve.

5. Drag the point down to darken or up to brighten the image, as shown in Figure 12-22.

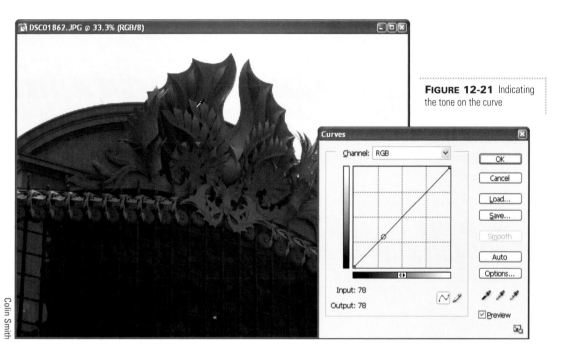

Colin Smith

FIGURE 12-21 Indicating the tone on the curve

Notice how much detail is now showing in the image as compared to the original.

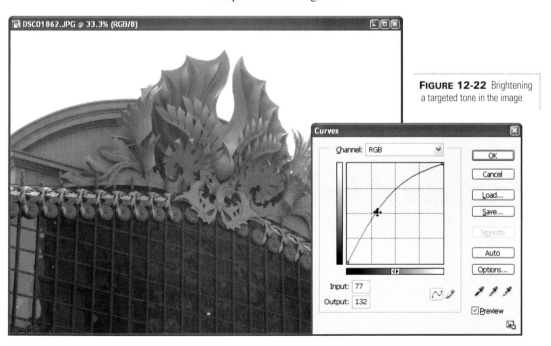

FIGURE 12-22 Brightening a targeted tone in the image

12

Color Correction

Without light, it would be impossible to take pictures. Different types of lights have different effects on our images. In general, light can be classified as two types: cool and warm (called *color temperature*). An example of cool light is moonlight, which is typically bluish. A warm light example is a lightbulb or incandescent light that gives off a warm, yellowish hue.

Most of the time, when you shoot photos under artificially lit conditions, you will experience *color shift*—that is, the appearance of color in your photograph is affected by the spectrum of light available in the artificial light. So while a color may appear a particular hue in natural light, under a fluorescent or incandescent light, the hue may appear a little different. The most common color shifts are toward yellow or green. We will examine several tools and methods you can use for correcting color shifts.

Variations Tool

Variations is a simple-to-use color correction tool. It lets you view several versions of the image side by side. The Variations dialog box shows your original image in the center, surrounded by versions that use different color tints. Simply click the thumbnail that you prefer and the image will take on the new color tint. This is a great way to correct the color in an image.

FIGURE 12-23 Image with a greenish tint

Colin Smith

Figure 12-23 shows an image with a green color shift; we will correct this using the Variations tool.

To open the Variations dialog box, choose Image | Adjustments | Variations. At the top of the Variations dialog box you will see two thumbnails:

- **Original (input)** Displays the open image before correction.

- **Current Pick (output)** Displays the result of the correction. This thumbnail will always display the last used setting. To reset, click the Original thumbnail.

Next to the thumbnails at the top are two sets of controls:

- **Range radio buttons** Allow you to target the Shadows, Midtones, Highlights, or Saturation.

- **Sensitivity slider** Sliding to the left (Fine) makes the change more subtle, and sliding to the right (Coarse) will make it more drastic. I recommend using a finer setting and applying it several times.

The Show Clipping checkbox (see Figure 12-24) will highlight colors that cannot be reproduced. In the rightmost column of the dialog box, you will see thumbnails with options to lighten or darken the current image.

Your current image appears in the center of the window, with six different color possibility thumbnails surrounding it. These thumbnails are arranged in a ring around the Current Pick and

FIGURE 12-24 The Variations dialog box

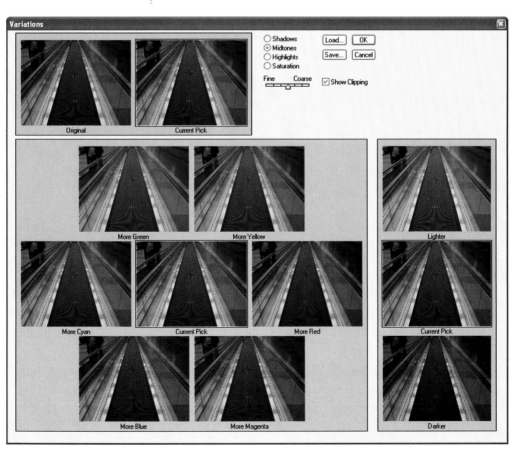

are opposites on either side, as shown in Figure 12-24. Choose the tone that best fixes your image color, and click the thumbnail to update the Current Pick.

Let's correct our image.

1. Choose Image | Adjustments | Variations.

2. Click the Original thumbnail at the top to reset the options.

3. Choose the Midtones radio button option, since our green color shift is in the midrange.

4. Lower the sensitivity slider one notch, and notice that the thumbnail variations update to reflect the new sensitivity setting.

5. Since our shift is to green, click the opposite variation thumbnail, which is More Magenta.

6. Lower the sensitivity and keep choosing options until you are happy with the view shown in the Current Pick.

7. Click OK when you're done.

FIGURE 12-25 The corrected image

Figure 12-25 shows the corrected image. Notice that the green color shift has now gone and the colors are looking more true to life.

Color Balance

Another tool used for color correction is the Color Balance tool, which consists of three sliders. The Color Balance tool produces a result similar to the Variations tool, but it is a bit more hands on.

Figure 12-26 shows an image with a significant warm color shift toward the yellow/reds.

1. Choose Image | Adjust | Color Balance.

2. In the Color Balance dialog box Tone Balance area, choose Midtones.

3. Move the color sliders in the opposite directions to the color shift to compensate, as shown in Figure 12-27.

4. Repeat for the highlights and shadows.

5. Click OK.

After the image is corrected, some oversaturation in the skin tones is still visible, but the overall image is looking better.

FIGURE 12-26 Uncorrected image is too warm

Note *This method is easy to use, but it lacks the ability to target a specific tone.*

FIGURE 12-27 Balancing the color

Hue/Saturation Tool

Another tool for color correction is the Hue/Saturation tool, which gives you control over three areas of the image:

- **Hue**   The actual color.
- **Saturation**   The quantity of the color.
- **Brightness/Lightness/Darkness**   Shifts everything across the board. I don't recommend using this control for correcting images; the Levels or Curves tools are much better for correcting lightness and darkness.

Figure 12-28 shows an image that is too yellow. The solution may not be adding blue to the image to compensate, because the old picture will lose its historic feel. Instead, we can just reduce the yellow a bit.

Sometimes all that is required to color correct an image is to reduce the *saturation*, the amount of color applied to an image. Oversaturated images have too much of a particular color or colors and appear unreal. The opposite end of the spectrum would be zero saturation—that would be grayscale with no color at all.

Colin Smith

FIGURE 12-28 Image before, with an oversaturation of yellow

1. Choose Image | Adjust | Hue/Saturation. You will see the Hue/Saturation dialog box shown in Figure 12-29.

2. Slide the Saturation slider to the left until the image looks more natural.

A quick way to correct color is to choose Image | Adjustments | Auto Color. This is a hit-or-miss approach, however, and is generally not the best solution.

You can make a huge difference just by reducing the saturation (see Figure 12-29). It's always a good thing to be creative when correcting images. This image still has a bit of a yellow cast, but it works for the antique effect that we want.

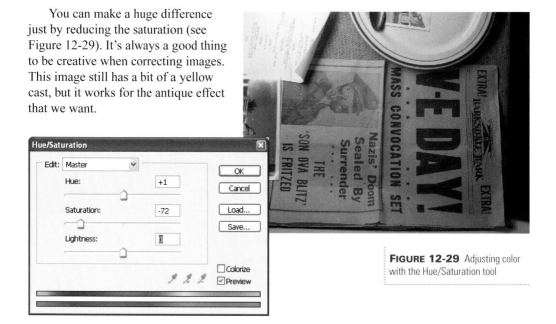

FIGURE 12-29 Adjusting color with the Hue/Saturation tool

FIGURE 12-30 Image with a yellow color cast

Adjusting Color with Curves

The most accurate way to correct the color on images is by using curves. See the section "Curves Tool" earlier in this chapter for an understanding of how curves work.

Figure 12-30 shows an image that has a warm color cast because of the lighting. The difficult part of this image is removing the color cast without affecting the blue glow too much, since we want to keep that color.

Using the Curves tool, you are not just limited to correcting the tones of grayscale. You can go into each color channel and adjust it individually.

1. Choose Image | Adjustments | Curves.

2. In the Curves dialog box, drag the mouse over the area with the most color cast, and you will see the circle on the curve indicating the range.

3. CTRL-SHIFT-click (CMD-SHIFT-click on the Mac) to add the adjustment point to each of the channels. (Note that the point will not show in the RGB composite channel.)

4. Click the Channel to open the drop-down list, and choose each channel one at a time to see the adjustment point on each channel. You'll see where that tone is for each color.

5. Make adjustments to each of the color channels.

6. You will notice that if the color shows high on a color curve, it should be darkened to neutralize it, as shown in Figure 12-31A in the Red channel. (Drag the point down.)

7. If the point is around the middle of the curve, it is already neutral and won't require any adjustment normally, as shown in the Green channel in Figure 12-31B.

8. If the point shows low on the curve, as in the Blue channel in Figure 12-31C, it should be brightened to neutralize the color. (Drag the point up.)

12

A.

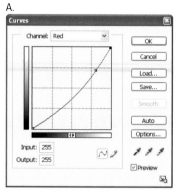

B.

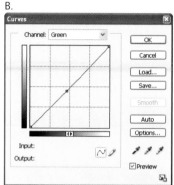

C.

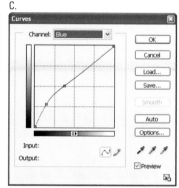

Figure 12-32 shows the image after making the correction with the Curves tool. Curves are the most accurate way to color correct images in Photoshop.

FIGURE 12-31 Making adjustments to the channels (A) Red channel (B) Green channel (C) Blue channel

Click the gray Eyedropper tool on an area of neutral gray in the image to remove any color casts.

FIGURE 12-32 The corrected image

Camera Raw

Most high-end digital cameras support a format called RAW. Unlike JPEG or TIFF images, RAW files contain the original unprocessed data stored by the camera. Basically, RAW files are the unadulterated data captured directly from your camera's sensor. Photoshop CS2 can open RAW images directly with a feature called Camera Raw.

The main advantage to using RAW is that image processing can be done after you have shot the photo, and the camera's processing is not permanently embedded in the image. The settings used on the camera at the time of capture can be recalled, or you can modify them. Other advantages include the ability to save 16-bit images, plus the RAW format is lossless and RAW images are a smaller file size than TIFF images.

If your camera doesn't support the RAW format, you won't be able to access this functionality or open the RAW settings.

Let's take a look at the Camera Raw window and then walk through processing an image. Figure 12-33A shows the Camera Raw window with four images open. The area on the left (the filmstrip) is visible only when more than one image is open. The histogram is just like other histograms discussed earlier in this chapter.

First, let's take a look at the tools in the Camera Raw window, as shown in Figure 12-33B.

FIGURE 12-33
(A) The Camera Raw window
(B) The Camera Raw tools

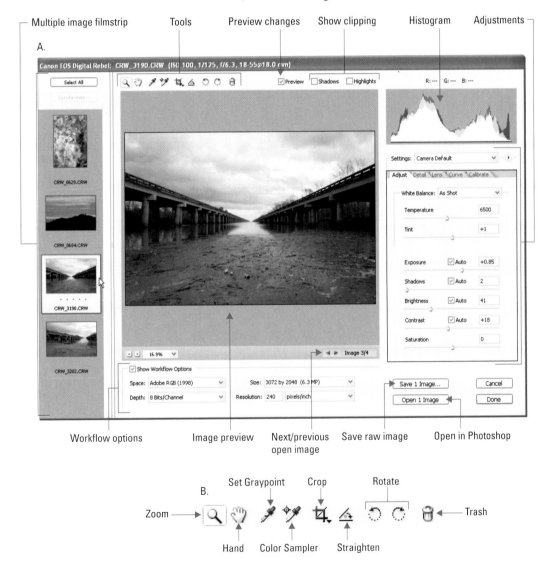

12

- **Zoom** Allows you to zoom in to the image (you can also change the magnification at the bottom-left corner of the Camera Raw window)

- **Hand** Allows you to move around in the image when it's too big to fit in the window

- **Set Graypoint** When clicked in an area that should be neutral gray, color corrects the image and removes any color casts

- **Color Sampler** When clicked on the image, leaves a marker that displays the RGB color values at that position

- **Crop** Allows you to crop the image, so only a portion will be processed

- **Straighten** Straightens crooked photos when you click and drag on the horizon line

- **Rotate** Changes the orientation of the photo

- **Trash** Deletes one or more of the images in the filmstrip

Processing an Image in Camera Raw

Let's start by processing an image in Camera Raw:

1. Open a RAW image by choosing File | Open; by selecting it in Bridge, right-clicking, and choosing Open Raw; or by pressing CTRL-R (CMD-R on the Mac).

2. Set the white balance to remove any color casts. Select the White Balance value from the drop-down menu shown in Figure 12-34. Experiment with the settings until you're happy with the coloring on your image.

3. Adjust the Temperature slider to fine tune the color—left is cooler (more blue) and right is warmer (more yellow).

4. Adjust the Tint if necessary.

FIGURE 12-34 Setting the white balance

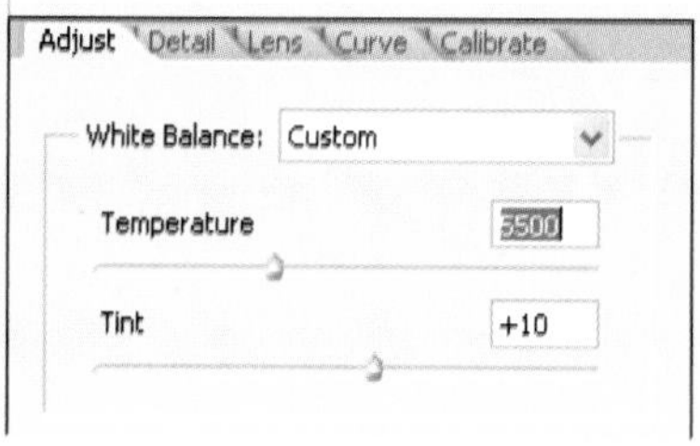

Adjusting the Brightness and Contrast

Let's adjust the luminosity of the image to produce nicely defined shadows that are not plugged and bright highlights that are not blown out. Areas that are plugged or blown out are called *clipped* areas because they are forced to white or black.

1. At the top of the Camera Raw window, select the Shadows and Highlights checkboxes to reveal areas that are potentially clipped in your image, which are shown in red and blue in Figure 12-35. (These indicator colors will not be revealed on the image after it's opened in Photoshop.)

FIGURE 12-35 Clipped areas are revealed on the image.

2. In the Adjust tab at the right side of the Camera Raw window, slide the Exposure slider until it is on the point where clipping begins (the point where the colored spots on the image begin to appear). (If you do not use the Clipping checkbox, you can hold down the ALT key [OPTION on the Mac] as you slide and the clipping will be revealed.)

3. Adjust the Shadows slider, taking it to the clipping threshold (the area where the image begins to clip). The shadows should be dark but not so dark that all detail is lost.

4. Brighten the image by sliding the Brightness slider.

5. Adjust the Contrast if the image looks too washed out (slide to the right) or too dense (slide to the left).

6. Adjust the Saturation slider if you want to increase or decrease the amount of color in the image. Figure 12-36 shows the adjusted image.

FIGURE 12-36 Adjusted image

Adjusting Sharpness and Noise Details

Noise in the digital imaging world refers to the grainy spots on an image. It's a good idea to zoom in to 100 percent to complete these tasks, so that you can closely view the results of the adjustments, as shown in Figure 12-37.

1. Click the Detail tab.

2. Zoom in to 100 percent.

3. Sharpen the image by increasing the Sharpness setting.

4. Luminance smoothing will reduce the grainy noise from the grayscale portion of the image; slide the slider to the right until the grain is gone, but not so much that the image blurs.

5. Color Noise Reduction removes the noise from the color; adjust the slider as needed.

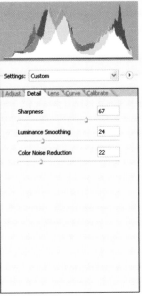

FIGURE 12-37 Adjusting the Detail settings

FIGURE 12-38 Curves histogram

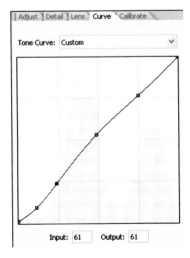

Adjusting the Lens Settings

The Lens settings repair any distortion caused by the camera's lens. If you use a wide angle lens, for example, these adjustments may be required.

1. Click the Lens tab.

2. Adjust the chromatic aberration to remove any color halos that may be present on the image; you will need to zoom in to 100 percent to see these. Adjusting the sliders will increase or reduce the size of the color channels to make the edges match.

3. Adjust the vignetting if the edges are brighter or darker than the rest of the image. Sometimes photographers purposely darken the edges to bring more focus to the center of the photo.

Adjusting Image Curves

Camera Raw now includes the ability to adjust image curves. The curves work in exactly the same way as the Photoshop curves we explored earlier in this chapter. The Camera Raw curve has a really cool feature, shown in Figure 12-38: a live histogram appears under the curve so that you can make any desired adjustments to your image.

Calibrating Color

This option is very unique and extremely handy. You can adjust the color calibration settings for each camera you use and save them, or you can use this feature for totally creative purposes.

 If you don't have much experience with color correction and don't know what to look for yet, it may be a good idea to wait until you're more familiar with color correction before using the Calibrate tab. If your eye is a little more seasoned and you want to get into the nitty-gritty, read on.

1. Choose the Calibrate tab.

2. Use the Shadow Tint slider to adjust the color balance in the shadow portion of the image.

3. Use the Hue sliders to shift the color in each of the primary colors. In Figure 12-39, the Blue Hue and Green Hue sliders were adjusted to make the grass look good and really make the trees pop out against the mountains.

FIGURE 12-39 Adjusting the Calibrate settings

4. Adjust the Saturation sliders to add or subtract color for each of the channels.

 Open the Settings drop-down menu and choose Save to save the custom settings so that they can be reused.

A.

Colin Smith

B.

FIGURE 12-40 Image taken
from Camera Raw
(A) As shot in the camera
(B) With adjustments made in
Camera Raw

Saving an Image

Click the Save Image button to save
the image to your hard disk. You can
choose any format or save the image
as a RAW image. Digital Negative
Format (DNG) is Adobe's RAW
format. Currently, efforts are under
way to make DNG the standard
across all cameras, because each
manufacturer now uses a proprietary
format, which can make exchanging
files in the RAW format difficult.

Opening an Image

Click the Open Image button to open
the image in Photoshop. If you find
that some options are grayed out
in Photoshop, change your image to
8-bit channels by choosing Image |
Mode | 8 Bits/Channel.

Figure 12-40 shows an image as
shot and processed in Camera Raw.
Notice the tree line and how the
processed image appears to have
more depth.

Determining Workflow Options

You can determine how a file will be opened in Photoshop
using the Workflow Options area in the Camera Raw window.
Figure 12-41 shows the Workflow Options optimum settings for
a 6 megapixel (mp) camera.

- **Space**   Choose a color profile. Adobe RGB (1998) is
  the most popular choice.
- **Depth**   Choose 8- or 16-bit channels; 16-bit channels
  will allow more adjustment without banding (stripes on
  the gradients).
- **Size**   Choose an image size.
- **Resolution**   Set the target resolution here.

12

Multiple Image Processing

Multiple images can be opened and processed in Camera Raw. Here's how:

FIGURE 12-41 Setting the Workflow Options

1. Launch Bridge.

2. Hold down the CTRL key (CMD on the Mac) as you click to select each of the images that you want to edit.

3. Right-click (CONTROL-click on the Mac) and choose Open Raw.

4. Select a thumbnail to make it the active image by clicking it in the filmstrip.

5. To share the active image's settings across multiple images, CTRL-click (CMD-click on the Mac) each of the images to be added, or click the Select All button above the filmstrip to select all the images.

FIGURE 12-42 Synchronize settings

6. Click Synchronize, and the Synchronize dialog box shown in Figure 12-42 will appear.

7. Choose the attributes to copy from the currently active image to all the selected images. Select a subset from the Synchronize drop-down menu or use the checkboxes.

8. Click OK to share the settings.

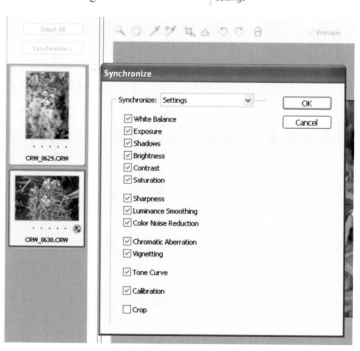

Straightening Images

Sometimes when you take a picture, you aren't holding the camera quite level. This can easily be fixed in Camera Raw.

1. Open the RAW image.

2. Choose the Straighten tool from the Camera Raw window tools area.

3. Drag across the desired horizontal line, as shown in Figure 12-43A.

4. Release the tool, and the new crop will preview, as shown in Figure 12-43B.

5. When you next open the image in Photoshop, it will be straightened.

FIGURE 12-43 Using the Straighten tool
(A) Applying the tool
(B) The result

A.

B.

Colin Smith

Sharpening

Face it, no matter how sharp the picture is, you can almost always make it look better with a little work. When you scan or resize an image, a little sharpening is usually in order to enhance things a bit.

Unsharp Mask

The best sharpening tool in Photoshop has the least likely name—the Unsharp Mask. The Unsharp Mask detects the image's edges and then enhances them by adding a tiny white halo. This may sound strange, but it is effective, and when sharpening is performed correctly, the viewer's eye will not notice the halo.

Instead, the eye will notice the more predominant edges, which create the illusion of a sharper image—most things you do in Photoshop are illusions.

The Unsharp Mask filter has three settings, all demonstrated in Figure 12-44. The final image in the figure shows a properly sharpened image. Notice that the effect is subtle; it just enhances the image and doesn't change it dramatically.

- **Amount**   The strength of the halo. If you turn up this setting, the edges become very predominant; if you turn it down, the effect is less pronounced.

- **Radius**   The size of the halo. As you turn up this setting, the white actually turns into a glow; a lower setting will create a more subtle effect.

- **Threshold**   Adjusts the sensitivity of the edge detection. Turning this up will soften the effect and cause only the most predominant edges to be detected. A 0 setting will cause the filter to work full strength on the entire image.

FIGURE 12-44 Unsharp Mask
(A) The amount turned up
(B) Increasing the radius
(C) Increasing the threshold
(D) Properly sharpened image

A.

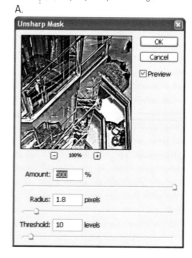

B.

C.

D.

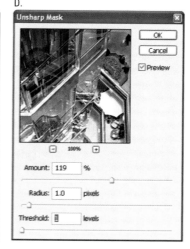

Using Unsharp Mask

Figure 12-45 shows an image in which the color balance and the tonal balance are good. A little bit of sharpening could further enhance the image.

Colin Smith

FIGURE 12-45 Image before sharpening

FIGURE 12-46 Image after Unsharp Mask

1. Choose Filter | Sharpen | Unsharp Mask.

2. In the Unsharp Mask dialog box, click Preview so that you can see the result on the main image.

3. Adjust the Amount and Radius sliders until you get a good balance. Turn the Preview on and off for a comparison of the effect before and after.

4. Set the Threshold slider to an acceptable level, affecting only the detail that you choose.

5. Click OK.

Figure 12-46 shows the sharpened image and the settings in the Unsharp Mask dialog box. These are pretty average settings to use on people.

Smart Sharpen

A new feature introduced in Photoshop CS2 is Smart Sharpen. This filter allows you to sharpen images in different ways. On the surface, this filter looks a little like the Unsharp Mask, but it's a lot more advanced. For example, you can use Smart

Sharpen to fade out the sharpening in the shadows, where most of the noise occurs, and avoid exaggerating the grain. You can also fade out the effect in the highlights and avoid the halos in the white portions of the image.

Choose Filter | Sharpen | Smart Sharpen to open the Smart Sharpen window. If you click the Remove drop-down menu, you'll see three options:

■ **Lens Blur** The blurriness caused by a lens; this is the most subtle option.

■ **Gaussian Blur** The best option for a generally out-of-focus photo.

■ **Motion Blur** Cancels out movement in a single direction, such as movement that occurs if the camera was not held still while the photo was taken (camera shake). Adjusts the angle to fix this problem.

Let's use Smart Sharpen to sharpen an image. Remember that subtlety is the key to good photo repair and retouching.

1. Open an image in Photoshop.

2. Choose Filter | Sharpen | Smart Sharpen.

3. Select a deblur type from the Remove drop-down menu—Lens Blur works well for most images.

FIGURE 12-47 Adjusting the settings in the Sharpen tab.

4. Adjust the Amount slider to control the amount of the effect.

5. Adjust the Radius slider to change the halo amount, just as you would using the Unsharp Mask.

6. Click the Advanced button. You will see three tabs, as shown in Figure 12-47.

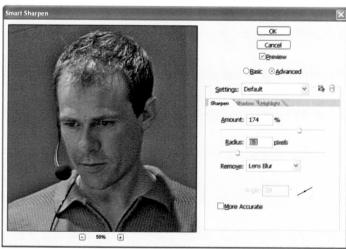

Tip   *If the filter is working too slowly, uncheck the More Accurate checkbox.*

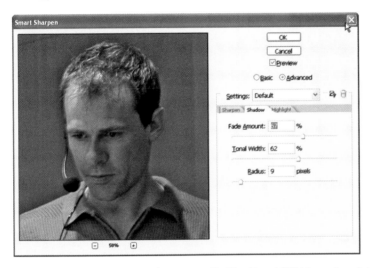

FIGURE 12-48 The Shadow sliders

FIGURE 12-49 Adjusting the highlights

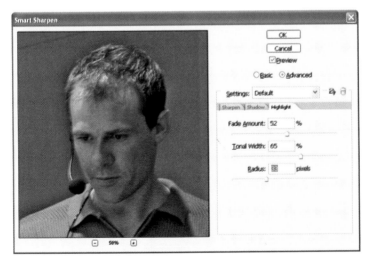

7. Choose the Shadow tab, as shown in Figure 12-48, to sharpen the image less in the shadows and thus avoid sharpening the noise that usually lurks in the shadows.

8. The Fade Amount setting will adjust the amount of sharpening that occurs in the shadows.

9. The Tonal Width setting determines the darkness of the shadows; move the slider to the right to affect lighter parts of the shadows, and move it to the left to affect the darkest shadows.

10. Use the Radius slider to control the distance of the blur; this setting is used to estimate which pixels will be adjusted.

11. Choose the Highlight tab.

12. Make the adjustments to the three sliders to lessen the sharpening effect in the highlights of the image, as shown in Figure 12-49.

13. Click OK to apply the sharpening to your image.

12

Figure 12-50 shows the image before and after the sharpening. Notice that the photo doesn't look filtered, but it does look sharper.

 Smart Sharpen is a very powerful filter; once you've mastered its use, you will probably never use Unsharp Mask again.

Reduce Noise

This filter's name sounds more like an order from a police officer than a Photoshop filter. In digital photography, noise, the equivalent of film grain, appears in low light conditions and rears its ugly head especially when shadowed areas are lightened up. Shooting with a high ISO setting on a camera will also increase the noise. You can remove noise by blurring the image; the challenge is blurring the noise and not the details of the image. The Reduce Noise filter does what it promises: it smoothens out a noisy image without losing image sharpness.

1. Open your image in Photoshop and choose Filter | Noise | Reduce Noise. You will see the Reduce Noise dialog box shown in Figure 12-51.

2. Adjust the Strength slider to control the amount of the effect.

3. The Preserve Details setting will localize the effect to areas without edges.

4. Adjust the Reduce Color Noise setting to reduce noise that has appeared in the color areas of the image. Two types of noise are affected: luminosity (in the grayscale portion of the image) and color noise, which is the result of the

A.

B.

FIGURE 12-50 The effects of Smart Sharpen
(A) The image before sharpening
(B) The image after sharpening

FIGURE 12-51 The Reduce Noise dialog box

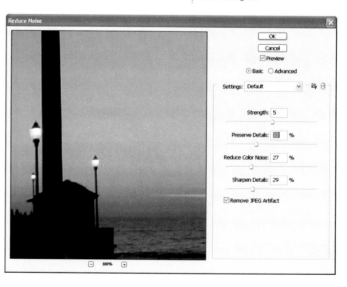

charge-coupled device (CCD), a chip that captures the image on digital cameras.

5. Use the Sharpen Details slider to sharpen the edges of the image.

6. Check the Remove JPEG Artifact checkbox to remove the damage caused by image compression.

The Advanced settings, shown in Figure 12-52, allow you to view each color channel and blur only the channels in which noise is present. Sometimes the noise will be stronger in a single channel.

 If you haven't read Chapter 6 yet, read it now so you'll understand how channels affect your image.

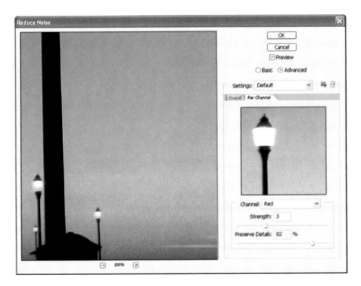

FIGURE 12-52 The Channel view

1. In the Reduce Noise dialog box, choose the Advanced radio button.

2. Click the Per Channel tab to open it.

3. Check out each of the Channel previews. Drag in the preview window until you find a portion of the image that contains some detail and some noise.

4. Once you have isolated the offending channels, increase the Strength setting to blur the noise.

5. Slide the Preserve Detail slider to restore the image detail.

6. If necessary, open the Overall tab and tweak the overall settings to compensate for the channel adjustments.

7. Click OK to apply.

Once you get used to this filter, you'll find it easy to use and a quick way to reduce the noise in images and produce a nice, smooth appearance. Figure 12-53 shows a before and after view of an image. Notice that the gradients in the sky are nice and smooth without the noise.

FIGURE 12-53 Applying the Reduce Noise filter to an image (A) Before (B) After

A.

B.

Colin Smith

Cropping

Cropping is another word for *trimming*. When you crop an image in Photoshop, it is the digital equivalent of taking out a pair of scissors and trimming away the portions of the image you want to discard. You may want to crop an image for several reasons:

■ **Remove unwanted subjects** Perhaps you love the photo of yourself but you don't want your ex to appear in the image. Or you may have shot an image on the beach, but the "porta-loo" on the edge of your photo ruins the shot. Whatever the subject, it can be cropped away.

■ **Emphasize a particular area** You can change the focus of an image by cropping the image into the subject tightly and discarding all the distracting scenery.

■ **Enhance the image creatively** You can turn a boring photo into a work of art by using some creative cropping.

■ **Adjust proportions** You may have set proportions within which the image needs to fit, such as within a layout, and you will need to trim some pixels off one or more of the edges.

Whatever your reason for cropping your image, Photoshop comes equipped with a powerful cropping tool that will help you out.

Cropping an Image

If you're working on an image that has a lot of distracting scenery that adds nothing to the image, you can use the Crop tool to make a more interesting composition.

FIGURE 12-54 The Crop tool in action

1. Choose the Crop tool from the toolbox.

2. Click and drag inside the image, as you would with the Rectangular Marquee tool.

3. Click and drag any of the eight resizing handles to change the size of the marquee. You can see the handles in Figure 12-54.

4. Click inside the selected window and drag to reposition the cropped area.

5. To apply the crop, double-click your mouse inside the cropped area or press ENTER (RETURN) on your keyboard. The crop is applied.

You can set a couple of settings in the options bar:

- **Shield**   Shows the area that is to be cropped away. You can change the color and opacity of this shield to provide a visual guide to the cropping.

- **Delete or Hide**   Available only if you are working on a layer. It gives you the option of cropping the image and discarding the pixels, or, if you use the Hide option, the canvas size will be reduced without deleting any pixels. You may reposition this layer later if you wish.

Straightening Photos

The Crop tool can do more than just trim an image. You can also use it to straighten crooked images while you are cropping them. This comes in handy, for example, if you scan an image that wasn't placed quite straight on the scanner or if you took a photo and the camera was crooked. Here's how to fix a crooked picture.

12

1. Choose the Crop tool from the toolbox.

2. Click and drag the rectangular marquee, as in the previous exercise.

3. If you hover your mouse outside of the cropped area over one of the corners, it will change into a curved, double-sided arrow.

4. Click and drag to rotate the crop selection to compensate for the crooked picture, remembering that the cropped image will fit the selected area, as shown in Figure 12-55.

5. Double-click inside the crop area to apply the crop. The image will now be straight, as shown in Figure 12-56.

FIGURE 12-55 Rotating the cropped area

FIGURE 12-56 Straightened picture

Correcting Perspective

Because of the curved shape of a camera lens, a phenomenon called *keystoning* can occur, in which the top of the image is narrower than the bottom. In the case of a tall building, this may be acceptable because of the *perspective*—as something is located further away, it appears smaller. Perspective allows us to judge size and distance. In the case of Figure 12-57, the perspective is caused more by the curvature of the lens and it is undesirable.

When you click and drag with the Crop tool, you will notice a Perspective checkbox in the options bar. Clicking this option allows you to change the perspective of an image. When applied, the cropped area will become rectangular and the entire image will be distorted to fit.

1. Click and drag with the Crop tool.

2. Drag the crop area until it covers the entire area that you want to keep in the image.

3. Click the Perspective checkbox to turn it on.

FIGURE 12-57 Original image with keystoning

FIGURE 12-58 Adjusting the perspective

4. In the image, click and drag the top-right corner a little toward the center of the picture. Drag it until the rightmost line is at the same angle as the desired straight line in the image. (I have used the windows in the buildings as a guide, as shown in Figure 12-58.)

5. Drag the top-left corner in until the side is aligned with the desired straight edge of the picture.

6. Apply the crop by double-clicking inside the image area.

Figure 12-59 shows the corrected image. Notice how much better the picture looks— it doesn't look like the sky is falling in.

Colin Smith

FIGURE 12-59 Corrected image

Automatically Crop and Straighten Photos

When scanning images, you can save a lot of time by placing
several images on the scanner platen and scanning them at once.
The drawback, however, is that you have to separate the images
to work with each one in Photoshop. This can be very time
consuming and cumbersome. A feature in Photoshop, aptly named
Crop and Straighten Photos, automates the entire process.

After you open the composite image, to break images apart,
choose File | Automate | Crop And Straighten Photos. That's all
you have to do; sit back and Photoshop will do the rest.

When Photoshop has finished, it will have created a new
document for each of the images in the composite. Each will be
perfectly cropped, and even if an image was askew in the scan,
it will be shown straightened out.

Lens Distortion

The Lens Correction filter is truly amazing, because this filter
can repair all kinds of distortions. Not only can it correct the
bulging created by a wide angle lens, or the weird distortion
created by taking a photo too close to the subject (such as the
bulging nose of a friend), it can also straighten images taken at
angles and make them appear as if they were shot straight on.
To demonstrate, let's use an image that suffers from many
problems and correct it.

1. Open an affected image and choose Filter | Distort | Lens Correction. Figure 12-60 shows the Lens Correction filter's dialog box. Notice the grid that assists you in lining things up.

FIGURE 12-60 Lens Correction dialog box

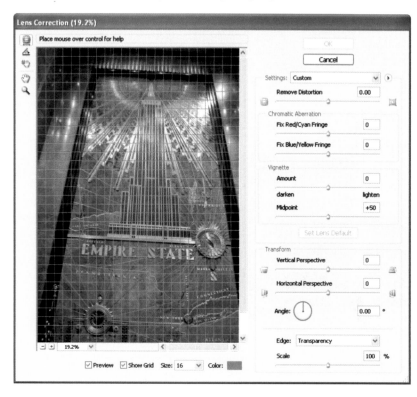

FIGURE 12-60 Lens Correction dialog box

2. Our first job is to straighten the image. It's impossible to fix all the other angles if the image is not straight first. Choose the Straighten tool on the left side of the dialog box, as shown in Figure 12-61.

3. Click and drag across the image to define the new horizon. Try to follow a horizontal line in the image to help guide you.

4. Because the image suffers from keystoning, we will fix the next most obvious defect. Adjust the Vertical Perspective slider to make the top and bottom the same width.

12

Straighten tool

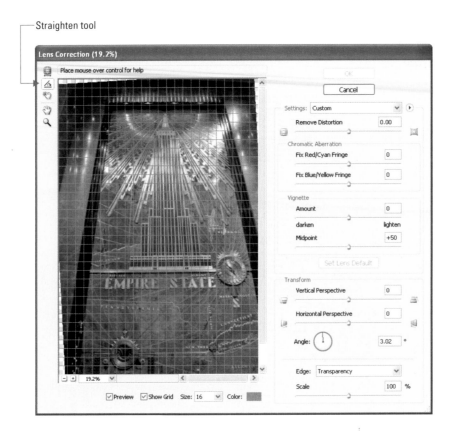

FIGURE 12-61 Straightening an image

5. Adjust the Horizontal Perspective slider; this appears to rotate the image through 3-D space. What is really happening is that we are making one side narrower than the other to counter perspective problems. You can also change the Angle to counter a diagonal distortion. Figure 12-62 shows the perspective repaired.

6. Notice that the image appears to bulge in the middle. Adjust the Remove Distortion slider, as shown in Figure 12-63. Slide it to the left to bulge out and move the slider to the right to pinch in. Alternatively, you can choose the Remove Distortion tool (the top tool on the left) and drag in the image, but the sliders give you more control.

7. After adjusting the distortion, you may need to go back and tweak the perspective again.

FIGURE 12-62 Fixing the perspective

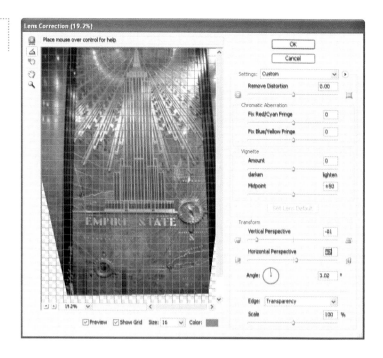

FIGURE 12-63 Adjusting the distortion

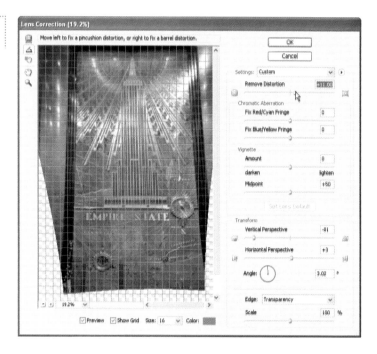

12

8. Choose an edge option:

- **Transparent** Produces transparent pixels outside of the distorted rectangle

- **Background Color** Fills the empty pixels with the current background color

- **Edge Extension** Stretches the edge pixels to fill the background, as shown in Figure 12-64

9. Click OK to apply the changes.

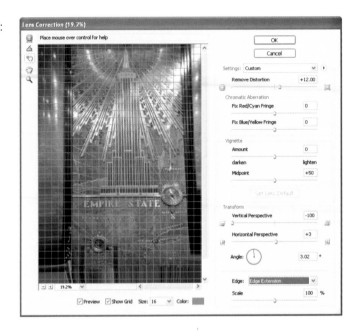

FIGURE 12-64 Extending the edges of the background

Figure 12-65 shows the power of the Lens Correction filter. To finish off the effect, you can crop the image to suit your needs. As you can see, this is a great tool for fixing distorted images.

FIGURE 12-65 Before and after lens correction (A) Before (B) After

A.

B.

Colin Smith

Repairing Images

Photoshop has long been the standard software used to "repair" damaged photos. Photoshop can "fix" anything from tears and scratches to creases and stains. Two tools stand out as almost magical in their application: the Healing brush and the Patch tool. These tools are unparalleled in any other application and almost too easy to use.

Healing Brush

The Healing brush is as simple to use as a standard paint brush. The brush is so intelligent that it samples the image where you are painting and compares it to another portion of the image that you choose. The Healing brush then simulates the texture and blends the brush stroke into the image seamlessly. The result is that you can effortlessly brush away all manner of damage in the image. It even works on wrinkles!

Figure 12-66 shows an image with heavy damage from scratches and chipping—a perfect target for the Healing brush. This image can be found on your Photoshop Install directory under *samples*. The nice people at Adobe have given us an image to use for practice.

FIGURE 12-66 A perfect target for the Healing brush

1. Choose the Healing brush from the toolbox.

2. Choose a brush size appropriate for the image. It's a good idea to use a small brush for small areas, but you can change the brush size while you're working.

3. Hold down the ALT key (OPTION on the Mac) and click in an undamaged portion of the image, close to where you want to make repairs. You have now taken a sample.

4. Click and drag the mouse to paint over the damaged portion of the image. You will see the cross hairs in the sampled region.

5. When you release the mouse button, you will see the brush stroke "morph" into the image, effectively brushing away the damage.

6. Continue repairing the image in the same manner, remembering to resample as often as possible; this is the key to good healing.

12

Figure 12-67 shows the image mostly repaired except for the top-left region. I have left this alone on purpose to experiment with a more heavy-duty tool, the Patch tool.

Spot Healing Brush

A new brush is included in Photoshop CS2 called the Spot Healing brush. This tool works exactly like the Healing brush except you don't have to take a sample. This brush estimates the fill by calculating the surrounding pixels. This works well for small blemishes and quick fixes on undetailed surfaces.

Patch Tool

The Patch tool is designed to sample a large area of texture and blend it into larger damaged areas. This tool works similarly to the Healing brush, but on a larger scale.

1. Choose the Patch tool from the toolbox.

2. Choose the Destination radio button from the tool options.

3. Draw a selection around a good, clean portion of uniform texture. (This portion of the tool works just like the Lasso tool.)

4. Release the mouse and you will see a selection.

5. Click and drag the selection on top of a damaged section of the image.

6. Release the mouse and the selected texture miraculously blends into the texture, eliminating all damage.

The selection is reusable; you can click and drag it again. Combined with the Healing brush, the Patch tool has made short work of the damaged picture. The image in Figure 12-68 is as good as the day it was taken.

Clone Stamp

When it comes to having fun with photos in Photoshop, it's pretty hard to beat the Clone Stamp tool, which allows you to sample a part of the image and then paint with the actual sampled pixels on another portion of the image. This is great for removing objects from pictures or duplicating objects.

FIGURE 12-67 The image after using the Healing brush

FIGURE 12-68 Restored image

Colin Smith

In the picture of Laguna Beach, California, in Figure 12-69, the ocean and beach look very inviting, but someone built a house right on the beach. This may be very nice for the people living in the house, but for everyone else, it is an eyesore. Hiring a bulldozer to tear it down would be a bit drastic; instead, we can remove it from the picture using the Clone Stamp tool.

FIGURE 12-69 The original image with the building

1. Choose the Clone Stamp tool from the toolbox.

2. To sample a portion of the image, hold down the ALT key (OPTION on the Mac) and click. You will see a target, as shown in Figure 12-70A; this is the area from which we will copy the pixels.

3. Click and drag through the unwanted portion of the image, as shown in Figure 12-70B. The cross hairs show the area to be cloned, and the circle shows the size of the brush. The brush will duplicate the pixels from the sampled region.

FIGURE 12-70 The Clone Stamp tool in operation
(A) Sampling
(B) Area to be cloned
(C) Painting with the clone stamp

4. Drag the Clone Stamp tool through the top of the house, replacing it with ocean and sky, as shown in Figure 12-70C. Resample as often as needed to make the image look real.

12

A.

B.

C.

5. Switch to a smaller brush size for the beach and rocks, because you will need more precision. Watch for obvious duplicated regions, as indicated in Figure 12-71.

6. In Figure 12-72, we have used a smaller brush and sampled sand from different parts of the image to avoid any obvious duplication of objects.

We have just performed magic by making an entire house disappear through the power of the Clone Stamp tool.

FIGURE 12-71 Duplicated regions

FIGURE 12-72 The house removed

Removing Red Eye

Red eye occurs when the camera flash is too close to the lens of the camera and it reflects in the eyes of a person when you are taking his or her picture. This is a common problem with flash photography and causes a demonic red glow to appear in the pupils of the subject's eyes. Figure 12-73 shows an image with some pretty bad red eye.

This is very easy to fix using the Red Eye tool. When we apply this tool,

FIGURE 12-73 Red eye with the tool in place

12

FIGURE 12-74 Removing the red eye

it will change the red part of the pupil into a darker color while maintaining the natural highlights.

1. Choose the Red Eye tool from the toolbox.

2. In the tool options, try the default setting for pupil size and darken amount. If it doesn't look right, make changes to these settings.

3. Zoom in to the image so that you can see the subject's eyes up close.

4. Drag the tool diagonally across the eye, so that the rectangle covers most of the eye. The red will be replaced by a dark pupil, as shown in Figure 12-74. On most images, you simply click once in the vicinity of each eye; experiment to see what works best for each image.

Replacing the Sky

Colin Smith

It's difficult to get a picture of a nice, blue sky unless you are using a polarizing filter on your camera lens. Even then, if you are in the big city, chances are that the sky will be gray. You are about to learn three ways to add a blue sky to your picture. Figure 12-75 shows a picture with an overcast sky. It's time for the sun to come out.

Using the Magic Wand tool, make a selection of the sky area. (See Chapter 10 for more on selections.)

1. Set the foreground color to blue, R=80, G=120, B=234.

2. Set the background color to white.

FIGURE 12-75 The original picture with a dull sky

3. Choose the Gradient tool.

4. Choose Foreground To Background and Linear.

We are now set up to create the sky.

Method 1: Clear Sky

1. Click the New Layer icon in the Layers palette. This will create a new layer with the selection still active.

2. Drag the Gradient tool from the top of the image to the bottom.

3. Your sky now fades from white to blue, as shown in Figure 12-76—a typical cloudless day.

Method 2: Cloudy Day

1. Select the sky area.

2. Create a new layer.

3. Choose Filter | Render | Clouds. Your image will now show a cloudy sky. If the clouds look too fake, add a bit of a blur to them.

Method 3: The Ultimate   This is the most realistic of the three methods. (Actually, it's a combination of the first two.)

1. Create a sky using Method 1.

2. Create a new layer, and then create the cloudy sky using Method 2.

3. Make sure that the cloudy layer is on top.

4. Change the blending mode to lighten.

5. To lessen the effect of the clouds, lower the opacity of the top layer. Our new sky is shown in Figure 12-77.

FIGURE 12-76 A cloudless sky

FIGURE 12-77 The best sky of all

Chapter 13 · Take It to the Web

How to...

- Use ImageReady
- Choose the best work flow
- Slice images
- Add links to slices
- Optimize images
- Use web-safe colors
- Create image maps
- Create rollovers
- Export as a web page
- Make images transparent
- Animate images
- Export as a Flash file

It seems everyone has a web page these days, and now that you are using Photoshop, there's no reason for you not to have a nice one, too. When it comes to building web sites, Photoshop is one of the best graphics programs to use. Several features are unique to web work, and we explore these in this chapter to start you on your journey. If you are already building web sites, you'll notice some features in Photoshop that will help you work more efficiently—such as a secret weapon called ImageReady, an application that's bundled with Photoshop. ImageReady and Photoshop work seamlessly together to help you produce artwork that can be sliced, optimized, and served on the World Wide Web.

Originally, the ImageReady product was released as a separate product for processing web graphics. Since Photoshop version 5.5, ImageReady comes bundled with Photoshop. The two programs have become tightly integrated. ImageReady offers features specifically for web work, such as image slicing and optimizing.

For a complete walkthrough of a site's construction, check out my book Photoshop and Dreamweaver Integration *(McGraw-Hill/Osborne, 2005).*

FIGURE 13-1 Launching ImageReady

To launch ImageReady, click the bottom button in the toolbox, as shown in Figure 13-1.

The ImageReady interface is shown in Figure 13-2.

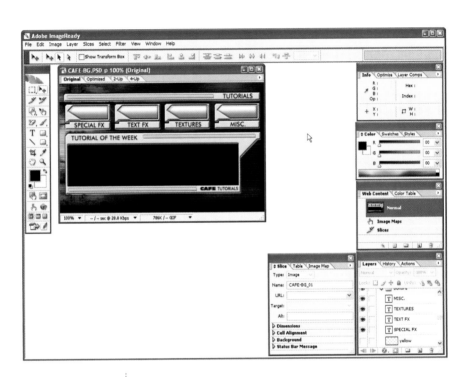

FIGURE 13-2 The ImageReady interface

The Work Flow

When you're preparing images for loading on the web, the most efficient work flow will go something like this:

1. Create the page in Photoshop.

2. Launch ImageReady.

13

3. Slice the image.

4. Add any special features, such as rollovers or image maps.

5. Optimize the image.

6. Export the page as an HTML page.

Your graphics are exported all ready for porting to the Web. We'll follow this work flow when working with ImageReady in this chapter.

Tip *When you create a web page, bear in mind that not everyone will be using the same screen resolution that you use, so plan accordingly. The lowest screen resolution commonly used is 800×600 pixels, so creating a page that is 775×550 pixels would work well. You need to allow some extra pixels to accommodate the toolbars and scroll bar in the web browser.*

Slicing Images

Slicing is a crafty technique commonly used by web designers. When you slice an image, you cut a large graphic into several smaller images that will be joined together seamlessly. This works in a similar way to a jigsaw puzzle, except you don't see any seams. You may want to slice an image for several reasons:

■ You want to make a slice clickable, allowing the visitor to move to another part of the web page.

■ You want to optimize each slice differently.

■ You want to add special features, such as rollovers and animations, to the slices.

■ You want to use slices to help your web page load faster.

You can do your slicing in either Photoshop or ImageReady. Usually, you produce your graphic in Photoshop and then launch ImageReady without closing the document. The ImageReady interface will load inside Photoshop. You can also slice from within Photoshop, but ImageReady has more robust features, such as allowing you to add a link to your slices.

ImageReady will construct an HTML page complete with an invisible table, with a cell for each slice. The images will be placed inside each cell so that they are all flush with one another.

When visitors view your web page, they will not see separate images; instead, they will see one image and the seams will be invisible.

User Slices

Let's walk through the process of slicing an image that will be used as an interface. You need to plan ahead a bit before you begin slicing. Consider the following:

■ Any button interfaces should take preference, because you want each button to be a single slice so that you can assign the click action to each button.

■ Try to separate important areas of detail versus nonessential portions of the image. This will allow you to optimize with a higher quality setting for essential portions of the image and a higher compression/lower quality for nonessential portions.

■ When you create slices, keep the number of slices to a minimum. If you create too many slices, they can cause the page to load more slowly because the computer will have to process all the data.

■ You may choose to use guides to help you slice the images. You can choose a snap-to guide to help define the slice placement. (See Chapter 1 for more on using guides.)

Let's begin slicing an image. We'll use an image that visitors to our web site can click to move from one page to another.

1. Choose the Slice tool from the toolbox.

2. Position your mouse pointer at one of the corners of your desired slice, as shown in Figure 13-3A.

3. Click and drag the mouse to define the slice in the same way that you would draw with a Marquee tool.

4. Release the mouse button and a numbered slice will appear, as shown in Figure 13-3B.

FIGURE 13-3 Using the Slice tool (A), and the finished slice (B)

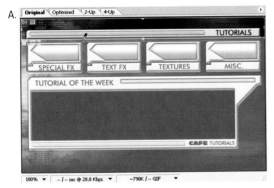

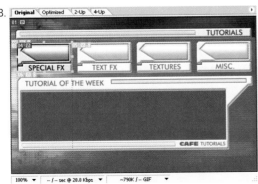

5. Photoshop automatically slices the rest of the image to accommodate your slice.

To hide the numbered slice, press CTRL-H (CMD-H *on the Mac).*

Whenever you create a slice, ImageReady assigns it a number. This helps you track the slices later on. When you export the page, each slice will become a separate image, labeled with the number by default. For example, an image named webpage.jpg that's been sliced three times will become webpage-01.jpg, webpage-02.jpg, and webpage-03.jpg. Figure 13-4 shows the interface with all the slices in place (A) and with the image hidden (B) so that you can get a good look at the slices.

You will notice that some of the slices' boundaries have a solid line and some have a dotted line. The solid lines are the slices that you have created yourself. The dotted lines are auto slices added by Photoshop. Whenever you modify one of your user slices (those you have created yourself), the auto slices will automatically adjust to make your slices work, like filling in the missing pieces of a jigsaw puzzle.

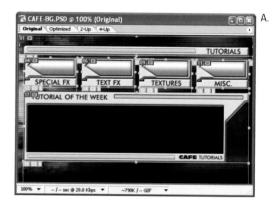

Modifying Slices

After you have created all your slices, you can modify them at a later time. The Slice Select tool is next to the Slice tool in the toolbox. Using the Slice Select tool, click inside any slice to make it active; you will see a bounding box around the selected slice. To adjust a slice, click and drag the bounding box.

You can also click and drag inside a slice's boundaries. The auto slices will adapt to fit your slice's new shape and/or position.

FIGURE 13-4 The image with the slices (A), and just the slices (B)

Converting an Auto Slice to a User Slice

If you click an auto slice, you'll notice that you cannot make modifications to it, as no bounding box or selection handles appear. If you want to make changes to an auto slice, you will need to convert it. In ImageReady vernacular, this is called *promoting* a slice. Here's how it's done.

1. Choose the Slice Select tool.

2. Click an auto slice to make it active.

3. Right-click (CONTROL-click on the Mac), and then choose Promote To User Slice. You will see the bounding box, with selection handles indicating that the slice is now a user slice.

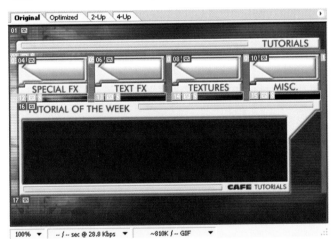

FIGURE 13-5 Selecting multiple slices

Combining Slices

When you are slicing an image, it's a good idea to cut down on any "stray" slices. For example, the selected slices in Figure 13-5 are disjointed, and a single strip would be much more efficient. The good news is that we can combine slices.

1. Select the first slice with the Slice Select tool.

2. Hold down the SHIFT key as you click each slice that you want to add to the selection. Figure 13-5 shows multiple slices selected.

3. Choose Slices | Combine Slices. The individual slices will be merged into one slice, as shown in Figure 13-6.

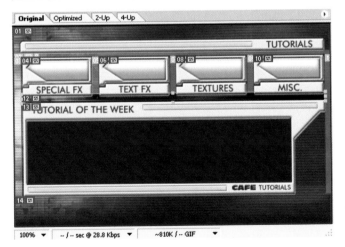

FIGURE 13-6 Combining the slices

Most of the slice options can be accessed by right-clicking the mouse (CONTROL-clicking on the Mac).

Splitting a Slice

You might want to divide a slice into segments—perhaps you need to insert a new image into a slice. You can use one of two methods for dividing a slice into segments: the first method uses the Divide Slice tool, and the second method involves resizing a slice and using auto slice.

The first method is great for dividing complex and precise slices:

1. Choose the Slice Select tool.

2. Select a slice to divide.

3. Choose Slice | Divide Slice.

4. In the Divide Slice dialog box shown in Figure 13-7, enter settings for the split.

5. Choose the Preview checkbox to see a live preview.

6. After you are satisfied with your changes, click OK, and your slice will be divided into multiple slices.

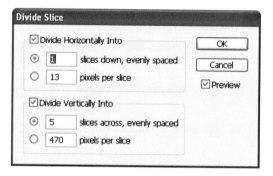

FIGURE 13-7 Divide Slice dialog box

The second method for splitting slices is not so scientific—it involves resizing an existing slice and allowing the auto slice feature to add the new slice.

1. Choose the Slice Select tool.

2. Select a slice to divide.

3. If you selected an auto slice, choose Promote To User Slice.

4. In the new user slice, click one of the bounding box handles.

5. Hold down the mouse and drag the handle of the slice to resize the slice. As you resize the slice, a new auto slice will be created.

6. To apply the changes, release the mouse button.

Hiding the Slices

You can toggle the view of slices on and off using the Show Slice toggle button in the toolbox, as shown in the illustration. Although the slices are still there, they are hidden from view. To show them again, click the same button.

Adding Links to Slices

You can turn any slice into a button, and you can assign web links to buttons on the image. When the user clicks this button, he will be taken to a new page or a new web site. You add links to slices in the Slice palette, shown in Figure 13-8, which offers access to several useful features:

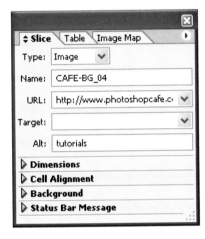

- **Name** Type in a name for the slice (renames the sliced image).

- **URL** Type in the web link, technically known as the uniform resource locator (URL), to which you want to jump when the slice is clicked.

- **Target** Tell the browser how to open the window with the new link—used mainly when a page is inside a frame set.

- **Alt** Type in the text that will appear on the page when the image is loading. The text will also show a *tool tip* if a user hovers the mouse over the button.

Here's how to assign a link to a slice:

1. Choose the Slice Select tool.

2. Click the slice that you want to use as a button.

3. Open the Slice palette.

4. Type the link into the URL field. You can type in one of two types of links:

- **Relative** Links to a page on an existing site, such as tutorials.htm.

- **Absolute** Links to a page on a different web site or to the full path on the existing site—for example, http://www.osborne.com or http://www.photoshopcafe .com/tutorials.htm.

When you export the page to the Web, these links will be assigned to the slices.

13

For more information on assigning links to images on your web page, see the section entitled "Setting Image Maps" later in this chapter.

Optimizing

When dealing with web pages, you want to make the file sizes as small as possible to accommodate modem speeds and the time it takes to transfer images. For example, you might want to adjust your images and web page content to accommodate the slowest modem speed found on most dial-up modems these days—56K (kilobytes).

You can shrink file sizes dramatically by using compression on the images. This compression process is called optimizing an image. When you compress an image, you will lose some quality— this is called lossy compression and is the most common type in use today. The trick to compressing an image is to balance the image quality with the image size. As you increase compression, the quality decreases. As you increase the quality of an image, the file size will also increase. A correctly optimized image will find the happy medium of quality and file size; finding this happy medium is a balancing act. Fortunately, ImageReady has some features that will help you find the right balance.

The two most common image compression formats are JPEG and GIF.

JPEG: Joint Photographic Experts Group

JPEG or JPG (pronounced *jay-peg*) is the preferred compression format for photos and images on the Web that contain a lot of *gradients*, or color progression. This format compresses images by discarding pixel detail and simplifying the image. The more you compress images using this format, the more the image quality will deteriorate. Even so, you can actually compress an image quite a bit before the degradation is noticeable to the naked eye. It is not uncommon to reduce a file size to a tenth of its original size, and most of us barely notice any difference as far as appearance.

Figure 13-9 shows an image that has been compressed using JPEG. At the highest compression, the image can look pretty bad. If you take into account the fact that the original image is 350KB in size, even the minimum compression still cuts the file size down a lot, and it doesn't change the image's appearance too much.

FIGURE 13-9 JPEG compression applied to an image:
(A) minimum compression, 74KB;
(B) medium compression, 32KB;
(C) maximum compression, 10KB

GIF: Graphics Interchange Format

GIF compresses images by breaking down the image into lines and then scanning the lines for repeating information. When it finds repeated information, it discards the repeating pixels. GIFs allow you to reduce the number of colors used in an image. As you reduce the colors, you'll get more "matches" and thus a smaller file size. GIFs work best for images that contain areas of flat color and for images with repeating patterns. GIFs also produce the sharpest results for text. A GIF can contain a maximum of 256 colors and a minimum of 2 colors. GIF is currently the only format that supports animation. It also supports transparency, in which you cut out an image and place it on a background that shows through.

FIGURE 13-10 GIF compression:
(A) 256 colors, 58KB;
(B) 64 colors, 37KB;
(C) 8 colors, 11KB;
(D) 2 colors, 2KB

Figure 13-10 shows an image that has gone through several GIF compression settings.

A.

B.

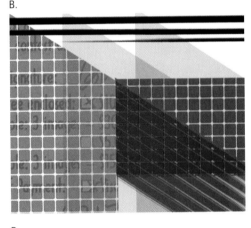

C.

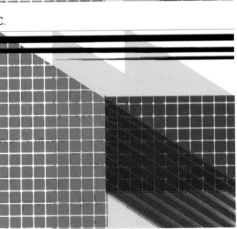

D.

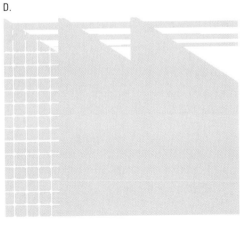

13

PNG: Portable Network Graphics

This file format will reduce the file size without any loss of quality to the image—PNG is a *lossless* compression. It also supports 256 levels of transparency; GIF supports only 1 level. The drawback to PNGs are that the files are larger in size compared to JPG, and older browsers don't support this format without special plug-ins. I suggest using this format only if you need complex transparency effects or you are exporting to another program such as Flash or video applications.

Optimizing in ImageReady

Let's take a look at how to optimize an image in ImageReady. You will notice four tabs at the top of the ImageReady image window; each tab represents a particular view:

- **Original**   This is the default view.
- **Optimized**   Perform your design work and slicing, and preview your image optimization (see Figure 13-11).
- **2-Up**   Compare the original versus optimized view.
- **4-Up**   View three different optimized settings versus the original.

FIGURE 13-11 Optimized view

First, let's optimize an image using JPG compression:

1. Open your image in ImageReady.
2. Choose the Optimized view.

A.

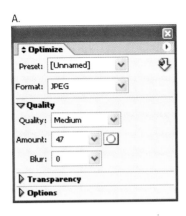

B.

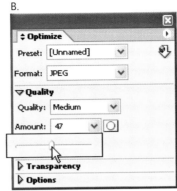

3. Open the Optimize palette, shown in Figure 13-12A.

4. In the Format drop-down box, choose JPEG.

5. In the Quality drop-down box, choose a preset.

FIGURE 13-12 Setting JPG compression: (A) Optimize palette; (B) Setting compression

6. Now slide the Amount slider, shown in Figure 13-12B. Slide to the left for lower quality and smaller file size; the most common settings used for web images are in the 30–50 range.

7. Check the image preview for visual quality and the statistics in the status bar at the bottom of the image window for file size, as shown in Figure 13-13.

FIGURE 13-13 Stats on the optimized image

8. Choose File | Save Optimized to save the optimized image.

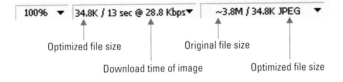

Optimized file size

Download time of image

Original file size

Optimized file size

 If you are working with slices, you can select each slice and optimize each individually using the same basic method.

 You will see a Blur option; adding a small amount of blur will help get the file size down even more.

Viewing Statistics

You can change the type of statistics shown for your images at any time by clicking the arrow to the right of the file size information along the status bar at the bottom of the ImageReady window, as shown in Figure 13-14. Simply choose a setting to display it in the status bar. You can choose from the following settings:

- Original/Optimized File Sizes
- Optimized Information
- Image Dimensions
- Watermark Strength
- Undo/Redo Status
- Original In Bytes
- Optimized In Bytes
- Optimized Savings
- Output Settings
- Size/Download Times

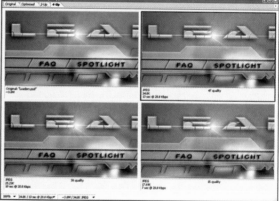

FIGURE 13-14 Changing the statistical information in the status bar

Optimizing Views

While optimizing an image, you may find it useful to compare the optimized image to the original. This gives you a visual cue as to whether the optimization looks OK, and it helps you to decide how much quality loss is acceptable. You can choose either the 2-Up or 4-Up tab to compare various settings simultaneously, as shown in Figure 13-15. To save your favorite view, simply click it and then choose File | Save Optimized.

FIGURE 13-15 Different optimized views: (A) 2-Up view; (B) 4-Up view

A.   B.

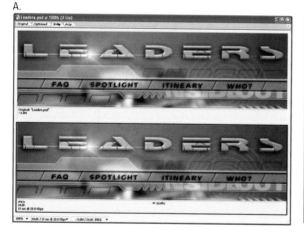

Optimizing GIFs

The process for optimizing GIFs is a little different from that for JPGs. You'll remember that optimizing GIFs means reducing the amount of color in an image. Figure 13-16 shows an image with the highest quality GIF, at 256 colors.

FIGURE 13-16 A GIF image with 256 colors

Let's reduce the file size using the GIF format:

1. Open the image in ImageReady.

2. Choose the Optimized view.

3. Open the Optimize palette.

4. In the Optimize palette's Format drop-down box, choose GIF.

5. Choose one of the following Reduction formats to build the color lookup table (CLUT):

   ■ **Perceptual**   Gives preference to colors that are predominant to the human eye

   ■ **Selective**   The default selection, which produces the most accurate color table

   ■ **Adaptive**   Uses the most common color in the images

   ■ **Restrictive Web**   Uses the 216 web-safe colors (see the sidebar, "About Web-Safe Colors")

6. From the Colors drop-down list, choose the number of colors. We chose 128 in Figure 13-17.

Dithering   In the Optimize palette, you can set the dithering options to smoothen out the transition between colors. Because we are reducing colors, the transitions can be very abrupt, especially in gradients. Dithering applies patterns to the transitions, simulating more colors and smoothing the transitions.

FIGURE 13-17 The same image reduced to 128 colors; the difference is hardly noticeable

Did you know?

About Web-Safe Colors

Because every computer and web browser displays colors differently, the W3C (World Wide Web Consortium) decided that a standard for 8-bit images (images of 256 colors) needed to be created. The web-safe palette was invented to solve some of these color issues. The palette consists of 216 colors that are deemed common for most web browsers on most computer operating systems. If your browser uses the web-safe palette and you view an image on a computer with 256 colors, no dithering will appear in the solid colors of the image, and the colors will be clean, sharp, and relatively accurate.

Reducing Colors Manually in the GIF Format   If you click the icon to the right of the Colors field on the Optimize tab, the Color Table will open, showing all the colors present in the image. You can choose to adjust the colors manually by using some of the options in the Color Table.

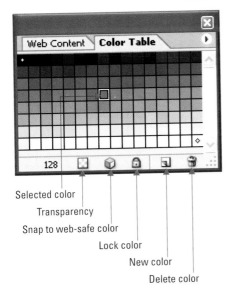

Selected color
Transparency
Snap to web-safe color
Lock color
New color
Delete color

Select the color by clicking on the color's box in the Color Table, as shown in Figure 13-18. Hold down the CTRL key (CMD on the Mac) to select multiple colors.

After you select a color, you can use the Delete Color button to remove the colors from the palette, thus removing them from the image and reducing its file size.

- **Transparency**   Turns selected colors into transparent areas.

- **Snap To Web-Safe Color**   Shifts the selected color to the nearest web-safe color. A diamond shape inside a color box indicates that it is a web-safe color.

- **Lock Color**   Prevents the color from shifting— indicated by a small square on the bottom right of a color box.

- **New Color**   Adds the current foreground color to the table.

- **Delete Color**   Deletes the selected color.

Tip   *If you find that you need to reuse the optimization settings, you can save them for a single-click recall. In the top corner of the Optimize palette, choose Save Settings from the drop-down menu. When you name the setting, it will be added to the Preset drop-down menu in the Optimize palette.*

Setting Image Maps

Image maps, sometimes known as *hot spots*, allow you to assign hyperlinks to portions of images. When the user clicks in the defined image map area, an assigned action will occur, such as moving the user to a new page. Image maps will appear invisible to the user until the mouse rolls over a hot spot. The mouse pointer will change to a pointing finger, which indicates that something will happen if the mouse button is clicked. Image maps are simple to create in ImageReady and can be used when you want to define an odd-shaped clickable region or you don't want to use slices. Image maps and slices can also be used together on the same web page or image.

Let's create an image map:

1. From the toolbox, choose one of the Image Map tool shapes, as shown in Figure 13-19.

2. Click and drag to create the image map area on your page. The image map is placed on the page wherever you let go of the mouse button. You may add as many image maps as you want to a page.

3. Open the Image Map palette.

4. Type the URL into the URL field, as shown in Figure 13-20.

5. Choose an Image Map tool shape to set the next image map area.

6. Repeat steps 2–4.

7. To test your new image map, click the Preview In Browser button in the toolbox.

8. The image will open in a web browser. Roll your mouse over the image map areas. The mouse pointer should change to a pointing finger when it hovers over the "hot" regions.

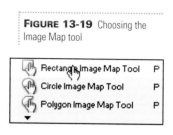

FIGURE 13-19 Choosing the Image Map tool

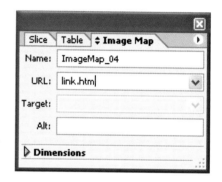

FIGURE 13-20 Setting the URL link

Creating Rollovers

Rollovers are used on web pages, in video games, and on DVD menus; when the mouse moves over a button or a portion of the image, the image changes—for example, the image may glow or appear depressed. It's common to use this technique with buttons on interactive web sites or other media.

Here's what actually happens behind the scenes to create this illusion: You create a slice that is set as a rollover. When the slice detects mouse activity, it swaps the sliced image for another image, which creates the illusion of the image changing. When the mouse moves out of the rollover region, the slice will switch back to the original image.

To create a rollover, you need two things:

- A slice with the original image (in its normal state)

- An "activated" image (in its rolled-over state) of exactly the same size as the slice

ImageReady takes all the hard work out of creating rollovers; you don't have to try to reproduce a small image at exactly the same size as the slice. Instead, you can simply create an effect on a layer and cause ImageReady to show or hide the layers when the mouse passes over them. ImageReady creates all the HTML and JavaScript code for you. Layer styles can also be used to create rollover effects, by showing or hiding the layer styles when the mouse hovers over them.

Preparing the Rollover Images

Before we can apply a rollover effect to a web page or interface, we first need to prepare all the graphics. Figure 13-21 shows the interface that we will use for this example. We'll make the buttons glow as the mouse rolls over them, to tempt the user to click the buttons.

FIGURE 13-21 The image without rollovers (normal state)

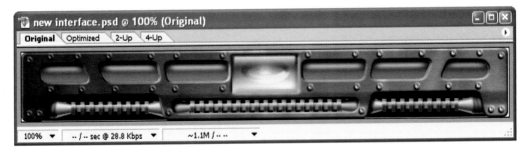

1. Create a new layer for each button, and create the effect of the buttons glowing in that layer—for the rollover state. The glows will be activated as the user rolls her mouse over each button. Figure 13-22 shows our interface with all the rollover states applied. (Chapter 11 told you how to create glows.)

13

FIGURE 13-22 The image with rollovers active (rollover state)

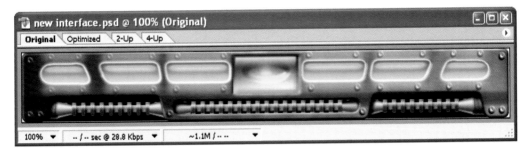

2. Turn off all the rollover layers. The image should now look as it did in Figure 13-21 in the normal state, but with all the glowing buttons hidden. Figure 13-23 shows the hidden layers in the Layers palette.

3. Slice the image using the method discussed in the section "Slicing Images" earlier in this chapter. Create a slice for each button and then optimize each slice.

Creating the Rollover Effect

Now that the images are prepared, we can use the tools in ImageReady to create the rollover effect. You don't have to know a single thing about the code to create and enjoy this effect, because ImageReady will create all the JavaScript code needed to make this effect work.

1. Using the Slice Select tool, choose one of the buttons.

2. Open the Web Content palette. You'll see your slice highlighted in the palette, as shown in Figure 13-24.

3. Right-click (CONTROL-click on the Mac) the layer thumbnail in the Web Content palette and choose Add Rollover State. You'll see a new thumbnail appear, called Rollover.

4. Now open the Layers palette and show the rollover layer for the glow on the selected button, as shown in Figure 13-25.

FIGURE 13-23 Hiding the rollovers in the Layers palette

FIGURE 13-24 The highlighted slice in the Web Content palette

FIGURE 13-25 Showing the layer

FIGURE 13-26 Setting the
rollover images

FIGURE 13-26 Setting the
rollover images

FIGURE 13-27 Setting the link

5. The effect will be reflected
in the Web Content palette,
as shown in Figure 13-26.

6. Set the hyperlink in the
Slice palette, as shown in
Figure 13-27.

7. Click the Preview In
Browser button in the
toolbox. Or toggle the
Rollover Visibility in
the toolbox.

8. The image will appear in
your web browser.

9. Roll the mouse over the button to test it.

Tip

*Whatever is visible in the Over state thumbnail
in the Web Content palette will appear when the
mouse rolls over the slice.*

The button should now glow, as shown in Figure 13-28.

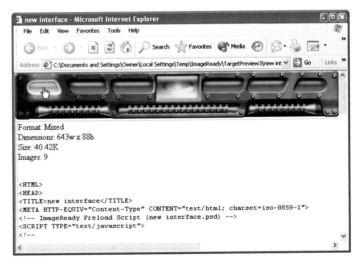

FIGURE 13-28 The image in
the browser

Exporting a Web Page

As you can see, we have followed a work flow to complete our
project. First, we created a web page in Photoshop, then we
sliced it, we optimized the slices, and then we created image

maps and rollovers and set the links. After you have tested the page in a browser and you are satisfied that everything works as you have planned, you are ready to create the final piece to post on the Web. ImageReady will create two parts:

- All the optimized slices will be turned into images and placed in a folder.
- The HTML page will be generated for you. This page will include all the tables, HTML code, and JavaScript to make everything work.

Let's get started:

1. Choose File | Save Optimized.

2. In the Save Optimized dialog box, choose a location on your hard drive to save the web site and create a new folder. Then click OK. All the files will be saved to the chosen folder.

3. Open the folder, and you will see all the parts of the web page, as shown in Figure 13-29.

FIGURE 13-29 All the files on the web page

interface_01.jpg   interface_01-over.jpg   interface_02.jpg   interface_03.jpg

interface_04.jpg   interface_05.jpg   interface_06.jpg   interface_07.jpg

4. Double-click the HTML file to launch the site in your browser, and you'll see the working web page.

5. Now transfer all the files to the Internet to have a fully functional web page.

Contact your web host or ISP for information about uploading files. Most web sites use FTP (File Transfer Protocol). Your web-hosting company should have all the information you need to upload the files and make them live on the Internet.

Using Transparent GIFs

A transparent GIF is an image that appears as a cut-out shape with a transparent background. You use a transparent GIF to create the illusion of a nonrectangular transparent shape that allows the background to show through in the transparent areas.

First, you need to create an image on a transparent background. We will crop the image as tightly as possible; even though the transparent pixels are invisible, they still increase the file size. To crop as tightly as possible quickly, choose Image | Trim from the Photoshop main menu. You'll see the Trim dialog box shown in Figure 13-30.

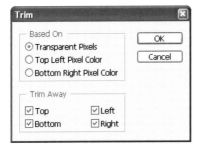

FIGURE 13-30 The Trim dialog box

To isolate an image from the background, place the image on a new layer and delete the background. Then you'll have a cropped image with a transparent background, as shown in Figure 13-31.

 For more on extracting images, see Chapter 10.

FIGURE 13-31 Transparent image

You can prepare the image in one of two ways:

- Open ImageReady and use the Optimize palette, which is best if you need to use advanced features such as rollovers, image maps, animation, and HTML pages.

- Use the Save For Web feature in Photoshop, which is best for images only.

For this example, we'll use the Save for Web feature in Photoshop. Choose Image | Save For Web, and in the Save For Web window shown in Figure 13-32, choose GIF from the Preset area at the right (or choose PNG 8, which works exactly the same as a GIF). You should recognize the controls in this window, because they are exactly the same as those in ImageReady, but they are presented in one palette instead of several palettes.

13

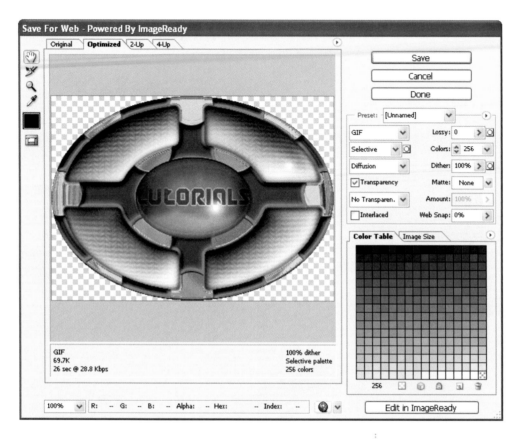

FIGURE 13-32 The Save For Web window

Matting

In the Presets area of the Save For Web window, you'll see a drop-down box next to an option called Matte. A *matte* is used to create a smooth edge around a transparent image. When the transparency is made, it can produce a rough edge around the image. A matte adds a thin border (called a halo) around all the edges in the chosen color. When the image is placed on a background of the same color, a very smooth edge will result.

Here's how to add a matte:

1. In the Save For Web window Preset area (Photoshop), or on the Optimize palette under Transparency (ImageReady), click the arrow to open the Matte drop-down list.

2. Choose Other.

3. You will see the Color Picker. Click the Only Web Colors checkbox.

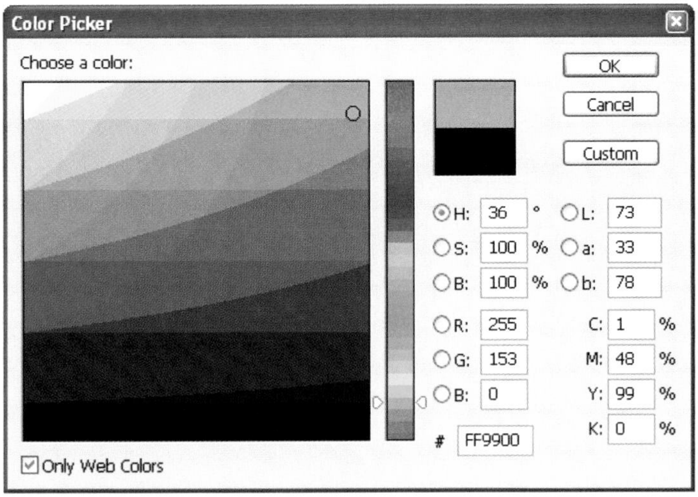

Color Picker

Choose a color:

OK

Cancel

Custom

- ⦿ H: 36 °   ○ L: 73
- ○ S: 100 %   ○ a: 33
- ○ B: 100 %   ○ b: 78
- ○ R: 255   C: 1 %
- ○ G: 153   M: 48 %
- ○ B: 0   Y: 99 %
- # FF9900   K: 0 %

☑ Only Web Colors

FIGURE 13-33 Choosing a color

FIGURE 13-34 The transparent GIF with a matte (left) and without (right)

4. Choose the color that you want to use for your web page background, as shown in Figure 13-33, and then click OK.

5. A thin halo will appear around your image. Click Save in the Save For Web window (in Photoshop), or choose File | Save Optimized (in ImageReady).

You can see the difference that matting makes. Figure 13-34 shows the image placed on a web page, with a matte on the left and without on the right. Notice how much smoother the matted edges look.

Using Animated GIFs

Animated GIFs are a series of images grouped together into one image. Each image in an animated GIF is called a *frame* and is displayed as part of a sequence of images, just like in traditional animation. When you quickly play the frames, it gives the illusion of movement. ImageReady and Photoshop CS2 are great programs to use for creating animations.

13

In this example, we will create an animated web banner.

1. Create a new file. Choose Web Banner for the preset size. (This preset is available only in ImageReady, although you can create your own for Photoshop.)

2. Type in some text on a new layer, as shown in Figure 13-35.

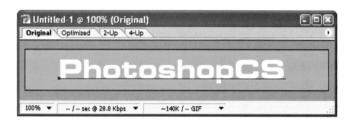

FIGURE 13-35 Text on a new layer

3. Drag the text, as shown in Figure 13-36, all the way to the left until it is just off the screen. The beginning of the text is the starting point of the banner animation.

FIGURE 13-36 Dragging the text off the screen

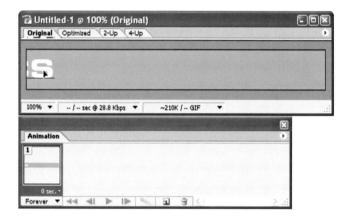

4. Open the Animation palette in Photoshop or ImageReady.

5. We now want to duplicate the frame. Click the Duplicate Frame button, as shown in Figure 13-37.

6. With the new frame still selected, drag the text until it is centered on the stage (Figure 13-38). This text phrase will mark the end point of the animation.

FIGURE 13-37 Duplicating a frame

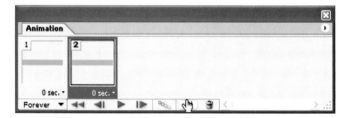

FIGURE 13-38 Moving the text to frame 2

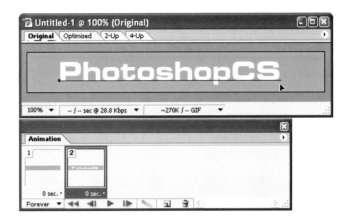

FIGURE 13-39 Setting the Tween options

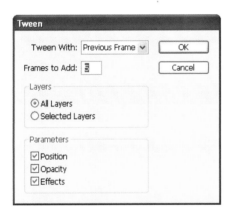

Tweening

To create smoother animations, we can add more frames between the start and finish points of the movement. Rather than make all the frames ourselves, the Animation palette has a feature called *tweening* that will automatically create all the in-between frames to smoothen our animation.

1. In the Animation palette, click the arrow at the far right (palette options) and choose Tweening.

2. In the Tween dialog box, set the Tween With option to Previous Frame, and type **5** in the Frames To Add text box, as shown in Figure 13-39. Then click OK.

3. Click the Play button and you will see that the animation runs. However, it is moving a bit rapidly; you can see that each frame shows for 0 seconds in the time indicators at the bottom of each frame, as shown in Figure 13-40. This is a bit too fast, so we will fix it in the next section by setting a delay.

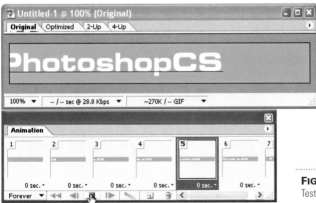

FIGURE 13-40 Testing the animation

Setting a Delay

The animation is now working. However, with the default settings, it happens so fast that it's hard to read what the banner says. The solution is to set the delay. We can tell the Animation palette how long to pause on each frame. We can either set a number of frames at once or we can set the frames individually. Let's set multiple frames at once:

1. Select the last frame in the animation.

2. Scroll to the first frame, and hold down the SHIFT key while you click frame 1.

FIGURE 13-41 All the frames are selected.

3. All the frames will now be highlighted, as shown in Figure 13-41.

4. Click on the characters *0 Sec* and choose a delay time. We chose 0.2 seconds in Figure 13-42.

5. Click any frame to unselect all the frames.

6. Select the last frame.

7. Set the delay to 5 seconds. This will keep the text visible for 5 seconds before looping back to the beginning of the animation.

FIGURE 13-42 Setting delay time

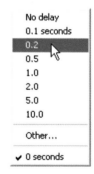

Creating a Fading Animation

So far, we have created an animation that moves from left to right, pauses for 5 seconds, and then jumps back to the start. It would be much smoother if the text faded out before restarting. We can easily create a fading effect with the Animation palette.

1. In the Animation palette, duplicate the last frame.

FIGURE 13-43 Hiding the text on the final frame

FIGURE 13-43 Hiding the text on the final frame

2. Hide the text layer on the final frame, as shown in Figure 13-43.

3. We now need to create the fade effect between the last two frames. Choose the Tween option from the pop-up menu at the top right of the Animation palette.

4. Set the tween to add 5 frames with the previous frame (see Figure 13-44).

5. Set the delay time for the new frames to 0.1 second.

6. Test the animation by clicking the Play button. The text should now fade out smoothly at the end of the animation.

7. Set the looping options in the bottom-left corner of the Animation palette. Choose any setting from Once to Forever for the playback.

FIGURE 13-44 Adding new tweened frames

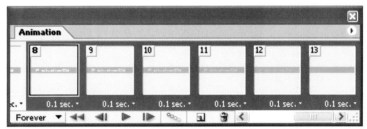

Saving Animations

Now we need to save our animation so that it can be used on a web page. Before you save an animation, make sure you optimize the file size, as we did earlier in this chapter under "Optimizing."

Saving as a GIF

GIF is the traditional web format for animations. Animated GIFs will work on any web page and in any web browser without the need for any plug-ins. GIFs work the best for raster graphics.

1. In ImageReady, choose File | Save Optimized. In Photoshop, choose File | Save For Web.

13

2. Navigate to the location at which you want to save the file.

3. Click Save.

4. Add the image to your web page by using an HTML editor, or do it by hand.

Exporting as a Flash File

ShockWave Flash (SWF) is the format used for Macromedia Flash animations. These animations are the best for vector formats. If you are working with vector shapes and text in ImageReady, these will be preserved when you export your animation as an SWF. This will result in a very small file size. The user's web browser will have to be equipped with the Flash Player plug-in for the SWF file to work. (No worries: at the time of this writing, more than 90 percent of web browsers in use are Flash equipped.)

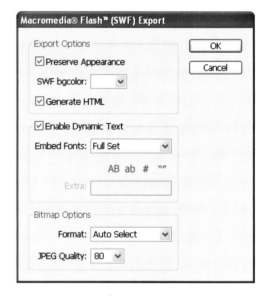

1. Create the animation.

2. Choose File | Export | Macromedia Flash SWF.

3. In the Macromedia Flash (SWF) Export dialog box, shown in Figure 13-45, use the settings shown in the figure. These work best for most cases.

4. Make sure that you choose the Generate HTML checkbox.

5. Choose a location in which to save the file.

6. Save the file.

7. Open the HTML page in a browser to watch the Flash animation. Our banner's file size was only 2KB! This is compared to 11KB for the GIF animation.

FIGURE 13-45 The Export dialog box

 Preserve Appearance will convert text to outlines. If you are using an exclusive vector image and you wish to update the text in Flash, turn this option off.

Chapter 14

Print Your Masterpiece

How to...

- Print in Photoshop
- Set the printing options
- Use the page setup
- Change the output size of the image
- Print a portion of a page
- Set visible printing options
- Print proofs for a professional print job
- Create printer's marks
- Set color management for predictable results
- Use color calibration

After you've spent hours working in Photoshop, the time will come when you'll need to print your masterpiece. At the least, a friend or client may ask you for a printout, or perhaps you just want to print out a single copy so you can pin it to your wall. On a grander scale, you may want to print a proof to look at before you rush it off to the printers to mass produce 100,000 color prints. In this chapter, we look at what you need to know to get a good print from Photoshop for all your printing purposes. We look into the dark realms of outputting for a printing press, and we touch on some color management issues as well.

Printing in Photoshop

If you want to simplify things, choose File | Print and walk away. The problem with this method, however, is that you may see a dialog box containing a message something like this: "Clipping will occur, proceed anyway?" If you are prone to panic attacks, reading such a message without knowing what is happening might not be good for you.

Another reason why you need to understand the printing features in Photoshop is because of what I call the "Cell Phone Principle." I admit that I love gadgets, but I hate to read manuals. I bought a fancy new cell phone because I liked all the buttons and the nice, big LCD display. It plays cute music and shows little animations on the screen. I had used this phone for a while when a friend purchased the same brand of phone. One day he said, "I love the way you can do this on the phone," and then proceeded to show me some clever new features. I didn't even realize that my phone had these features, because I never took the time to read the manual.

That's how it is with the Print options in Photoshop. If you just choose Print and walk away, you miss all the exciting features. (By the way, when Photoshop says that an image will "clip," it means that the image is too big for the piece of paper onto which you want to print.) You can click OK and hope for the best or, better yet, use some of the following information to make the most of this feature.

FIGURE 14-1 Image ready to be printed

Printing Options

Figure 14-1 shows the front panel art for a CD. After spending some time experimenting with a design, you'll need to print it out to see how it looks on paper. For some reason, things always look a little different after they are printed.

When you are ready to print, choose File | Print With Preview. You'll see the Print dialog box, offering quite a few options. You'll also see a preview window that gives you an idea of what, exactly, will be printed (see Figure 14-2).

14

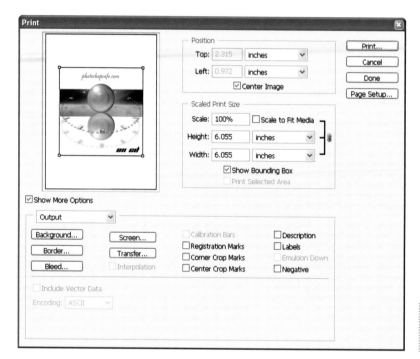

FIGURE 14-2 Print dialog box with print preview

Setting Up the Page

You may want your image to print at the actual size, or you may want to change the size of the image to match the size of the paper. Let's set the options for the paper size.

FIGURE 14-3 Page Setup dialog box

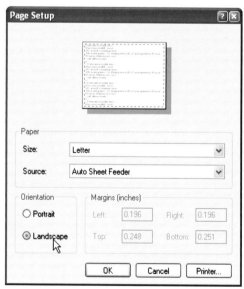

1. Click the Page Setup button. You'll see the Page Setup dialog box shown in Figure 14-3.

2. Choose the paper size from the Size drop-down list.

3. Choose the Orientation of the paper—either Portrait (tall) or Landscape (wide).

4. Click Printer to select the printer if more than one are connected to your computer.

5. Click OK to close the dialog.

Back in the Print dialog box, check your settings and the preview to make sure everything is as you want it, and then click the Print button. Or read on to make other adjustments.

Tip

For printing to an inkjet printer, your resolution should be set to a minimum of 150ppi (pixels per inch). For a photo printer, it should be set to 300ppi.

Note

You may also be a bit confused with the terms ppi and dpi (dots per inch). They are basically the same when it comes to units of measure. Pixels refer to the pixels on screen and dots refers to printed dots. A printer does not use pixels, but tiny dots make up the image. If you fit 300 dots into an inch space, the resolution of the printer is 300dpi. For more about resolution, see Chapter 2.

Changing the Output Size of the Image

One of the Print With Preview option's best features is that it lets you control how large the image will print. Here's an example using this feature:

1. In the Print dialog box, click the Show Bounding Box option in the Scaled Print Size area.

2. Click a corner point in the preview and drag to make the preview larger or smaller, as shown in Figure 14-4. Or you can enter a percentage setting in the Scale field.

FIGURE 14-4 Scaling the preview

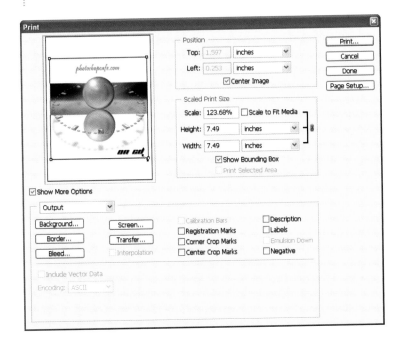

3. You can also change the position of the image in the window. This will cause it to print on a position of the paper that you choose. Uncheck the Center Image checkbox in the Position area.

4. Either drag the image to a new position on the preview page or enter the coordinates into the Top and Left position fields (see Figure 14-5).

5. Recheck the Center Image checkbox to center the image again if you change your mind.

FIGURE 14-5 Changing the image position

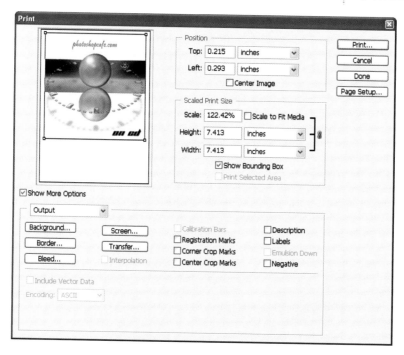

If you don't want to mess with settings, you can let Photoshop do the work for you. You can force the image to print at the largest possible size for the paper and printer you are using. The image will be printed as large as possible without any of the edges being cut off the page.

Most printers cannot print all the way to the edge of the page; a small margin is needed for the printer to feed the paper. Also, the top and bottom page margins are generally larger than the side margins.

To let Photoshop do all the thinking for you, choose the Scale To Fit Media checkbox. Whenever you are ready to print the image, click Print.

Media is a fancy word for paper. Sometimes, people may use transparent sheets for overhead projectors of clear plastic sheets, so media is an all-encompassing word for "whatever you put in the printer."

Print a Portion of the Page

When printing, you may find that you need to tweak the image a bit because it doesn't print as you expect. Perhaps you're like me and have wasted mountains of paper and gallons of ink. Here is a way to print just a selected portion of the page. This is a great way to proof your images before committing to a full-page print.

1. Using the Marquee tool, make a selection around the portion of the image that you want to print.
2. Choose File | Print With Preview.
3. Click the Print Selected Area option.
4. Click Print, and only the selected area will be printed.

Choosing Visible Printing Options

If you don't want your image to be printed on a plain background—perhaps you want to make a greeting card or you just want to display your proof with a nice background—you can change the background color. Here's how:

1. In the bottom half of the Print dialog box, you will see a drop-down menu that has two options: Color Management and Output. Choose Output.
2. Click the Background button.
3. You will see a Color Picker. Choose the color you want to appear on the background.
4. Click OK.

The color is displayed behind the image in the preview, as shown in Figure 14-6. You can also set a border around the image by clicking the Border button and choosing a border thickness. This feature is especially useful if you are printing an image with a white background on white paper and you want to show where the image ends.

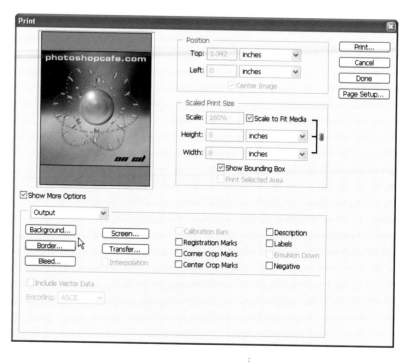

FIGURE 14-6 Color background

Printing Proofs for a Professional Print Job

Remember that before you print on a professional press, you must have your image set at 300ppi for a good quality print. You'll also need to convert it to CMYK mode—choose Image | Mode | CMYK. This makes the image ready to be printed on a printing press. Let's look at the print options.

The next couple of options are meant to prepare proofs for a professional printing press. You won't need to be concerned with this set of options if you are printing on an inkjet or laser printer for your own use.

Setting Bleeds

You know that desktop printers cannot print all the way to the edge of the page. But with some professionally printed jobs, you may want your image to print all the way to the edge of the paper, as you often see in posters, postcards, CD inserts, and brochures. What you need to do is set up something called a *bleed.*

When you're printing a bleed in Photoshop, you take a larger piece of paper than your target size. You then create the image slightly larger than what is needed, and trim it to the exact size you want. The excess will be trimmed away on the edges and guarantee that your image prints all the way to the edges of the trimmed page.

 Never place any important design information all the way to the edge of the page, because it may get trimmed off in a bleed.

FIGURE 14-7 Setting a bleed

frozen-journey.jpg

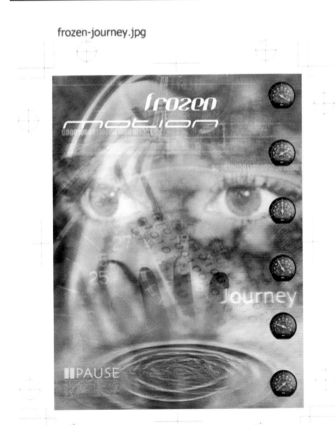

Photoshop can create a bleed for you:

1. In the Print dialog box, select More Options if it's not already checked.

2. Choose the Output option in the drop-down menu at the top of this area.

3. Click the Bleed button. A Bleed dialog box will open, as shown in Figure 14-7.

4. Set the Width in inches or whatever measure you choose. The standard for most bleed purposes is .125 inches (1/8 of an inch).

5. Click OK.

6. Click Print to print the page.

Adding Printer's Marks

Printer's marks are added to a printed sheet to help the printer accurately align and crop the image (see Figure 14-8). The following checkboxes should be

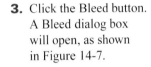

FIGURE 14-8 The printed document showing crop marks and registration marks

14

selected in the lower section of the Print dialog box to set up printer's marks.

- **Registration Marks** These marks are needed for a *color separation*. The professional printer will break the image into four separate files, one for each ink color. The registration marks, which look like circles with crossbars in the middle, show the printer where to align the separations.

- **Corner Crop Marks and Center Crop Marks** These marks show the printer where to trim the image. The crop marks are a trimming guide to help the printer cut the image to size.

- **Description** This can print the description from the image's metadata (File | File Info).

- **Labels** Prints information for the printer's reference, such as filenames and other information.

 If you are making a final print, it's a good idea to set the image scaling to 100 percent.

Color Management for Predictable Results

One thing's for sure: just about every computer displays colors differently. Monitors, printers, and scanners all play a part in how the colors are displayed. To try to bring a standard to the print and design industry, *color management* was invented. It sets a standard for measuring color and attempts to bring some consistency across the board—to keep printers and designers happy. ICC, the International Color Consortium, is a group whose goal is to set color standards in the color world.

Calibrating Color

When you buy a piece of computer equipment, check its documentation for information about its ICC profile. Some printers, monitors, and scanners come with calibration software. If this is the case, follow the directions and calibrate your hardware. During calibration, you match the ICC color with your device's colors to produce consistent and predictable results.

The calibration process can range from simple to complex. For example, a less expensive monitor may come with software or perhaps even a color strip that you hold against the monitor and match the colors by eye. The Kodak Colorific devices are inexpensive color calibration devices. On the other end of the scale are electronic devices that sit against your screen and take measurements, such as the ColorVision Spyder 2, shown in Figure 4-19. This device reads the colors on your screen as you follow the onscreen instructions. When you have finished, your monitor will be calibrated. The Spyder 2 is quick and simple to use.

FIGURE 14-9 The ColorVision Spyder 2 in operation

Be sure you're using typical work lighting conditions before you run calibration software.

Using the Color Settings in Photoshop

Photoshop allows you to set up your color management and allows you to assign color *profiles* to your images. These color profiles help you produce consistent colors even when using different systems. First, we will look at the color settings in Photoshop.

Choose Edit | Color Settings, and you'll see the dialog box shown in Figure 14-10.

Let's start with the Settings drop-down menu. Here, you can choose regional settings—for example, U.S. Prepress Defaults sets up your colors to match most prepress requirements for printers in the United States.

- If you are using Photoshop for printing to a commercial printing

FIGURE 14-10 Color Settings dialog box

press, choose the prepress region that is closest to your country.

- For general work and printing to an inkjet printer, choose a General Purpose default; for example, in North America, you'd choose North American General Purpose Defaults.

- If you are creating mainly online graphics, choose Web Graphics Defaults.

You can customize these settings further. In the Working Spaces area, change the RGB settings for your specific purpose; these are the three that probably concern your project:

- **Adobe RGB** Best choice for photographic and print work

- **Monitor RGB** Best choice if you want your web images to look consistent with Photoshop

- **sRGB** Best choice if you are putting your images on the Web and want consistent color with other types of monitors

Whenever you create a Photoshop document, the profiles you have created will be embedded in the document. If you try to open a document with a different color profile embedded, Photoshop will give you the choice of using the embedded profile or replacing it with your working profile (the settings you have just made). The best choice generally is to keep the embedded profile of the image, because that way it will maintain the appearance the original designer intended.

You can turn on and off the profile mismatches in the Color Settings dialog box. If accurate color is not important to you, you can turn off these warnings so that they don't bug you whenever you open a document. If accurate color is important, turn on these options.

When you are saving a document, it will give you the option to include the color profile. It's a good idea to use this option if you are using color management. To use it, just click the checkbox. If you don't want to add a color profile, uncheck the box.

You have just finished your crash course on printing and color management. If you want to get serious about color management, entire books are devoted to the subject, such as Tim Grey's excellent book, *Color Confidence: The Digital Photographer's Guide to Color Management* (Sybex, 2004).

Behind the Scenes

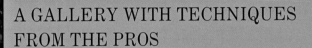

A GALLERY WITH TECHNIQUES FROM THE PROS

Some of the most gifted and recognized digital artists working with Photoshop have submitted examples of their art to include in this gallery. Each piece of art is accompanied by step-by-step tutorials that show you how to create at least one aspect of the composition, offering a behind-the-scenes look at how professional artists use Photoshop in their work. Here you get a glimpse of the range of techniques that can be applied using the tools you learned about in this book. More than likely, most readers will not have reached the level at which these artists have arrived. The purpose of including such stunning art is not to intimidate you, but rather to give you something to aspire to. Enjoy!

Texture

Oliver Ottner

Vienna native Oliver Ottner is the owner of advertising agency iService, which works with clients such as Estée Lauder and Clinique. His popular web site, at http://www.effectlab.com, displays some of his work, such as the *Naturemorphosis* series, as well as his Photoshop tutorials.

Ottner approached creating this piece, entitled *Naturemorphosis XII*, by playing with different techniques and discovering what works through trial and error. He says that while there is "no major trick to teach" in creating such a piece, he can teach you to understand how to use the best paths and techniques as a good starting point from which you can explore various methods that work for you. In each of his pieces, he uses a different blending mode in combination with various opacity settings for the layers. (Refer to Chapter 5 for more on blending modes and layers.)

Naturemorphosis XII

To prepare the image, Oliver opened a photo of a face in a .psd file with a texture on its own layer.

He reduced the opacity of the texture layer so the face beneath shows. Oliver used his favorite Photoshop selection tool (Chapter 10) to delete all unwanted Texture areas.

He used the Rubber Stamp tool for the final touch-ups, zooming into the image and moving it around, deleting with various brush sizes until it fit perfectly.

3

Next, he activated the texture layer by clicking it and cycled slowly through the layer blending modes. (In most cases, one blending mode will look best, letting the face shine through but at the same time showing enough texture.) Oliver decided "soft light" was a good start, because it allows the wood structure to show through but the highlights and shadows of the face are still visible.

4

Oliver wanted the cracks in the image to look realistic. To accomplish this, he first duplicated the texture layer. Next, he cycled through the blend modes again. The blend mode Multiply brings back what he lost before.

5

Since the image now looked much too dark, he chose Image | Adjustments | Curves (explained in Chapter 12) to make the layer lighter. Notice how the cracks keep their highlights and shadows, the colors are realistic, and the face behind shows its depth again.

6

Oliver wanted to correct the light to make the image look real and to give the piece more drama. To accomplish this, he made a copy of the face layer, and then he chose Image | Adjustments | Desaturate to turn the layer to grayscale. Next, he loaded the selection of the texture layer, and then he inverted the selection by choosing Select | Inverse.

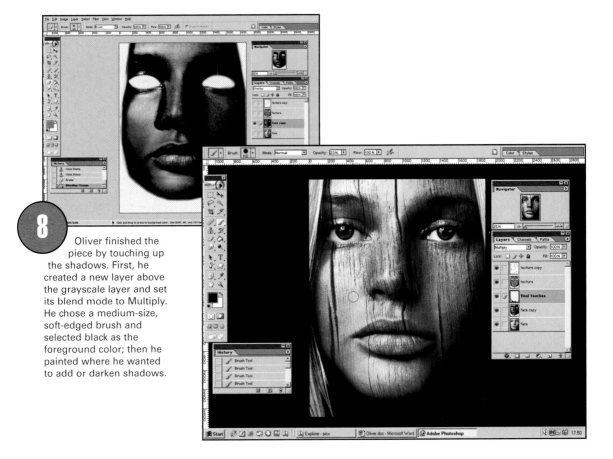

Then, to ensure that the grayscale face layer was still active, he pressed delete to leave just the texture area. He brought up the curves again to darken the grayscale and set its blending mode to Overlay (after again cycling through the modes to see what could fit best). Note the good contrast and dramatic lighting. Oliver then reduced the opacity of this layer to 60 percent so the effect wasn't overly dramatic.

Oliver finished the piece by touching up the shadows. First, he created a new layer above the grayscale layer and set its blend mode to Multiply. He chose a medium-size, soft-edged brush and selected black as the foreground color; then he painted where he wanted to add or darken shadows.

Hair

Malachi Maloney

Arizona-native Malachi Maloney first tapped into his artistic talent as a boy, when he began drawing monsters as a way of coping with his nightmares. As an adult, he frequently applies his training in traditional media to a subject far less frightening than monsters: pin-up models, created using Photoshop. Malachi has developed a reputation as one of the most impressive pin-up artists to come along in decades, working with Playboy Playmates, Penthouse Pets, Perfect 10 models, and various sci-fi and fantasy cover models, among others.

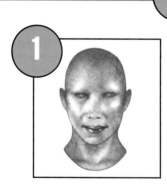

1 To accommodate this demonstration, Malachi quickly made a mannequin head on which to paint the hair.

2 Next, he sketched in the hair—just enough to give him a rough idea of the type of hair style he wants her to have. For sketching, he used a 2-pixel airbrush set to multiply at an opacity of 70 percent and a hardness of +50. Next, he set the layer style to multiply and duplicated the layer. Finally, he merged the two sketch layers together and lowered its opacity to around 50 percent.

Army Brat

Malachi is constantly experimenting with techniques to improve his work. His method for painting hair, shown in this tutorial, is the result of a couple of years' worth of experimentation. Even after investing this much time to get the process right, he claims it's possible he won't use it forever, since he might discover a better method as he continues to play with processes and learn. For this technique, Malachi suggests you use a graphics tablet and that you paint at a high resolution—the higher the better. For this example, he painted at 2x2 inches at a resolution of 300ppi.

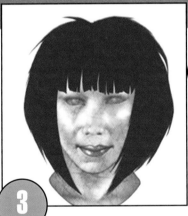

3 He created a new layer under the sketch layer, which he named "Hair." He started blocking in the shape of the hair with a paintbrush at an opacity of 100 percent. After he got the shape he wanted, he cleaned up the edges with a hard eraser at 100 percent opacity and a fine tipped smudge tool at an opacity of around 90–95 percent.

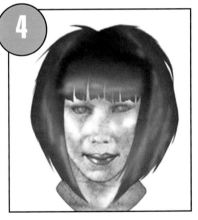

4 He locked the layer transparency so he could paint on just the part that's blocked in without affecting the rest of the layer's surface. Then, to establish the lighting, he used a soft airbrush at an opacity of 3–7 percent to paint in the basic shadows and highlights, making sure to vary the colors every so often for a realistic effect.

5

6

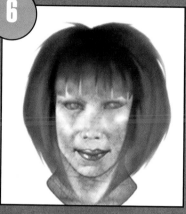

To form the basic shapes, he first used a soft smudge tool set to an opacity of around 65–70 percent to form the shapes and clumps of hair. Then he went in with a High Opacity Blur tool to soften everything, including the edges.

To prepare to paint the individual hairs, Malachi used a soft low opacity airbrush and lightly erased around edges and at the tips of the hair to make them slightly transparent, which makes the hair look lighter and more natural. Malachi painted the individual

hairs by first creating another layer above the main hair layer. With a 2-pixel paintbrush, set to an opacity of 90 percent and a hardness of +50, his brush options all set to Stylus except for color, he started to paint in the individual strands of hair.

9

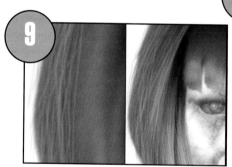

Again, he repeated the process described above over the entire surface of the hair.

10

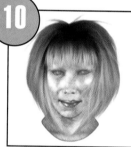

Malachi painted in some loose strands of hair on two layers: one above the main hair layer and one below it. After they were painted, he merged them to the main hair layer and used a Low Opacity Blur tool to soften areas of the hair and a little bit of Low Opacity Sponge tool to increase the saturation in certain areas.

11

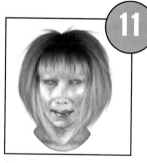

Next he added a shadow. First he made another layer beneath the hair layer. Then, he CTRL-clicked the hair layer to select its shape and filled it with a dark color on the layer below. Malachi usually chooses a dark color that corresponds with the color of the skin/surface on which he's casting a shadow.

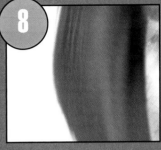

7 Next, Malachi locked the transparency of the layer on which he painted the strands. Using a large, soft airbrush set to an opacity of 10 percent, he painted in the appropriate colors and highlights. After the strands had been colored, he unlocked the layer's transparency and went over the strands with a Soft Blur tool set to around 15–20 percent. Next, he used a soft, low opacity eraser to make the tips of the strands slightly transparent. After the strands of hair were painted, he lowered the layer's opacity to 85–90 percent and merged it with the main hair layer, as shown here.

8 The same process was repeated over the area a few times to build volume.

12 After the shadow was done, he moved it and distorted it using free-transform to get it into a position that corresponded with the light source. After a little light blurring, and a little light erasing, it was done.

Depth

Philip H. Williams

Philip Williams began his professional career as a commissioned portrait painter after graduating from a coordinated program between the Pennsylvania Academy of Fine Art and the Graduate School of Fine Arts at the University of Pennsylvania. In the early 90s, when desktop computers began to show promise as creative tools for the visual arts, Phil migrated toward web site design and illustration. Today, he spends most of his time on commissioned illustration work and his personal artwork, all of which is created digitally.

1 Phil started by laying out a rough composition.

2 He then constructed some of the foreground buildings, as shown here. Phil approached his "epic" pictures almost like an engineer approaches the design of a complex object: he started with an overall concept and then built the elements and stuck them together. Photoshop, with all its adjustment capabilities, is the perfect tool for working this way.

Cityscape

Phil had the movie *Blade Runner* in mind when he designed the building in the foreground of *Cityscape*. The other large buildings are his own creations, while most of the small buildings are based on existing buildings in New York City.

3

To help with the perspective of the image, Phil created grids on a new layer using the Line tool. The Free Transform and Perspective Transform tools were used to shape the grids. After the larger objects were built, Phil started to add some detail in the foreground.

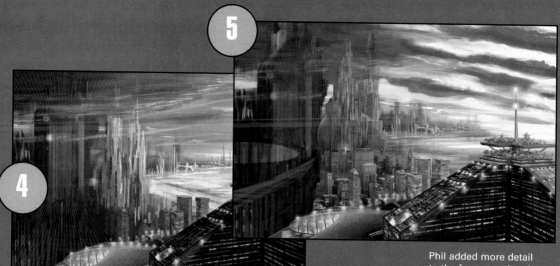

5

4

Phil roughed in the background and the sky. Here you can see how Phil achieved depth by placing objects in the foreground and background and by using the Brush tool to airbrush at different thickness settings.

Phil added more detail to the foreground and background and began to rough in the mid sections of the image.

8

9

Phil added lighting and touched up the color, to finish off the image.

To bring all the foreground and background together, Phil created a bridge to "bridge the gap," so to speak.

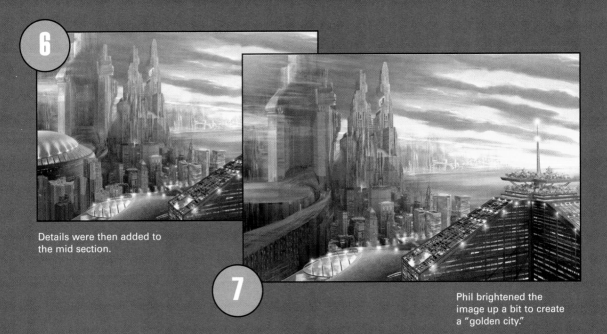

6 Details were then added to the mid section.

7 Phil brightened the image up a bit to create a "golden city."

10 Here is a close up of the grid system that Phil developed to help keep everything in perspective. Lines and grids can be stored in a layer set to make it easy to turn them on and off as needed.

Shadows

Bert Monroy

Bert Monroy was born and raised in New York City, where he spent 20 years in the advertising industry as an art director and creative director for various agencies, including his own. He now lives in Berkeley, California. Bert embraced the computer as an artistic medium early on, with the introduction of the Macintosh 128 in 1984; he is considered one of the pioneers of digital art. He has written numerous articles and books, including co-authoring the award-winning *The Official Adobe Photoshop Handbook* (Bantam Books, 1991), the first book written on Photoshop.

In addition to writing and lecturing, Bert continues to serve his installed base of clients, which includes Apple Computer, Adobe Systems, Pioneer Electronics, Fujitsu, SONY, AT&T, Chevron, and American Express. Since May 2001, Bert has shared Photoshop tips and techniques as a regular guest on the TechTV channel show "The Screen Savers."

In *Shadowplay*, Bert uses shadow to achieve realism. The cast shadows, so-called because they are produced by light cast on an object, have been distorted and wrapped around different objects. In the tutorial that follows, I applied the technique Bert used in *Shadowplay* for creating cast shadows to a simple object, a flower.

Shadowplay

1

To start, I created an image in its own layer using the Custom Shape tool.

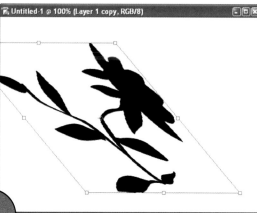

2

I duplicated the layer and hid the original so I could see what I was doing. Then, using Free Transform, I chose Skew and distorted the layer in the direction I wanted the shadow to fall.

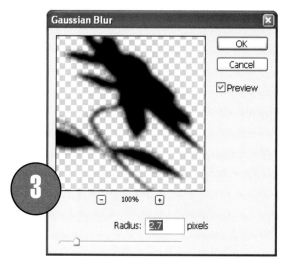

3

To soften the shadow a bit, I chose Filter | Blur | Gaussian Blur.

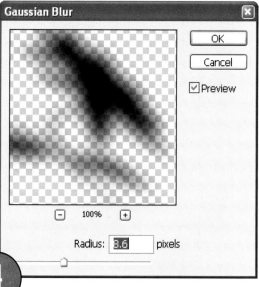

4

As shadows get further away from the object casting them, they soften. To achieve this effect in my image, I needed to create a softer shadow. First, I duplicated the shadow layer, and then I hid the original shadow layer.

5

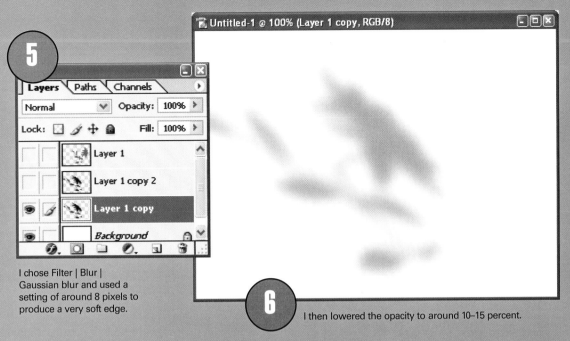

I chose Filter | Blur | Gaussian blur and used a setting of around 8 pixels to produce a very soft edge.

6

I then lowered the opacity to around 10–15 percent.

7

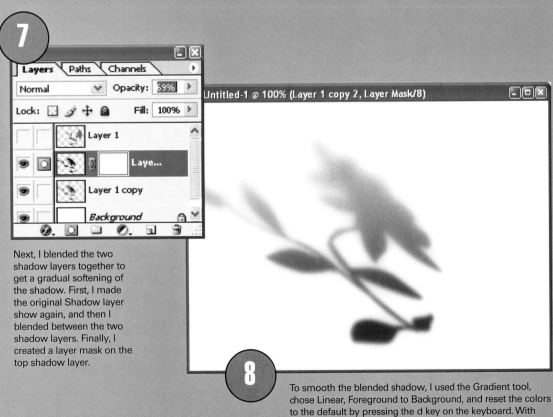

Next, I blended the two shadow layers together to get a gradual softening of the shadow. First, I made the original Shadow layer show again, and then I blended between the two shadow layers. Finally, I created a layer mask on the top shadow layer.

8

To smooth the blended shadow, I used the Gradient tool, chose Linear, Foreground to Background, and reset the colors to the default by pressing the d key on the keyboard. With the layer mask still selected, I dragged the gradient from the top to the bottom of the shadow area.

Imported Images

Jens Karlsson

Born in Sweden, Jens Karlsson now resides in Beverly Hills, California, where he works as a Senior Designer at DNA Studio. After discovering a love for photography, Jens studied media communications, graduating with a degree from Hyerisland School of New Media Design, Scandinavia's most prominent school in this field. In addition to founding two design companies and working for various design firms in New York and Los Angeles, Jens manages his personal web project, Chapter3.net. Chapter3 is a ubiquitous name in the online design scene as a result of Jens's success in both his noncommercial and professional work, as well as his dedication to making the digital tool accepted in the art world.

The foreground environment in *Pegasus* was modeled in 3ds max and imported into Photoshop. You can import 3D images created by other artists into Photoshop if you don't know how to use 3D programs yourself—see Chapter 2.

Before Jens modeled the foreground environment, he planned where the sky in the background would be really bright. Knowing where the main light source was going to be placed in the image, he set up the lights in his environment to cast shadows that would match the surroundings once composited in Photoshop.

Pegasus

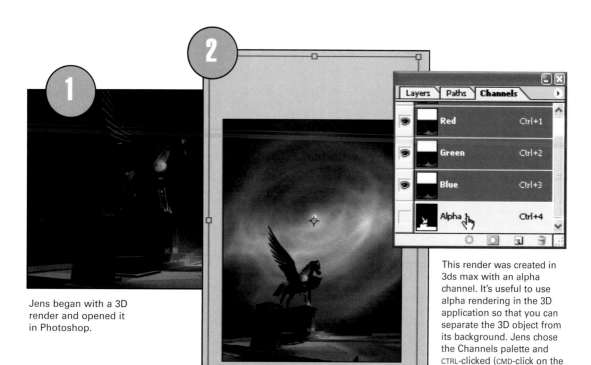

Jens began with a 3D render and opened it in Photoshop.

This render was created in 3ds max with an alpha channel. It's useful to use alpha rendering in the 3D application so that you can separate the 3D object from its background. Jens chose the Channels palette and CTRL-clicked (CMD-click on the Mac) the channel thumbnail to turn on the selection. He returned to the Layers palette and copied the selected object to a new layer. The effect for the sky was also a 3D render. Jens brought it into Photoshop and sized it on a new layer.

Jens used the Hue/Saturation adjustments to add some color. He chose the Colorize option.

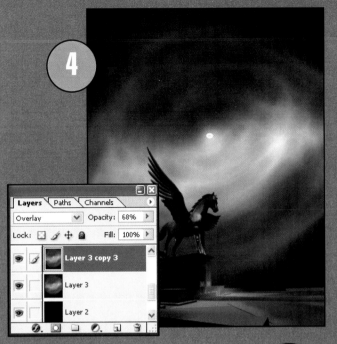

4

Jens duplicated the cloud render, added 10px of Gaussian blur to the duplicate, and erased some parts of the duplicated layer to add texture. He duplicated the original cloud render layer once again and set the New Layers Blending mode to Multiply, and then scaled it down to cover some parts of the underlying layers to achieve the contrast-rich explosion.

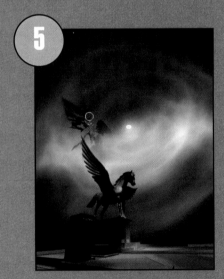

5

Next, Jens brought in some more 3D renders for the particles in the sky, used layer masks or the Eraser tool to softly blend them into the background and remove the harsh edges.

6

7

He duplicated one of the objects, filled it with white, and added a radial blur to begin the process of creating the light rays.

Jens duplicated the light rays, resized and added a blur, and added some color with Hue/Saturation and experimented with the blending modes. He continued to build up the image by adding objects, duplicating, and blurring. He continuously experimented with the blending modes to produced a nice result. Also, he added dodging and burning to the layers using the Dodge and Burn tools to build up the shadow, highlights, and texture.

Creating a Split Neutral Density Filter

Tim Cooper

A big problem with photography is that film and digital sensors cannot capture in one exposure the complete range of tones that our eyes see. With film photography, we overcome film's shortcomings by using a split neutral density filter. With digital cameras, we can overcome this by exposing the scene twice and then combining the exposure that renders the shadows properly and another that renders the highlights properly.

When shooting a scene to composite, it's important to minimize movement between exposures by using a tripod and cable release. Analyze the scene and determine what your different exposures will be. If the scene requires more than a two-stop change of exposure, I shoot three exposures at one-stop increments and then combine the first two together using the following technique. When I am finished, I add in the third exposure using the same technique again. This ensures a smooth graduation between dissimilar tones.

1 Good highlights

2 Good shadows

To create a split neutral density filter, I opened up both images in Photoshop and selected the Move tool from the toolbar. I clicked and held and dragged the darker image on top of the lighter image. I pressed the SHIFT key before I dropped the image to center and align it on top of the destination image. I checked to see if my images were aligned by dropping the opacity to about 50% on the upper layer and enlarging my image to 100%. It wasn't aligned perfectly, so I used the Move tool to align it properly. I then returned the opacity to 100% and closed the darker scan or image file.

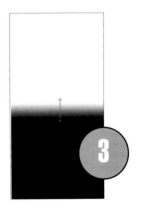

3 I clicked the Add A Layer Mask button at the bottom of the Layers palette and chose the Gradient tool from the toolbar. I then wanted to draw out the split neutral density filter. This tool is used by defining the gradient zone.

4 I started at the top and went to the bottom. (If I don't like my first attempt, no problem—I just redraw the line.)

5 When I was satisfied with the effect, I chose Layer | Flatten Image.

Wrapping a Shape Around a Cylinder

Colin Smith

I constructed this camera image 100 percent in Photoshop using no photos or scans. A big part of making things look convincing is the ability to wrap a shape onto a surface in a convincing fashion. Here I'll show you the technique used for wrapping the grip onto a camera lens. I used a more simplified shape for this example so that you can follow along easily.

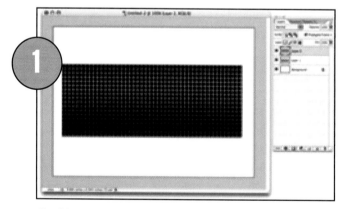

First I began my cylinder on its own layer. Then I created a new layer, placed my soon-to-be wrapped shape on this layer, and made a tight selection around it using the Marquee tool.

I chose Filter | Distort | Spherize to distort the layer into a spherical shape; however, I constrained this distortion to vertical by changing the mode to Vertical only. I cranked the amount all the way up to 100% and clicked OK to apply the effect.

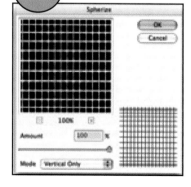

Photo-Realistic Camera Image

3

Notice that the object now wraps around the shape. I added some layer effects such as drop shadows and bevels to add to the dimensional feel. This effect works equally as well for photos and text.

Artists

Tim Cooper

tim@timcooperphotography.com

timcooperphotography.com

Jens Karlsson

jens@chapter3.net

www.chapter3.net

Malachi Maloney

malachi@liquidwerx.com

www.liquidwerx.com

Bert Monroy

bert@bertmonroy.com

www.bertmonroy.com

Oliver Ottner

info@naturemorphosis.com

www.effectlab.com

www.naturemorphosis.com

www.iservice.at

Colin Smith

colin@photoshopcafe.com

www.photoshopcafe.com

www.pixeloverload.com

Philip H. Williams

phil@eyewoo.com

www.eyewoo.com

Index